BREAKING

✝HE

CHAINS

Overcoming the Spiritual Abuse

of a False Gospel

Shari L. Howerton

All scripture quotations, unless otherwise indicated, are taken from The Holy Bible, English Standard Version®, copyright © 2001 by Crossway Bibles, a publishing ministry of Good News Publishers. Used by permission. All rights reserved.

Scripture quotations marked (NIV) are taken from the Holy Bible, New International Version®, NIV®. Copyright © 1973, 1978, 1984 by Biblica, Inc.™ Used by permission of Zondervan. All rights reserved worldwide.

Published in Nashville, Tennessee by Shari L. Howerton

ISBN: 978-0-9713499-4-0

Printed in the United States of America

To my sister-in-law, Cheryl Mears Morrell,
I didn't have a sister growing up, but I have
a sister now. I love you, Cheryl.

Table of Contents

Acknowledgments

My whole life is a testimony of God's faithfulness and redeeming love. I thank Him, first of all, for His amazing grace.

I thank my husband, John, for his love and devotion. I once heard a sermon using the love of a spouse to emphasize the power of our love and acceptance in Christ—how a spouse's opinion can outweigh the opinions of all others. For instance, if my husband thinks I am beautiful, I will *feel* beautiful. While feeling *beautiful* has never been my great longing, I have always wanted to feel *lovable*. John makes me feel lovable and adored. And through the magnitude of John's love for me, I have been blessed to experience the richness of God's love; *because as deep as John's love is for me, I know that God loves me even more.* My husband has been a rock of stability for me as I have struggled to heal from the many wounds of my past. Without his constant encouragement, support, and patience, I might never have written this book.

I thank my son, Danny, for consistently focusing me on God's grace and the cross of Christ throughout the process of writing this book and for introducing me to the online sermons of Tim Keller. And I need to thank Tim Keller. Although I don't know him personally, he has been instrumental in helping me to understand what the cross truly means in my life. Listening to his online sermons revealed to me how the entire Bible is the story of Jesus. As I struggled to break the chains of false doctrine, and before I could believe the simplicity of the Gospel, I had to be *convinced* that it was true. Tim Keller convinced me that God's grace was true and real, and I could trust in Jesus for my complete salvation.

I thank my friend and pastor, Allen Jackson. He has been not only a teacher but an example to me of how to become a more fully devoted follower of Jesus Christ. He has been patient and kind when I have needed gentle guidance and spiritual encouragement. His counsel helped me to overcome my unbelief in God's promise of eternal life through faith in Christ. He ministers to our congregation from a posture of humility rather than superiority, which I have greatly appreciated. And he has cultivated a love for Israel in my heart that I never had before.

I am indebted to the friends who devoted time and energy to reading this book as I wrote it, chapter by chapter, rewrite upon rewrite, offering their unique insight and feedback. They prayed for me. They propped me up when I occasionally succumbed to fear and anxiety anticipating the possibility of painful repercussions. Ann and Eric Brenton, Donna and Lee Synnott, Karen Jones, Robin Hanloh, Dr. Frank Scott, Andrew Osenga, and my husband, John: you have my heartfelt gratitude for your contribution to making this a better book.

Thank you, Jennifer, for telling me—in no uncertain terms—to stop apologizing for my convictions.

I thank my editor, Geoffrey Stone, not only for his skill and expertise in editing but for making the process less painful than I anticipated. After finishing the original manuscript, I didn't imagine that I could think any more deeply about any of these past experiences. However, as a result of his thoughtful questions and comments, I gained even further insight into my past through the editing process of this book.

I don't know how I could ever effectively convey in words my deep gratitude to my friend, Charlie Daniels, for agreeing to write the foreword to my book. We have only been friends for a short time, but he and his wife, Hazel, have so impressed me in their love for Jesus, their humility and their boundless generosity. When I asked Charlie if he would consider writing the foreword, I never dreamed he would respond, "I would be *honored* to write your foreword." Charlie, the honor is truly mine.

Terra Mears, I want to acknowledge you and thank you for the beautiful cover you created for me. I have always admired your artistic talent.

However, considering the subject matter and content of this book, as the granddaughter of Cornelius Mears, your involvement and contribution to this effort are extremely meaningful to me far beyond the blessing of your obvious talent.

I want to thank my sister-in-law, Cheryl, and the many friends who gave me permission to tell their very personal stories in this book, using real names. I am thankful that I have not been alone on this journey of deliverance and I do not stand alone in proclaiming the truth of our shared past because of *your* willingness to go on record in this book.

Foreword

There are many interpretations of the Holy Bible. There are many mysteries which are more or less left to our own discernment. Eschatology, geographical locations of events, and trying to imagine when the second coming will take place can burn gallons of midnight oil and quite a few brain cells. But one thing is made very plain on the pages of the Holy Scriptures. Jesus Christ is the Son of God, He is eternal in that He has always existed and created everything that exists. The Bible says that everything that was made was made by Jesus. He is also the only path to forgiveness of sin, redemption of the soul, and eternal life with God in Heaven. He is *the* way, *the* truth, and *the* light, not *a* way, *a* truth and *a* light.

Any group that believes Jesus is less than God is a cult and is usually centered around a human being instead of the King of kings and the Lord of lords. They cherry pick the Scriptures, adopting parts that fit their interpretation and deemphasizing or leaving out completely the passages that don't. The result is false doctrine, pure and simple. Either we accept the *full* truth about Jesus Christ, or, if we don't, it's tantamount to calling the Holy Scriptures a lie. I don't mean to infer that all the people who belong to these cults are evil or devious, but when one generation misleads the next, over time the untruths become church doctrine; the young ones unsuspectingly follow the lies they are being told, and on it goes.

This is the story of one woman's struggle with the cracks she began to see in her church as she grew up and the difficulty she had in breaking the chains of the doctrine of perfection—that she had to achieve perfection in this life before she would be eligible for eternal life. Her church was one of those, "we're right and everybody else is wrong" denominations. They discouraged individual discernment of the Word of God and fraternizing with other Christians who didn't belong to their exclusive denomination.

Jesus said that He came to bring a sword and families would be divided over Him. There is a lot of hurt on these pages as Shari had to turn her back on family and friends and as they ostracized her for daring to question their beliefs. This story is her journey into truth and light and spiritual rebirth. It's about being able to love deeply the very people who are persecuting you, to put aside the malice and turn the other cheek. It's about forgiveness and the joy of coming to the realization that it is not perfection but the blood of Jesus Christ that seals our salvation.

I met John and Shari Howerton on a trip to Israel with the church we both attend and quickly developed a friendship. It was the first trip to the Holy Land for all of us, and it didn't take long to realize what a very special place it is. In the last part of this book, Shari writes about being baptized in the Jordan River. Well my whole family and I were a part of that joyous event. John and Shari are our brother and sister in Christ, and I know that it is Shari's deep desire that by sharing her story of overcoming she will give others the courage to question what they are afraid might not be sound biblical teaching, to read and discern the Word of God for themselves, and to step out on their own in boldness, no matter how uncomfortable it may be.

Charlie Daniels

Preface

Every time I seriously considered writing a book, I would wonder why anyone would want to read my story. Numerous friends and acquaintances with whom I have shared my personal testimony over the years have asked me, "Why don't you write a book about your testimony?" I usually shrugged it off but sometimes would answer by saying that someday I just might. Someday finally happened, and this is my story.

My aunt has hosted a weekly women's prayer group for more than twenty years. In that time, many prayers have been answered. One day my aunt asked if I would be willing to share my testimony with her friends. We spent an entire afternoon exploring my past. One question led to another, and someone suggested I write a book. As we concluded our time together, my aunt and her friends prayed for me. One of their specific prayers was that God would use my testimony for His glory and the deliverance of others.

That experience came at the beginning of 2009. As I write this introduction, it is still January. Not a great deal of time has elapsed. However, that afternoon has stayed with me. I believe it was an ordained appointment.

Why *would* anyone want to read my story? There may be any number of reasons, I suppose. Although my story of deliverance is not typical for most Christians, deliverance in itself promotes hope and strengthens faith. Most of us do not anticipate being thrown into a pit by our brothers and sold into slavery, but reading Joseph's story should encourage our own personal faith as we see that God delivers even in the direst of situations. I am certainly not comparing my life to Joseph's. Rather, I am suggesting that it doesn't matter what your circumstance. We are all in need of deliverance, redemption, and a Savior.

There are many Christians held captive in spiritual bondage, oppression, and deception. Some of you may be able to relate more specifically to my story than I realize. For all of you who have been through or are going through similar struggles, I desire the same deliverance God has mercifully brought to my life through the Gospel of Jesus Christ. His deliverance and abundant redemption are the best experiences we can share on this earth.

Mine is not the story of someone whose chains were worldly passions or a life descended into the gutters of sinful living. My chains were a false religious system and crippling spiritual deception. I believed I was a Christian, but did not know the Gospel. Robbed of God's promises by men who added their own set of requirements to faith in Christ, legalism prevailed. I had no joy. I envied Christians not exposed to this "truth."

Despite my desire to live for God all those years, I was a prisoner of my chains. I needed deliverance as much as any sinner in the gutter. I knew nothing of the freedom Christ had died to provide for me.

There are aspects of my personal testimony that are unique, but I am just an ordinary person. I do not think of myself as particularly interesting. However, when I have the opportunity to share my testimony with others, it often sparks endless questions. Whether they relate to my story or not, many do seem genuinely interested in the details. My husband has told me he cannot imagine anyone, let alone a Christian, believing the things I was taught. Although it is a foreign concept to him and others I have talked to, it was my life for forty-three years.

I have no desire to author an exposé or a "tell all" type of book. This is my spiritual journey and my testimony of deliverance. However, I cannot share my deliverance without revisiting my captivity. I intend to leave out unnecessarily salacious details, focusing on the events that had the greatest impact upon my life. Unfortunately, some of those details include scandal. My story overlaps with many other people's stories, and the best illustrations are often real-life examples. I will make every attempt to write with precision and accuracy, verifying my memories through other sources. I deliberately conceal the personal identity of victims. Where I give someone's identity, the details are a matter of public record or the person has given me express permission.

Since this book is about a personal journey, I cannot avoid revisiting conversations, interactions and experiences that have shaped and influenced my life. It is not my desire to hurt or embarrass anyone. Therefore, I will struggle with that aspect of my writing from beginning to end. I am well aware that my book will create different levels of discomfort for many. *I genuinely grieve that unavoidable consequence.*

I grew up in a religious cult. It is difficult for me to use that word in print because it is inflammatory. I am aware that the word conjures up images of mass suicide, burning buildings, polygamy, and such. Those extremes are not part of my story, nor do I have any expectation that those dangers exist today for others within my former church. However, because of my love for the Gospel, I know I cannot be shy about confronting the deception and bondage that is so pervasive in all false religious systems, such as the one in which I grew up. Sometimes we must take a bold stand, accepting whatever personal consequences come as a result. Love and apathy cannot harmoniously coexist.

Those of us who have walked this path of deception are uniquely able to relate to one another. For some, trust becomes virtually impossible after confronting the deception of our past. Others do not want to set foot in another church because they are hurt and angry. We react to our wounds differently, but we are all keenly aware of how difficult it is for other Christians to understand or relate to our experiences. I want to help those who are hurting and lacking the emotional support they need to find healing. I want to say to those of you I have never met, "I understand your pain. I have been where you are."

While I cannot personally reach out to every hurting person, I can educate. In sharing my testimony, I hope to equip you with a deeper level of understanding. As children of God, we need genuine compassion for others, even those with whom we may not necessarily be able to relate or with whom we don't have shared experience. God mends broken hearts and spirits. More often than not, He chooses to do this through us. We are His instruments.

I would like to convey this message; do not ever lose sight of the reality that God wants to use *you*, whoever you are, to comfort and encourage others who cross your path. It is an important part of our calling to be salt and light. I believe that reading my deeply personal story may help you to recognize a ministry or friendship opportunity you might otherwise have missed.

Self-disclosure comes easily for me. God made me a communicator. However, not everyone is able to share as freely and openly as I do. Several friends have shared with me that they feel reluctant to reveal their experiences to other Christians. They fear being viewed as strange or gullible. All those held captive in spiritual prisons carry wounds. I have made tremendous progress in my healing process, but I still bear many scars. They are just not as visible as they once were.

For those of you who may one day cross paths with someone struggling to heal from spiritual abuse, I hope that reading my story will help you to better understand and minister to these wounded souls. For those who have left, or recognize the need to leave a similar environment, I hope I can convey hope and provide encouragement. You are not alone in your journey. Others, like me, have walked in your shoes. I want you to find comfort and emotional support in this book. More importantly, I want you to grasp the truth that Christ died for your redemption and freedom. You must simply put your faith in Him and take hold of that freedom. It is yours in Christ!

Growing up, I knew nothing of that freedom. I did not know what it meant to be in Christ. I only knew what it meant to be in church.

My sincere hope is that my story of deliverance might play even the smallest role in another soul coming to know the freedom and the hope found only through Christ and the true Gospel.

ℒ

"The richest testimonies come from people whom Christ has made whole and who still remember what it was like to be broken."

— *Beth Moore*

1

Growing Up

I was the first and only daughter born to parents in their early twenties. My brother Todd came along two years after me. My brother Chris did not make his appearance until I was eleven. Our parents raised the three of us in a strict, religious home. I thought they were *too* strict, especially on me. However, I did not have much to complain about other than that. Even when I occasionally entertained the common teenage notion that my parents hated me and wanted to ruin my life, I knew they loved me.

While I do believe my parents should have done some things differently, I give them credit for doing more right than wrong. My parents had our best interests at heart as we were growing up. When it came to the church they raised us in, I know they were convinced it was the best spiritual environment they could provide for us. I do not struggle with anger or resentment connected to the past or any of their choices.

My mother and I were different in temperament and coping styles. She was introverted, guarded, reserved and private. I am the polar opposite. I am an extrovert, an open book. I am unguarded and rarely think of my privacy. I am likely to be the first one to tell you anything you want to know about me. This is disconcerting to a guarded person. Because of my mom's discomfort with open, honest expression, I could have pleased her more had I been able to effectively internalize my emotion and be a better actor. My mom's way of coping was withdrawal and avoidance. When hurt, she would retreat to her room, close the door and cry privately. In the presence of others, she would appear to be fine. She did not like to talk about anything unpleasant if she could avoid it. She could pour her heart out to only a few. The unspoken message I received was that it was better to act as if everything was fine, whether it was or not. Unfortunately, that coping style has never worked for me. I do not put my feelings on display for the purpose of display, but I see no virtue in wearing a mask or pretending I have no problems. Because of our differences, my mom and I did not communicate well.

While my mother and I have different coping *styles*, we do have many similarities. I inherited from her a great deal of inner strength and the ability to endure difficult circumstances. I also inherited her grateful heart. I will never forget hearing her recite all of her blessings to me even as she faced an extremely premature death. She inspired me to be thankful.

My dad firmly planted me in the reality that life would not be fair. Therefore, fairness was never my expectation. I accepted life's inequities with relative ease because of this outlook. My dad emphasized that we should not run from our problems, nor go through life exchanging one set of problems for another. Whenever he had the opportunity, he reminded me that the best approach to life was to accept responsibility for my actions and take my consequences on the chin, facing them head on and getting them behind me as quickly as possible. I remember once telling him that he gave great advice, but I wondered if he could "walk the walk" were he in my shoes. He responded, "You don't have to be a great player to be a good coach."

Whether or not he practiced what he preached, his words of wisdom served me well in adulthood. However, I believe my ability to apply these principles came from the inner determination my mother passed down to me. I will never forget her expression and one raised eyebrow, as she told me, "I can psych myself into anything." I think the more accurate translation of her statement was that she possessed resilience and the ability to rise above challenges by focusing on her blessings. That is the part of my mother in me that I am the most thankful for today.

My mom passed away on June 14, 1987, just after her forty-ninth birthday. I was twenty-eight. During the seven months of her illness, we became close and spent a great deal of time together. That chapter is a major part of my story and one I will share in great detail. For now, I will simply say that I finally felt like my mother knew me and realized how much I had always loved her. For the first time, I enjoyed the bond and connection I had always longed for with her. That was and is a great comfort to me in her absence.

My basic personality has not changed since I was young. I have always been expressive, emotional, assertive, opinionated, and strong willed; yet vulnerable and sometimes needy when it comes to seeking acceptance and approval from others. Because of my assertiveness and strong personality, many never saw my insecurities and vulnerabilities. Yet they were always present and I made no effort to conceal them. I frequently see evidence of how much my need for validation and affirmation drives me. The spiritual environment I grew up in cultivated people pleasing in me from an early age.

I was born into a church that was like a family. We were a tight-knit group. It was unusual for anyone raised there to leave after being convinced we could not find God or truth in any other church. Our lives revolved around our congregation and our church friends. Loyalty and allegiance to our pastor was expected.

If you asked members of the community about us, most would have said that we kept to ourselves. In all my years there, I cannot remember a time when we engaged with other Christians or our community in any meaningful way. We were even encouraged *not* to have Bible studies in our homes without the pastor's presence. He held the view that people might begin to come up with their own interpretations of the Bible or merely get together to share grievances.

The pastor's approval was required for just about any type of social gathering from bridal showers and birthday parties to wedding anniversary celebrations. Sometimes the pastor would veto a certain guest or eliminate someone from your wedding party if that person had not been attending services regularly. I was forbidden to serve as an attendant in a close friend's wedding party because I had missed services.

We learned to deal with the control over our lives and choices. There are those today who outright deny this control ever existed, or contend that we did not *have* to submit to it. Although it is true that no one held a gun to our heads and we could have left, most of us would not have considered challenging the man of God or his authority. It was unacceptable.

At an early age, I was aware that we were different from other Christians. We went to church four times a week. Participation in any school activity that required us to miss a church service was not permissible. We were not to miss services for other activities. We did not miss a service unless we were physically ill or out of town. Attending all services indicated faithfulness and dedication, to God *and* our pastor. I remember the admonition that when you failed to show up every time the doors were open and the people of God were gathered "you cast a vote to close them." Our pastor took note of those who were not present in services.

As a young adult, I was questioned by my pastor because I missed a few services. "Are you not for me?" my pastor asked. I remember thinking *what a strange question.* I was struggling through a painful time. I was discouraged. He knew that. The services I missed or attended had nothing to do with being for or against *him*, except in his mind.

Our services were long. Evening services began at 7:30 and were supposed to end by 10:00 p.m. However, the pastor frequently spoke until 10:30 or later. Sometimes the younger children would go to sleep on the floor because they could not stay awake. Our pastor made light of any suggestion that children who had to get up the next morning for school should be home in bed, getting their rest. We understood that being in church was a greater necessity for us than sleep.

~

Although there was an unspoken order in which our services progressed, we placed great value on spontaneity. It was often said that we were "led by the Spirit, not by a program." Everyone who spoke in our services did so extemporaneously. The spontaneity of being "prompted by the Spirit" was more highly valued than preparation. Even at a young age, I assumed the view that a written or prepared sermon was something to be frowned upon. This was just one of the many biases I would have to overcome in the future.

Our worship was different as well. Although we sang occasional hymns, we often changed words to fit our specific doctrines. We also sang choruses written by those within the group to fit our theology. We sang about our thankfulness for being a part of this particular group. We sang about being different. We sang about perfection. We even sang songs about the ministers. I'm reminded of one song in particular when I consider the reverence and worship paid to the pastors: "Let's all lift the hands of God's ministry. *If it had not been for them*, look where you and I might be" (emphasis added). Here is another one that we sang that emphasized man over God: "Since I found *the Body of Christ*, life's worth living."

We sang the same choruses endlessly at times. Our way of thinking—and worshiping—was that we had to "bring in the Spirit" through our focus and effort. We had to attract God's attention. We often sang until we *felt* something. Our *feelings* were the barometer for whether or not *we* had touched God in our praise and worship.

When you grow up spending many hours in church services, your thoughts and emotions are cultivated through the things you sing and hear. In our church the emphasis was on feelings. We repeated choruses over and over until spiritual feelings were produced. This style of worship was more than a preference; it was almost addictive. We would depend on those feelings. An attachment to a familiar *feeling* prevents many from being able to worship in any other style or setting. Thinking that we were seeking a superior style of worship, we were completely unaware that we were elevating our feelings above what worship is intended to be, giving glory and Honor to God as opposed to providing a feeling for us. I was searching for that familiar feeling as well until God showed me that worship was about Him, not me.

During the forty-three years I spent there, the church handed down many of its own distinct doctrinal revelations. These were significant beliefs, which differed from mainstream Christianity. I will address more of those teachings in a subsequent chapter. We believed that God had revealed His "truths" to us as a group; "truths" He had not revealed to Christianity as a whole. As God's special people, we were called to restore the church to its former purity and ultimate latter day glory; we were not called to evangelize.

One "truth" in particular affected me deeply even as a child, the teaching on perfection. This belief set us apart from most, if not all, other Christians. We were taught that no believer had eternal life based on faith alone in Christ. Initial salvation had to result in the same sinless, perfect life that Jesus lived in order to qualify for heaven. Only the souls of those who attained sinless perfection in this life would go to be with the Lord immediately following death.

We were taught that perfection was possible in this life, and it had been accomplished by a small number throughout the centuries up to our day. This number represented the high calling, the bride of Christ. At one time, the ministry taught that there would only be 144,000 bride members from all of human history. Few would find this narrow path.

This theology begs the question of what happens to the souls of believers who are not perfect when they die. Short of sinless perfection, I was taught that we remain in the grave after death—spirit, soul, and body—awaiting a resurrection at the end of the thousand year reign of Christ. That resurrection is not a resurrection to eternal life, however. It was taught as an extended opportunity to reach perfection.

I was told that I could still spend eternity in the grave if I did not go on to attain perfection following this resurrection. The requirement was still the same. I wondered how I would be able to achieve perfection after a resurrection if I had not been able to do it in this life. On the other hand, we were taught that hell was simply the grave and eternal separation from God. Based on my indoctrination, I had no fear of hell. I simply believed this life was probably all I had. Believing these "truths" greatly inhibited my desire to share my faith with others as well. I did not consider it *good news* to inform someone they had to be perfect to go to heaven, and I wasn't concerned about anyone going to hell. I was convinced that all Christians would resurrect at the end of the thousand years—no matter what they believed— and find out *then* about the requirement of perfection.

You may be wondering how in the world I accepted these teachings as truth. It was all I knew of Christianity. I was taught these beliefs from a young child well into adulthood. I was told I had been given "precious truths," and they were to be treasured as "the pearl of great price." Anyone who left our group had lost their vision.

My parents reinforced these beliefs. My immediate family and extended family had deep roots in this group. Both of my parents were committed to the group's beliefs when they married. I did not have an opportunity to consider anything else. I was sheltered from all other influences. Even listening to contemporary Christian music was off limits most of my years there.

I believed what I was taught based on my faith in the people telling me. I had only one pastor my entire life. It was instilled in us to revere the original founder of our movement, who died before I was born. Our pastor faithfully carried the founder's message forward. This was the spiritual heritage handed down to me. I did not choose it for myself; I accepted it because I could not see anything outside those walls. I have never seen the movie, *"The Village,"* but I am told by friends that there are many parallels between the movie and our lives growing up in that group.

I lived a sheltered life. We were discouraged from attending college. Most of us considered college to be a worldly influence, one that would surely take a young person away from God and the church. Some believed it was a waste of time because Jesus would return within a matter of years, and there was not enough time for an education to pay off. I must admit, I was not interested in school at that age anyway. However, I do remember believing that if I went to college, I might displease God. Therefore, I never considered it an option.

I do not remember having any understanding of what other Christians believed. What I do remember hearing repeatedly was that other Christians did not think it mattered how they lived. They were looking for "an easy way." The basis for these statements was that other Christians believed salvation was *accomplished* for us on the cross and was a gift we could not earn. Other Christians did not believe in the requirement of perfection. "Christians aren't perfect, just forgiven."

The perfection message and pervasive legalism went hand in hand. Grace was little more than a word. It had no meaning for me. The list of rules we were expected to follow and enforce upon our children was long.

There were many restrictions as a child, especially for the girls. We were forbidden to wear pants to school, except on rare occasions. Shorts of any length were unacceptable. My dresses had to be longer than the girls I went to school with. Our elbows were supposed to be covered, although I do not remember my parents enforcing this particular rule. Short hair (above the shoulders) for girls was considered displeasing to God. Make-up was frowned upon. Pierced ears were considered worldly and unacceptable. At one time, the pastor even prohibited necklaces.

Men were expected to wear long sleeves year-round and in all settings. Men's hair was to be short. Any type of facial hair was strictly prohibited; a mustache or beard signified rebellion against the pastor. I remember a specific person who did wear a mustache as an adult. He was a little older than I was. On different occasions, when the pastor would ask that he shave it off, he would respond, "When you can show me that rule in the Bible, I'll shave it off." To which the pastor replied, "Would you do it *for me?*"

As a teenager, I remember feeling confused when maxi or midi skirts and boots were disapproved. All three were popular at the same time. I had been excited, thinking I could follow the rules, be modest in appearance, and finally wear something that did not make me stand out as strange. Our pastor, however, said these items of clothing were worldly trends and fashions that we were not to follow (even though they were modest). As far as the boot ban, I heard that the pastor personally disliked boots on women. The pastor's approval was a high priority for most of us.

Legalism and abuses of power are problems in many churches. However, legalism combined with the requirement of perfection caused me to focus entirely on my shortcomings, placing the weight of all my failures and inadequacies upon my own shoulders. I felt that weight even as a young child. The cross did not remove this weight from me because I was taught that only my "past sins" were forgiven at the cross. After that, perfection was the requirement. I clearly remember thinking *What were the "past sins" of a young child who had been raised in church?*

I remember feeling shortchanged by the cross because of this theology. I never stood in the promise of *all* my sin being covered by the blood of Jesus, the assurance of salvation, or the hope of heaven. What I was taught felt like a prison and a death sentence to me.

In about the fifth or sixth grade, I remember praying and asking God, "Why did I have to be born in this church and know the 'truth' that I will not go to heaven when I die? Why could I not have been a Christian who believed I was going to heaven, even if I was wrong? At least then I could have had hope and joy in this life."

During my mid-teens, my pastor began to talk more specifically about the year that could mark the beginning of the last days. I remember a great deal of teaching on the book of Revelation. When I was a teenager our pastor proposed the theory that "the last prophetic hour," according to his calculation, might begin in 1989. According to him, a prophetic hour was fifteen years. We were taught that Jesus would return in the middle of the last prophetic hour. Assuming my former pastor's calculation and teachings were correct; if the last hour began in 1989, Jesus would then return in 1996. I do not remember my pastor ever specifically saying 1996 was the year, but I do remember him citing the year 1989. It made an indelible impression on me, perhaps because it produced such fear and anxiety.

In all the years I spent in this environment, I remember greatly anticipating the Lord's return, but with a sense of dread not joy. I did not believe I would ever be perfect, and, therefore, He would not be coming for me. As a young adult, I wrote songs containing words I did not fully believe. I tried to believe I could be perfect. Occasionally, in spiritually high moments of intense emotion, I felt a ray of hope. I told myself I could do it. However, deep down, I was always profoundly aware of my inadequacy. The coming of Christ meant for me an abrupt end. I feared that time was so short I might not have the opportunity to raise a family. I married at the age of sixteen and became a mother at eighteen. I remember counting the years, wondering if my son would reach adulthood. I lived under many such clouds.

My son graduated from high school in 1996, obtained his BA in 2000 and his MA in 2004. He is happily married and the father of two little boys. These are just a few of the surprises God had for me.

2

Roots and Revelations

William Sowders died in 1952, seven years before I was born, but his name has always been familiar to me. He was the original founder of the Gospel Assembly Churches and the Gospel of the Kingdom Campground. My former pastor was ordained to the ministry by Sowders, and our church had its roots firmly in the Sowders movement.

I never knew William Sowders personally. I have only heard and read *about* him. Our unique revelations originated with Sowders. We were taught deep reverence for this uniquely called man of God for this dispensation. My pastor and his wife spoke of William Sowders with affection, admiration, and honor; declaring an allegiance to his teachings as "the original" they would never depart from.

As I was growing up, I heard my pastor tell the story of William Sowders' calling to the ministry many times. I have substantiated my memories through other witnesses and online research. The details of his testimony are recorded in a document called "*A Man Called Out.*"

In the early days of the twentieth century, there was a nationwide revival. This revival gave birth to the Pentecostal Movement. According to the accounts I have read, William Sowders was converted around 1912 and received the Pentecostal experience of Spirit baptism with the evidence of speaking in other tongues nine months following his conversion. Subsequent to this, he claimed an audible calling from God.

I heard about God speaking audibly to William Sowders repeatedly throughout my life. My former pastor knew William Sowders personally and seemed to enjoy retelling the story. He spoke of his dear Brother Sowders with fondness. I never doubted this man's experience or his calling because of the confidence I placed in my own pastor.

The story goes like this: One day, while working on his boat, Brother Sowders heard a voice thunder from heaven. The Lord said repeatedly, "I want you to do something." Finally, in desperation, Brother Sowders responded, "Lord, what is it you want me to do?" A voice like a clap of thunder said back to him, "I want you to preach MY GOSPEL!" He later recalled that the voice was so loud it about took the life out of his body and almost burst his eardrums, especially the words, "MY GOSPEL!" When he came to himself, he looked up. Light was all around him. Strength returned to his body, and he got up off the ground.

According to the story, William Sowders had never considered preaching prior to this experience. However, following the experience, he began to study God's Word diligently both day and night. He only had a fourth grade education and did not attend formal seminary. He claimed special knowledge, directly from God Himself, by way of experience. Those who followed him regarded this as superior to any type of formal education. The special knowledge he received, however, was a departure from the teachings of the Pentecostal movements of his day and entirely different from the teachings of historical Christianity. The "gospel" that was being *revealed* to him was a different gospel.

According to my former pastor, God restored to this man the original doctrines of the early church. According to my pastor, the "truths" Sowders received had been lost in the years of apostasy during the dark ages. Through William Sowders, however, God had chosen to reveal these lost "truths" for our day and for the beginning of the restoration of His true church.

Sowders claimed revelation after revelation. He eagerly shared these "truths" with other preachers, but to his dismay, many of his contemporaries did not share his enthusiasm. Some advised him that he was falling into heresy and pointed him back to more traditional Christian teachings. He was disappointed and heartbroken, but he remained determined to preach what God was revealing to him.

In hindsight, he believed that God had intentionally isolated him from these other men in order to prevent him from becoming a part of the newly formed denominations within the Pentecostal churches. He claimed that God showed him in a dream that those who were organizing were following the beast described in the book of Revelation. He believed that these men were being carried away into Babylon. To this day, the churches following Sowders' teachings call themselves an "affiliation" or "fellowship," as opposed to an official denomination. However, they were—and are—a very distinct group of churches.

In all the years I spent in this group, the terms "religious world," the "church world," and "Babylon" were used synonymously to describe Christians and churches outside of our affiliation. We exclusively claimed the title "The Body of Christ."

According to Sowders, one could not baptize in the name of Jesus if he himself belonged to and operated in a particular denomination. He explained that when Peter said to baptize in the name of Jesus in Acts 2:38, Peter was not addressing what men were to *say* over a candidate for baptism; instead, Sowders taught, Peter was telling them *how* to do it. In order to baptize correctly, one had to be doing it *in* the name of Jesus and not in the name of any organization.

The doctrine of perfection was another of William Sowders' revelations. Sowders taught that the bride of Christ would comprise literally 144,000 people. Based on his understanding of the book of Revelation, only the people who overcame all sin in this life would be "caught away" with Jesus when He returned. (We did not use the word rapture, since it was not found in the Bible.) They were "the overcomers" mentioned in Revelation who would rule and reign with Christ for a thousand years. The souls of perfected believers who were alive at Christ's return would never taste death, and the bodies of those who died "perfect" would come forth from the grave at Christ's return, or the first resurrection. Only the souls of perfect Christians did not die when their physical bodies died. Only *as a perfect overcomer*, would your soul leave your body following death immediately to be with the Lord. The imperfect believers' souls died along with the body. They would come forth in a second resurrection and inhabit the new earth *after* attaining perfection following their resurrection. However, the bride would rule and reign over all *those* for eternity. There was an eternal distinction made between those in the bride (the high calling) and those on the new earth— even though all had to attain perfection to receive eternal life.

William Sowders viewed the Godhead differently than other believers as well. He believed God led him to take the middle ground on the doctrine of the Godhead. Sowders contended that there were not three, not one, but two separate persons in the Godhead. God the Father was a spirit being and Jesus the Son was a heavenly creature, God's first creation. The Holy Spirit was not believed by Sowders to be a person or member of the Godhead, but rather a spirit or force emanating from God. Despite the Bible's consistent reference to the Holy Spirit as "He," we referred to the Holy Spirit as "it."

I remember being taught that the doctrine of the Trinity was not only false it was absurd. This understanding of the Godhead was dismissed as nonsensical, and it was belittled from the pulpit. Without any understanding of why other Christians believed in a triune God, I accepted that anyone who believed in the Trinity was lacking in common sense.

Sowders taught that the doctrine of a burning hell for the wicked was false. Hell was nothing more than the grave. He taught that "Babylon's" interpretation of Lucifer as a fallen angel was false, and that Satan was simply our carnal mind. (I remember being told from the pulpit to go look in the mirror and I would see the Devil. This was usually said by my former pastor with a hearty chuckle.) There was never a mutiny in heaven, according to Sowders, because the Bible tells us that God's will is done in heaven.

Therefore, my former pastor would pose the question to our congregation, "Why would God tell us that God's will was done in heaven if the heavenly angels had been capable of rebellion against Him?" That made sense to me at the time, and I did not question Brother Sowders' revelations.

We did not believe in any judgment for the wicked other than the grave. According to my understanding, Sowders taught that the soul died when the body died, and there was no resurrection for the ungodly. We also believed that life did not begin at conception; an unborn child did not have a soul until it took a breath on its own. This was based on the KJV of Genesis 2:7: "And the LORD God formed man of the dust of the ground, and breathed into his nostrils the breath of life; and man became a living soul." All Scriptures addressing us in our mother's wombs were apparently disregarded.

My pastor did not believe that abortion was wrong. I personally know of several married women in the church who went to him seeking counsel regarding an unplanned pregnancy. According to them, the pastor said they were not sinning if they terminated the life of their unborn child. I even heard he told one woman that terminating a pregnancy was no more significant than squishing a sperm. My heart breaks for these mothers. How sad it is to think that a pastor would not counsel a mother against terminating the life of her unborn child but would condemn her for wearing lipstick.

This same man who did not consider abortion to be wrong thought it was shameful to go to a theater and sinful to attend a professional sporting event. I remember struggling to understand his priorities and values and had some understanding when I looked into his past.

৯৹

My pastor was Cornelius Mears. His father, Reva Mears, was a contemporary of William Sowders. I always had the impression that the two of them were instrumental in the formation of "the Body," including the revealed "truths" we were taught. My understanding was confirmed when I read in William H. Wallender's book *Why the Holy Spirit Was Poured Out in 1900* the following:

> God gave him men to work close to him like Reva Mears. . . . In 1925, Bro. Sowders ordained Bro. Reva Mears to the ministry, and he went to Martinsville, Indiana to pastor (Bro. Cornelius Mears was 2 years old at the time). Bro. Mears had a dream. . . . He saw fishermen coming up along the shore of the riverbank pulling a rowboat. A net was stretched on the bank that was all torn up. Bro. Sowders got a big needle for himself, and got another one and handed it to Bro. Mears and said, 'Let's mend this net.' Bro. Mears began to work on the net with Bro. Sowders. He awoke.
>
> When he began to get active in the schools and in the meetings, different doctrines (that men cherished) would come up. Bro. Mears would get up and say, 'This is the way I see it.' Bro. Sowders took him aside and told him, 'Look here boy, don't tell them this is the way you see it, just tell them the way it is.'
>
> Bro. Reva Mears became one of the key men around Bro. Sowders and was a great help and blessing to him and the Body as a whole in restoring many truths. He could stand by the hour and unravel many types and shadows of the Old Testament.

Numerous accounts of William Sowders—his revelations, his life, and his ministry—corroborate my own memories. While exploring websites, I found this paragraph, entitled "Body of Christ Roots," in the closing remarks of an affiliated church's webpage:

> "Presently, *Brother Sowders'* work goes on. His teachings are the foundation stones for revealed truth in the **Body of Jesus Christ**. Brother Sowders instilled a spirit for finding the <u>absolute truth of the Word of God </u>which is now working in **The Body** *today*. Now, as the last remaining members are being made up to be in the Bride of Jesus Christ, Brother Sowders' work is being completed. We appreciate Brother Sowders' commitment to the service of our Lord and Savior. We thank God for the Founder of our work in the last days of the gentile dispensation." www.geocities.com/gacbloomington/roots_2.html.

Cornelius Mears is now deceased. I have many conflicting emotions when I reflect on his life and ministry. I no longer believe I received the truth from him, nor do I view him as a modern day apostle (a title some gave to him publicly, which I never heard him reject). On the other hand, I view him as someone who was himself a product of *his* environment and conditioning.

MEARS FAMILY TREE

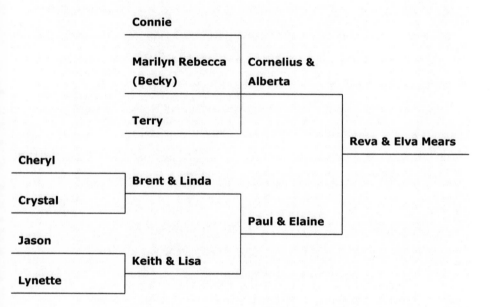

3

Following Moses

What you read, what you hear, what fills your mind shapes you into who you are. What you meditate on is what you become, which is why the Bible says to meditate on what is true and worthy and of good report. This is true of what you hear in church. The words and stories you hear *should* build you into Christ, but sometimes they build you into men. We are human beings and there is a human tendency to put more faith in people than we should. In 1 Samuel 8, the Israelites asked for a king to lead them as kings led other nations and went out before them to fight their battles.

God told Samuel that the people were rejecting *Him* by asking for a king, but then He granted their request. Sometimes God gives us what we ask for even when it is to our own detriment. When He gives us clear warnings and we do not heed them, we experience the consequences; we learn the hard way. These consequences aren't punishment for disobedience; rather, they are the evidence that He told us the truth. He wants only His best for us. We are deceived when we fail to believe and put our trust in Him, which we do all the time. But the wonder and beauty in the face of our bad choices is God's grace. Even when we make choices to our own detriment, we have the assurance that all things work together for the good of those who love Him and are called according to His purpose (Romans 8:28). I have learned to rest in this passage through every challenge I have faced. I know that God's redemptive purposes in my life will eventually prevail. Every wrong will one day be made right through the coming of Christ and His Kingdom. I can say in my heart what Joseph was able to say to his brothers in Genesis 50:20, "You intended to harm me, but God intended it for good to accomplish what is now being done, the saving of many lives" (NIV).

Although my life's circumstances have been different from Joseph's I can also look back over my life and see God's deliverance in miraculous ways. I see those many places where someone intended to harm me and God used it for my good. Through those experiences, my trust in God has grown. At the same time, my expectations of other people have diminished because my faith and confidence is no longer in *them*.

Learning to remove my faith in other people has been a difficult struggle. I was *taught* to put my faith in men. I was taught that if I obeyed my pastor, and his advice turned out to be wrong, God would not hold me accountable. God would bless me for honoring and obeying my pastor. I was taught to trust my pastor with my soul. I was taught that God would speak to my pastor, not directly to me. I was taught to put more faith in the *man* of God than in God. Our pastor stood between God and us. We could not trust God to speak directly to us. This produces the kind of soil that is fertile ground for the seeds of deception and manipulation. The soil of *my* heart was cultivated to accept whatever the man of God said. For many years, I did just that.

Cornelius Mears was born in Evansville, Indiana, in 1923. He did not become a pastor until 1947, when he was almost twenty-four. His family was living in California by then. Cornelius believed he was destined to become a preacher as William Sowders himself prophetically declared God's call on him when he was a baby. As the story goes William Sowders visited the Evansville home after Cornelius was born. Sowders held the newborn baby boy in his arms and declared, "This is a proper child; a little Moses." Cornelius was proud of this fact and told the story often. I first heard it as a child, and I was still hearing it in my forties. My former pastor told it about himself, and others told it about him as evidence of God's call on his life from birth. The fact that it was William Sowders who made this declaration added to the authenticity of the words spoken. Then, in 1947, William Sowders confirmed Cornelius's calling by ordaining him to the ministry at the graveside of his father and personally appointing him to carry on his father's ministry in California. This graveside story was also periodically retold.

(I always referred to my pastor as Brother Mears. Since leaving the church, I have tried to discard this term of respect and endearment, but it is unnatural. "Brother Mears" is who he was and who he will always be in my memory. Therefore, from this point on, I will refer to him as Brother Mears simply because it takes such a conscious effort on my part to refer to him any other way.)

ço

We had a beautiful church building in South San Gabriel, California. At that time, our church was called *San Gabriel Gospel Temple*. It was common for the Sowders churches to have "Gospel" as a part of their independent church names. Among other variations were "Gospel Tabernacle" and "Gospel Assembly."

I was a baby when the San Gabriel church was under construction. The members of the church provided most of the labor. The men worked on the church every Saturday, and the women would provide lunch. Sometimes I feel like I can remember those days, but I have simply heard stories and seen pictures. I was too young to remember. The building was completed in the early sixties. I remember being a flower girl in several weddings throughout the sixties. I have many clear memories of church services, Sunday school, and even funerals at that location. My paternal grandmother died in March of 1970, and her funeral was held in that church.

The first time I remember the topic of moving being proposed I was not even a teenager, around 1971. I was a young girl when Brother Mears called a business meeting one night to make a major announcement. I can still picture the scene in my mind. He explained to the congregation that he felt led to move the church to Evansville, Indiana. I do not remember details of this meeting as well as I do subsequent "moving meetings" because of my young age at that time. What I do remember is feeling scared. I did not want to move to Indiana. All I knew of the Midwest was the small town my grandparents lived in, Mt. Carmel, Illinois. I knew Mt. Carmel was close to Evansville. The Midwest felt like a different world compared to California. It was fine for a visit, but I could not fathom living there. From the little bit of Evansville I had seen, I did not understand the draw. After all, we were living in sunny California. Indiana would mean cold winters with snow and ice. However, I knew that if Brother Mears wanted us to move, we would move.

When the decision was made, I do not remember anyone challenging the decision. Everyone seemed willing to go. Then again, I was very young and would not have been aware of dissenting conversations. What stands out most in my memory is the family who was the first to sell their home and load up their furniture. They hit the road with everything they owned and were in transit, between California and Indiana, when Brother Mears changed his mind and called off the move. This family was literally pulled over by a highway patrolman and given a message from Cornelius Mears to return to California. I could not imagine what that must have felt like to them. I have tried to put myself in their shoes many times. That experience should have served as a red flag, but it did not. We were so compliant. Our trust was in a man.

The church ended up selling the building in San Gabriel before Brother Mears made a decision about where to go next. He often took a long time to make decisions. My parents sold our home in South San Gabriel, even though we were not sure where we were going yet.

Brother Mears was considering several different areas of the country. Among them were Oregon and Colorado. A number of families moved to each of these locations in the early seventies, hoping they were in the spot that would be chosen for a permanent relocation. Ultimately, all of these families were asked to return to California. This was difficult for some because they had grown to like those areas and would have preferred to stay. One friend recounted the phone conversation she and her husband had with Brother Mears when he instructed them to pack up and return. They informed him that they had prayed and did not feel that God wanted them to return to California from Oregon. Brother Mears responded, "Well, He did not tell me. So I am expecting you to come back." And they did.

While these families were in Oregon and Colorado, another group of us held down the fort in California in a rented facility. Nobody wanted to buy a home until Brother Mears bought church property because we were all encouraged to live close to the church. I remember Escondido as one option under consideration. Based on the expectation that we might be headed further south, our family rented an apartment in Anaheim, California, and I enrolled in junior high school. I attended the eighth and ninth grades at Brookhurst Junior High School in Anaheim.

Several other church people also lived in the same complex. I recall a handful of them right off the top of my head. We all tried to get apartments close to one another. My church friends and I often walked to school together. Our apartment complex was catty corner to the school. It was a short walk, but we had to cross two intersecting streets. I had to wear skirts and dresses to school. I preferred skirts because I could roll up the waistband and make my long skirts short. Of course, all of my friends knew I did this.

I would start rolling up my skirt as I crossed the first street. One morning, I looked up and saw my friend's dad sitting at the light watching me as I significantly shortened the length of my skirt. He was grinning. He and my dad were friends, and I remember my initial panic as I anticipated him telling on me. His daughters assured me he would not, and, to my relief, he never did. It must have been comical to him.

❧

While we lived in Anaheim we attended church services in a temporary building, located in El Monte, California. El Monte is about twenty-five miles from Anaheim. The church held four services a week. We made the long drive to church nearly every service. On Sundays, we did not go home between the afternoon and evening service. We went to dinner and then straight back to the church. A few people rented homes in the El Monte area, but most of us drove a long distance from somewhere else.

When Brother Mears finally did purchase land for a new church, it was not in Escondido, or Denver, or Portland, or any of the other possible locations. He chose Chino, California, a community about twenty-five miles east of El Monte. I remember being disappointed at first. My dad had fallen in love with a house in Anaheim Hills during the long wait for a decision. He even threatened to go ahead and buy it—which would have meant not moving to Chino with everyone else. I loved the house in Anaheim Hills, and part of me wanted to live there. Anaheim was urban, and I liked it a lot better than the dairy farms of Chino. Chino felt like "Hicksville" to me. It was so small and "country" compared to Orange County. On the other hand, it was hard to imagine being far away from my church friends.

My mom wanted to live near the church. She was never in favor of following through with the Anaheim Hills purchase. My parents did not normally have those kinds of conversations in the presence of their children, but I remember her persuading my father to look at several new homes in Chino as a family. I remember exploring the models, admiring the mirrored wardrobe doors, the openness of the stairway and even the room I wanted. My dad was reluctant, but he ended up going with the program. We bought the Chino house and let the other one go.

In 1974, we began to build the new church in Chino. It was completed in 1975. I was sixteen years old the night of the first service, and I remember thinking that now we could finally stop living in limbo; no more rumors about the church moving. We had done it. It was over. Finally, we could just live our lives. I was so wrong.

We did have several years without the threat of moving, but the rumors eventually started up again. Over the course of several years, Brother Mears took regular trips to various parts of the country. He loved to look at property. It was a hobby for him. For quite a while, he explored Tacoma and Seattle, Washington, as well as Nashville, Tennessee. I cannot describe what it was like to live constantly under the threat of an impending move; a move you do not have any desire to make. What was almost more disconcerting was the possibility of moving only to then be asked to move back, like what happened to the family in the seventies.

I cannot remember exactly how long we were in Chino before the talk of moving began. I really did not think it could ever happen again. After all, how many times can you ask people to do this and expect to receive their undivided cooperation? Apparently, more times than I would have thought because as it turned out, it could *and would* happen again.

4

A Peculiar People

An important part of our spiritual identity was found in three words from the King James Version of Titus 2:14: "*a peculiar people.*" Almost every time I heard my pastor define us by this verse, emphasizing the word *peculiar,* I remember thinking to myself, "We're peculiar alright." Our appearance was peculiar. Our beliefs were peculiar. Our ways were peculiar. If peculiar was intended to mean strange, we certainly did fit the bill.

Another verse I remember hearing quoted quite often was "Obey them that have the rule over you, and submit yourselves: for they watch for your souls, as they that must give account, that they may do it with joy, and not with grief: for that is unprofitable for you" (Hebrews 13:17 KJV). If someone questioned a rule that was not supported by Scripture, Brother Mears would quote Hebrews 13:17. He would say it at times with a smile and other times quite sternly: "I'll give you the Scripture right here; 'Obey them that have the rule over you, and submit yourselves: for they watch for your souls.'" He explained that *he* would give an account for us one day. Did we not want him to be able do it with joy? This was one way the pastor lulled us into submission. As long as we heeded our pastor's instruction, God would honor our obedience, *even if our pastor advised us to sin.* I distinctly remember my dad telling me that I could not go wrong by following Brother Mears' counsel because God would hold *him* responsible if he had been wrong, not me.

࿐

As I have mentioned, we followed strict dress codes and standards, best described as old school Pentecostal. In the early days of the Sowders movement, even the color red was forbidden as worldly. I have heard stories about the prohibition of open-toed shoes. Our churches embraced the standards (for women) of long dresses, long sleeves, no pants, no make-up (or very little), minimal jewelry, and long hair. Being set apart was analogous with being a peculiar people. We believed, as I assume a few other Holiness groups did, that we were observing these appearance guidelines in order to set ourselves apart.

When I say "we," I am referring to the mindset of the group as a whole. I was never convinced in my heart that *looking* so different from other people was the appropriate or ideal way to set ourselves apart. But I was in the minority when it came to such thinking. I remember debating the importance of our sleeves covering our elbows with Becky, the pastor's daughter. She argued that we were to be different and not resemble the world. I claimed that it was not that important, that worldliness and godliness were not an inch apart (the distance from above my elbow to just below my elbow).

A woman's hair was another sacred area that made us a peculiar people. A young woman in our fellowship who was visiting our church at the time overheard someone comment about needing a haircut. The visiting woman said, "Oh! Our pastor would *never* let us cut our hair! Our hair is our godliness." We *were* taught that it was displeasing to God for a woman to have short hair. I remember someone asking specifically what hair length our pastor considered "long enough." He indicated that hair reaching the shoulder blades or middle of the back qualified as long hair in his view. However, he pointed out that *his wife* did not cut her hair *at all;* her hair was well below her waist.

One time a distant cousin of mine from another congregation explained to me why she was taught married women should wear their hair up. (I never understood the point of growing your hair long so you could pile it up on top of your head.) She said her pastor had emphasized that long, flowing hair was sensual and sexy. He had quite effectively planted the idea in her mind that it was a special thing for only your husband to see you with your hair down after you were married.

While we were expected to wear our hair up after we were married, Brother Mears didn't strictly enforce it; he never told us that only our husbands should see us with our hair down, *thank goodness*. The only time I remember feeling actual pressure to wear my hair up was prior to our conventions, when people from other churches in our fellowship would be present. The majority of the women within the group wore their hair up on top of their heads, so before the convention our pastor's wife would always give us what I considered a "pep talk" on standards. I remember how she would instruct us on our appearance. I played in the band and the band was seated behind the piano on the platform. Anyone sitting on the platform was considered to be sitting in a prominent place and we were expected to be an example when it came to standards. Sitting on the platform and playing in the band was *a privilege*. We were taught that our appearance and conduct should reflect that.

On a few occasions, I remember people being "put out" of the band for disobedience of church rules, even minor infractions like sleeves above the elbow or a female cutting her hair. One time a teenager was told harshly to go sit in the congregation because her sleeves were too short. The band director, Sister Mears, threatened her, "Brother Mears is getting ready to put some people out of the band." Those remarks made me want out of the band in the worst way. The only thing that kept me there for years was that I did not want to disappoint Sister Mears by telling her I did not want to sit up there anymore. I knew she would not understand since she was the one who often made me feel discouraged. Her words to others frequently were harsh and disapproving. I felt bad for the younger girls when Sister Mears would embarrass and openly rebuke them. Sometimes it ruined the whole service for me.

When in California, I remember a specific statement that brought to my attention for the first time the superficiality of the rules on our appearance. I was confronted by the lack of integrity that was being cultivated in me. Sister Mears was lecturing the women in the band about our hair. She was explaining why we should be wearing our hair up for the meeting. She said, "You married women need to be wearing your hair up; *especially if it's too short!*" I remember thinking that she might as well have said that if we were not what we should be, we should at least be faking it. When I heard those words, I physically cringed. I thought to myself, what kind of message is she sending to these girls? If you are not doing the right thing, *pretend that you are?* That is so wrong! We were being encouraged to create a façade of obedience in order to please her and other people. If hair length was important to God, would God be fooled by pinning it up, making it appear longer than it was? Much earlier in my life, our pastor's daughter was imploring a few of us younger girls to wear less make-up and not cut our hair. She said, "How will my dad have any credibility with the other ministers if the women in his church don't do right?" I knew then that Sister Mears was more concerned about appearances than about actually doing right.

Not everyone grew their hair to the middle of their back or put their hair up, as was the "Body" custom. But shoulder length hair was definitely considered too short by our pastor. Brother Mears was, for the most part, a soft-spoken man. I would not describe him as easygoing, but he had a reputation for being gentle and meek because he did not raise his voice. Compared with other ministers in "the Body" he was considered lenient. He typically did not rail against us or dictate to the congregation in a harsh way, as some other ministers did, but he would lay down the law in certain situations; especially when he felt provoked.

On a Sunday afternoon in 1985 or 1986, Brother Mears lost patience and laid down the law to the women of the church. Brother Mears began to address the topic of hair length that Sunday. He started talking about how lenient he had been with us and how he felt we women had abused his leniency. He had *allowed us* to trim our hair, have a few layers in it and wear bangs, but we had responded to his leniency by pushing him and his boundaries further and further. He was not happy with us. He mentioned that there had been women in the church who had come to him and asked privately if they could trim their hair "this much" (very little). Then, after he gave his permission, they would go out and cut it shorter than he had consented to. Therefore, he issued a directive to all of us that day that we were not to cut or trim our hair at all until he said we could do so again. He was teaching us a lesson.

Someone asked if we could just trim our bangs. No scissors were permitted to touch our hair, period, final answer. Several women tried to talk to him after the service anyway and reported that he refused to have a conversation with them. By the time church was dismissed, I was very upset. It is hard to believe I felt obligated to obey his orders; it is downright embarrassing to admit I allowed someone to have this kind of control over my personal choices. But in order to convey how far God has brought me, I *must* reflect on where I have been.

I was in my mid-twenties and had never pierced my ears because wearing earrings would have meant enduring public disapproval and judgment from others. I could not wear pants without the fear of similar unwanted consequences. And I allowed someone to tell me, as a grown woman, that I could not trim my hair. I believe this single event portrays, in a nutshell, how we allowed our lives to be thoroughly governed by the authority of a man.

Our pastor was treating every woman in the church with utter contempt, yet we were all reluctant to challenge his authority. I realize how outlandish this sounds, but many of us left church that day feeling considerable stress. The only ones who felt no stress at all were those who already wore their hair extremely long by choice. Some women can wear that style well. I cannot. I did not believe I had to make myself look bad or plain in order to please

God. As a teenager, I had vowed to myself that I would never intentionally make myself dowdy and unattractive.

The collective mood was somber. As I headed for the car, I did not want to talk to anyone. I knew that tears would come quickly to my eyes if I tried to express my feelings. I did express my frustration in the car on the way home. I talked to a friend of mine on the phone shortly afterward. She was out of town and had not been present to hear the ruling handed down. She said, "Why did you tell me? I could have gone ahead with my hair appointment this week in ignorance, since I wasn't there." Since I had told her, she felt constrained by the ruling as well. I remember feeling bad that I had not thought that through and spared her.

For many months (it seemed like an eternity) Brother Mears would not lift the ban on cutting our hair. I *hated* the way I looked. I tried to obey my pastor. I did not take the situation lightly. On the other hand, I did not believe God gave my pastor the authority to issue these kinds of orders. It was clear to me that this new law had more to do with his personal indignation than anything else. His response was over the top—today I call it spiritually abusive. I do not have a clear memory of *exactly* how long we endured this restriction. However, I have pictures of myself from my dad's fiftieth birthday party in March of '86. Whenever I see my hair in those pictures, I am reminded of that "trial."

The pressure I felt had little to do with believing *God* expected my compliance; it was primarily about peer pressure. What would other people think if I did not obey? Would I be labeled as rebellious, disobedient, and disrespectful toward Brother Mears?

One Saturday evening, I attended a barbeque along with other church friends. The hair subject came up, as it always did. By this time, I had trimmed my bangs in absolute desperation. My hair looked terrible and I was spending way too much time trying to make it look decent. So I gave in to temptation and trimmed my bangs ever so slightly. I did not cut as much as I wanted to. At this gathering, I openly admitted I had done this. I did not take pride in my disobedience or display an attitude of defiance. I simply made an honest confession.

The next day in church, Brother Mears received a written question from someone in the congregation while he was speaking. Written questions were common. An usher would deliver notes to our pastor while he was at the pulpit. He would open them and pause. Sometimes he would read and answer them on the spot. Other times, he would set them aside. On this occasion, he read the question aloud.

"Brother Mears, what do you think about someone who has gone ahead and cut their hair after you said not to, and then goes around *telling people* that they did?" The wording implied that the very least someone like this should do was *hide their disobedience* from others. It seemed pointed and judgmental, and I believed it was directed at me. I will never forget his response: "If you are someone who has done this, how can you call yourself my friend?" I could not believe he was responding to a note clearly *targeting* another person in the church. Yet he not only read it, he declared to the whole church that I must not be his friend simply because I had dared to trim my bangs. I was angry and hurt. How could he say to the whole church that I was not his friend? I had tried so hard to follow this rule. I wondered how in the world he could question my *friendship* based on such a minor thing.

My pastor had drawn a line in the sand, which served ultimately to divide people, including close friends. The women who had strictly complied and not touched their hair with scissors felt betrayed by those of us who were weak. Some felt that if they had to look bad, everyone else should look bad. Other women became self-righteous in their obedience (such as the woman who wrote the note to the pastor). I heard that one woman visually inspected another woman's hair with a disapproving look; as if to suggest it did not *look* like it had grown much. Some of the women who had always worn their hair long made condescending remarks suggesting they did not understand what was so hard about not cutting your hair. Everyone was in some way comparing herself with someone else and exhibiting a form of pettiness. I felt like our pastor had accomplished little more than bringing out the worst in everyone.

Ultimately, the ban was lifted. It seemed like a year but may have been only six months, before Brother Mears once again gave us permission to trim our hair, along with the opportunity to show him the proper respect by not taking advantage of his goodness this time. I was relieved that the ordeal was finally behind us, but it left me with fresh wounds. I am sure Brother Mears hoped we had learned a valuable lesson about modesty and obedience through this experience. I did in fact learn valuable lessons, but not the ones he intended.

Our pastor had wronged the women in our church. He made this situation all about him, ensuring that the women appeared holy. He sowed seeds of dissension and contempt between friends. Cutting our hair was either wrong or it was *not* wrong. Something did not become wrong when he called it wrong, then permissible when he decided to exercise leniency. God did not appoint him to set an ambiguous bar for us; raising or lowering it as he saw fit and throwing out Hebrews 13:17 as a shield of protection. God's Word is not something to be manipulated.

I have never forgotten the way this experience affected me. Brother Mears wasn't typically this controlling; that's why the event had such impact on me. I viewed the ordeal as a complete abuse of power, yet I never considered leaving. I suspect you wonder why anyone would remain in this type of environment willingly. There are a number of reasons. First, controlling groups claim special knowledge of God that cannot be found outside the group. Where would I go? The best illustration of this mindset I can think of is a song we sang. It goes like this:

> If from God's order, now I should wander; where could I go,
> Lord, where could I go? I know that Babylon no longer wants me;

for too many things about her now I know. I guess the world would take me back, but I'm glad I'm off that track; for I've had enough of sin, and I love this peace within. So keep me, Jesus, here in God's order; for if I should leave you now where could I go?

There is not one shred of worship in that song. It is an indoctrinating message. We sang such choruses repeatedly. People would have emotional experiences while singing songs like this. It gets in your head; especially if you have experienced nothing else from the day you were born. Allegiance to the group is cultivated in a multitude of ways, including songs accepted as a part of worship. *Brainwashed* seems to me to be such a harsh word. I prefer to describe my thinking as *conditioned* instead; but I know that is simply a euphemism.

Second, my family and my dearest friends were also deeply rooted and invested in this group. Leaving the church meant leaving them. How could I do that? I was certainly not independent enough to do it while I was young. I was taught my whole life that there was nowhere else I could go to find God, the truth of His Word, or people who genuinely loved me the way those people loved me. I believed that if I ever left and tried to serve God anywhere else, I would never be happy or satisfied. I would always look back with longing. Leaving the church was synonymous with leaving God in my heart and mind. Therefore, it was not something I ever seriously contemplated.

5

God's Will

We were in Chino from 1975 to 1992. I saw a lot and grew up a lot during those years. I had many painful events from the ages of sixteen to thirty-three. However, one agonizing experience eclipses all the others, the process of losing my mother. Not only was my mother's terminal illness painful emotionally, it also was the impetus for a major turning point in my spiritual journey. Though I remained in the Christian Gospel Temple (CGT) for years, God used this experience to begin chipping away at my absolute confidence in a man. This period of my life is a multi-faceted and deeply personal part of my story.

Our first relational view of God is defined by our relationship with our parents. For some, their concept of God is shaped primarily by their relationship with their earthly father. I transferred the one common thread in both relationships—father *and* mother—to my relationship with God.

Although I loved her so much, my mom and I were never close. I wanted to please her, but I don't think I ever did. I never felt like I was the daughter she would have chosen off the showroom floor. She could not understand or relate to me. I was a frustration. At times, I felt that she did not try to understand me, but I am sure she did. We were just very different in temperament and personality. She was an introvert and I am an extrovert. We each had obstacles and limitations to overcome in understanding one another. I do not fault her for our lack of closeness. We simply did not have enough time to overcome our obstacles.

Words, however innocently spoken, can have a significant impact. Parents' words can really wound their children even without them having any idea that is what they are doing. I am sure I have done it to my own son, though I have made a conscious effort not to. I remember something my mom said to me in jest. I am sure she had no idea she was wounding me. In my mind's eye, I can see her face and almost hear her laughter as I recall her telling me that if she ever got old and sick, I would probably just put her in her room and close the door. I was in my early twenties at the time. To this day, I do not know what I ever did to make her think I was so uncaring or shallow. I remember thinking, *What kind of a person does she think I am? Why can she not see how much I love her and long for her approval?* However, I never said those things. I just laughed and said, "I would not."

My dad has always been a jokester. I learned to be a good sport about this and take his teasing in stride at an early age. However, my laughter sometimes concealed pain and embarrassment. My dad made up a joke about what would happen when *he* got old. In it he described the differences among his three children. When he becomes old and sick his oldest son will take him in and care for him; his daughter will put him in the best nursing home money can buy; and his youngest son will talk to him about the advantages of euthanasia. In the joke he said essentially the same thing my mom had said: Shari would not want to be bothered.

As far as I was concerned, he might as well have said that only his oldest son really loved him. My youngest brother and I have laughed about this as adults. I did not get the slightest impression that Chris felt wounded, but I remember again wondering why both of my parents seemed to believe I would not want to be bothered with them in illness or old age. What was it about me that conveyed such indifference and selfishness? What they saw of me externally was so different from what was in my heart.

When I was in my early teens and feeling independent, my mom would often get frustrated with me. My brother, Todd, was far more compliant than I was. In Mom's words, I was "mouthy." During one heated conversation, she blurted out in exasperation, "You're such a disappointment! Why can't you be more like Todd?" I was thirteen at the time. To say this crushed me would be a monumental understatement. She must have seen the wounded look in my eyes because she apologized immediately and said she had not meant what she said; I was not a disappointment to her. I could tell she genuinely regretted the remark, and I had no problem forgiving her. However, the words could not be unspoken. They became a lasting part of my self-image. Those words helped foster my identity as a "disappointing child." I spent much of my life, well into adulthood, believing that perhaps I was defective and not easy to love. In hindsight, I am certain my parents always loved me. In some ways, I think they were even proud of me. However, I never felt like either of them knew me—or wanted to, for that matter. I believed my own parents had a difficult time loving me. This belief created within me a deep insecurity and fear that I was an unlovable person.

Words of affirmation are my primary love language, or the way that I get rejuvenated and energized. I needed to be affirmed by my family. However, my needs were a seemingly unwanted imposition on every significant person in my life. Even my first marriage was unhealthy and turbulent from beginning to end. I never felt unconditionally loved by anyone, including God.

My early church environment also contributed greatly to my belief that I was defective and a disappointment to others because I would be chastised for trimming my hair or wearing lipstick. I knew that God loved me, but I feared even He was continually disappointed in me. I felt like I could never be good enough to please anyone. And the truth is I could not. I just had not learned that pleasing people was not God's desire for me.

ప

My mom had battled colon problems for quite a while. After a diagnosis of diverticulitis in 1985, she had failed to pursue follow-up care. My mother was not one to "baby" herself. She told me that no matter how bad she felt, she would never lie down on the couch until after all her housework was done. My mother virtually never stopped cleaning. If she noticed the smallest fingerprint on a window or appliance, she had a paper towel and Windex in her hand the next moment.

Mental, physical, and emotional *toughness* have never been traits I identified with. I am not like my mother in this way. I do not care if my house is imperfect or my bed is unmade. I am not task-driven; I am relationship driven. If I had been in the kind of pain and discomfort my mother was in, my focus would not have been on my spotless house or work ethic. I am much more likely to baby myself by resting and seeing a doctor. I do not pride myself on silent suffering either. I am a communicator. Therefore, I did not grasp how sick my mother was while she kept up the façade of being fine.

By autumn of 1986, Mom was definitely getting worse. She had dropped ten pounds quickly and effortlessly. This was not a good sign in combination with her other symptoms, but they were ten pounds she had wanted to shed. Therefore, she did not seem alarmed. I remember her striking a pose with a wide grin as she announced her weight loss. If she was worried about her health, she hid it well.

Our church was hosting a convention that November for the churches in our fellowship. Anyone wanting to come was welcome, and many came from various parts of the country. There were similar gatherings in different states and there was always a schedule of upcoming meetings. When we hosted one of these events, we had longer services than usual and served hot meals to our guests in the dining room. Much work and preparation went into these gatherings.

My mom had been in charge of the dining room for years. She would oversee everything pertaining to the seating and serving of our guests. All of us who served were under her direction and supervision. She took this role very seriously, as she did all of her responsibilities. As the November meeting approached, my mother was in a lot of pain. She needed to go back to the doctor. However, since she felt needed in the dining room, she did not attend to her own health. She promised she would make an appointment with the doctor as soon as the meeting ended. She was very sick that week, but she worked as hard as ever. Several people expressed their concern to me, noticing that she did not look well at all. One of her best friends mentioned the word cancer. I knew something was wrong with my mom, but I thought this friend was being an alarmist.

My mom willed herself to get through that meeting and do her duty for the church. After it was over, she woke up in such excruciating pain that she could not walk from her bed to her adjoining bathroom. She went to see the doctor that day. He immediately admitted her to the hospital and began to prepare her for surgery. He told her that he was sure she had a tumor and he was almost certain it was malignant. He told us that he would remove the tumor and as much of her colon as necessary. Depending upon how much of the colon was involved, he might have to perform a temporary colostomy. However, he assured us that once she had recovered and regained her strength, it would be completely reversible. I remember hoping, as she went into surgery, that she would not have to endure the colostomy and thinking of that as the worst-case scenario.

I do not remember how many hours the surgery lasted, but I will never forget the surgeon giving us the news we had never anticipated. The tumor was malignant, but the reason she had been in such excruciating pain was that it had ruptured. Unfortunately, once that occurred, the cancer had spread throughout her abdominal cavity and all of her major organs were now affected, including her liver. Her cancer was terminal and no treatment would help her. It would only weaken her without any possibility of curing her. The doctor was sending her home to die. He gave her about a year. I was devastated.

My mom was forty-eight years old. She was strong and healthy apart from the cancer. The peritonitis—inflammation caused by the invasion of bacteria—alone should have been fatal. However, the surgeon said that her strong constitution kept her from dying on the table. He did not think it was a good idea to tell her she was terminal for a few days, until she had recovered from the surgery. I remember going in to see her before she came out from under the sedation. I stared at the tubes and the paleness of her face in utter disbelief. *How could this possibly be happening to her? Why had she chosen not to take care of herself? If she had seen the doctor prior to the meeting, she would not be in this grave condition.* Her belief that the meeting could not go on without her would result in all future meetings *having* to go on without her. It did not make sense. I think I could have felt angry with her in that moment had I not felt such overwhelming compassion and sadness.

A few days later, very early on Thanksgiving morning, the surgeon went in to see my mother and told her she was not going to get well. He did not tell any of the family that he was going to do this. None of us had a chance to be there because it was so early in the morning. We had not told her the truth because we were following the surgeon's advice about letting her recover first. My mom received this news completely alone and in the coldest possible manner. I was so mad at that doctor. The nurses told us later that my mom showed no visible reaction and no emotion. She just stopped talking to any of them. That did not surprise me. My mother was very private about her emotions.

Before her release from the hospital, Brother Mears came to see her. I will never forget what he said when he arrived. He openly declared that he had been praying for my mom that day and God told him that Sister Jane was not going to die; it was *God's will* for her to be healed. I heard him say it with my own ears. I had never heard my pastor make such a claim. We had prayed for people's healings on many occasions. I knew of people who had received miraculous healings and others who had not, but I had never heard Brother Mears say that God *told him* someone was definitely going to be healed. At that time I trusted Brother Mears so much that hearing those words from him was as good as hearing them from God directly. A feeling of hope and euphoria swept over me. My mother was not going to die. Brother Mears said so! And Brother Mears would never say such a thing if God had not spoken to him. *Great was my faith in Brother Mears.*

༄

My mom came home from the hospital and went into the Christmas season very weak. I remember not wanting to leave her side. Not only did I want to spend every moment I could with her, I wanted to *prove* to her how much I loved her and wouldn't abandon her in her dying days. I would prove to her that she had been wrong about me. I was determined to be the best and most devoted daughter any mother could have. If she did get well, as Brother Mears had assured us she would, our relationship would hopefully be changed forever.

For the next seven months, I spent almost the whole day, every day, taking care of my mom. I cooked for her, hoping she would be able to eat. I cooked meals for my dad. I did the laundry and the grocery shopping. I tried to keep things running as smoothly as possible for both of them. I wanted to be the perfect daughter for my dad almost as much as for my mom. Everything in my own life became a low priority. I could not enjoy a single ordinary pleasure while my mom was going through this. I remember how meaningless the trivialities of life became during this time. Things I normally would have taken pride or satisfaction in, like my son's perfect report card, did not touch me at all. Nothing seemed important. Everything seemed hollow and pointless. My own life stopped as I invested all my emotions in my mother.

My grandma lived in Illinois, but she made several trips back and forth while my mom, her only daughter, was ill. She knew my mom wanted and needed her, and her visits were long. Nevertheless, she would occasionally have to go home and take care of my grandpa too. As hard as it was for me to witness what my mother was going through, I could only imagine what it must have been like for my grandmother to watch this happen to her child. My mom and my grandma had always been close. I knew my grandma was suffering as much, if not more, than I was.

Christmas was hard. As great as the physical pain was for my mom, I could see the surpassing emotional pain in her countenance, and I believed that was the hardest part. She had three grandsons. My son, Danny, was eight years old. He adored his Grandma Jane. Jared and Justin, Todd's two boys, were adorable little tots. She loved all of them so much, and they loved her. I watched her look at them and I assumed she was thinking *I might not be here next Christmas. I might not see them grow up.* After everyone finished opening their gifts, my mom quietly and somberly left the room to go back to the family room sofa. I remember feeling such deep anguish as I watched her that morning.

We all tried to stay focused on Brother Mears' words. It was important for us to have the faith that God would heal her. Our faith was an important element in the healing equation. At first, I really believed she would be healed.

It was difficult for me to leave my mom for any reason during this time. There was no place else I wanted to be. However, sometimes she would insist that I go to church. I just wanted to do whatever she asked. On one occasion she asked if I would be willing to go on to church that night, allowing a family friend to stay. I said, "Mom, I will do anything you ask. Whatever you want me to do, that's what I'll do." My mom looked at me and said three words, "You're so sweet." To this day, those are the most precious words my mother ever spoke to me. I felt like she could finally see how much I loved her. That meant everything to me *and it still does.* I had longed to hear affirming words like that from my mother. I never stopped needing my mother's approval, no matter how old I was.

All the services I attended during that time were hard for me. I didn't attend every service but many of them revolved around my mom and her anticipated healing. Individual testimonies were a large part of our services. Anyone was at liberty to stand to his or her feet and speak extemporaneously. My mother was loved and admired. Losing her was simply unacceptable. No one was willing to give her up. Therefore, everyone took hold of Brother Mears' words and clung to the belief that she would not die. There were many testimonies about how God was going to heal her. Not only were there testimonies, there were endless personal experiences. People had dreams and received words from the Lord almost daily. One person approached me at church and told me that God had told her, "Jane is healed." Then she proceeded to tell me the exact time it was—she had looked at a clock—as God was speaking those words to her heart. It was as if her noticing the time added emphasis or authenticity to her experience. I remember her grabbing hold of my arms and firmly telling me, "Your mother is healed! Just believe it!"

Those emotional experiences came from loving hearts. No one ever intended to do harm. In spite of the good intentions and sincere hearts, however, I do not believe today that God told *anyone* my mother would be healed. God is not a liar.

Another person, someone I have always dearly loved, approached me after a church service and strongly admonished me about the importance of our family having the same strong faith that the rest of the church had. She was trying to convey to me how important *my* faith was in the healing process, but unknowingly and unintentionally, she was inflicting guilt and a perception of responsibility because I was seeing my mother every day. Mom was not getting better. I had to face that reality. People in the church did not.

One of the most challenging aspects of this experience was trying to reconcile all of these experiences with the reality of my mother's decline. Not one person ever had an experience that revealed my mother would not get well. My mom began to blame herself and believe that perhaps she did not have enough faith. Maybe it was *her* fault or lack of faith. I will never forget watching her force herself to eat an egg and a piece of toast. She had no desire for food and it was such a struggle to get food down. She was trying with everything in her to have faith that she was getting well.

One day she said to me, "I feel like I must be doing something wrong because God is telling everyone it is His will to heal me, yet I am not getting better. I'm trying so hard to believe. I'm doing everything I can. I'm even making myself eat. I don't know what else to do." She felt like she was letting other people down. It tore me apart to see her carry this weight of responsibility when I knew she believed God could heal her. Then I would go to church and hear someone say, "I heard a report that Jane is so much better, she is eating bacon and eggs for breakfast!" I thought to myself, *Yeah, she is gagging down an egg, but that is a complete distortion of the truth.* I felt like I was surrounded by a wall of denial and I could not fathom how these reports were getting started in the first place. I wanted to know what God was *really* saying. I did not want to be caught up in a wave of emotion. If I was going to lose my mom, I wanted to be able to prepare myself (an impossibility I was later to learn). At a certain point, people's experiences were no longer comforting me or giving me hope. They were confusing me and adding another layer of anxiety to my distress. We observed a couple of weeklong, corporate fasts and at the end of each, it seemed like Mom was always worse instead of better. I longed for Mom to have peace. I wanted peace. I wondered if God was trying to tell us something that we were simply unwilling to hear.

Because of this experience, to this very day I am sensitive to comments concerning my faith as it relates to physical healing. Although I don't doubt God's ability to heal, I know that He does not always choose to do so. Death is a part of life. We live in a fallen world. If it is not God's will for someone to be miraculously healed, then it doesn't matter how strong his or her faith.

Faith is not the power of positive thinking; it is believing in God and trusting that His will is always best even when you cannot understand why. He has not promised to shield me from all pain and loss. He has not promised that *others* will never leave me. He has promised that *He* will never leave me. My acceptance of God's will, even when it is not in line with my own, is not an indication of a lack of faith. Whenever that is suggested, I feel my scars.

While struggling desperately to find the peace I needed, I prayed one morning that God would give me a Bible verse. I remember sitting on the edge of my bed and telling Him, "You've given all these verses, experiences, and dreams to others. Would you please give me something to strengthen and encourage me? I know you *can* heal my mother. But I am not as convinced as everyone else that you're telling us you're going to." I then opened my Bible randomly, expecting to find words specifically pertinent to this situation.

I had my eyes closed as I opened my Bible. When I opened my eyes, I stared in amazement. I had turned to the blank pages between the Old and New Testaments. I could not have done this if I had tried. My heart sank. "Oh God," I pleaded, "*please* give me something." On the next attempt, I opened to a passage that had no application whatsoever. I did not try a third time. God was not telling me what He seemed to be telling everyone else. Therefore, I could believe one of two things: either God was not responsible for all of those experiences or He did not care enough to give me the same encouragement. But I knew God cared.

6

Sin in the Camp

The emotional stress was building as my mother's illness progressed. There were better days, but they were few and far between at that point. She had one week that was so good, she wanted to make an appointment for tests. She hoped to receive confirmation of healing, and then go ahead with the reversal of her colostomy. In anticipation of this, the church fasted and prayed. Mom again got worse. She was never strong enough to follow through with the tests, and it became obvious, even without the tests, that she still had cancer. Mom was beginning to deteriorate more rapidly now. She recognized the physical signs that her body had begun the process of shutting down. I remember her showing me the swelling in her legs, telling me she had seen that and knew what it meant. My mom helped care for my dad's mother when she was dying of cancer many years earlier.

One day my mom told me I was the only one who would let her talk about dying. She said, "Nobody will let me talk about it. Everyone insists I am not going to die." My mom never desired open communication like I had. If a conversation became difficult, she would shut down and withdraw, which made me feel as though I had hurt her by trying to talk to her. It was ironic that my desire for open, honest communication was a comfort to her during that time, and she was drawn to me by the very trait that had previously caused her such discomfort. Nobody could have been more surprised by that than me.

There are things you can avoid by not having conversations. Death is not one of those. Everyone else could choose not to accept the possibility of her death until after it was written in stone. She, however, did not have that luxury. There were things she needed to say. And I am so thankful for those conversations. She said only one thing that troubled me. She said, "If I don't get well, please don't lose your faith in Brother Mears." I remember feeling a little stunned. I was expecting her to encourage me not to lose my faith in God.

ஒ

One of my biggest fears during those long months had to do with the upcoming camp meeting in Shepherdsville, Kentucky, in June 1987. The camp meeting was an important part of our roots. In 1935, William Sowders purchased 350 acres of land near Shepherdsville, Kentucky. He called it the Gospel of the Kingdom Campground, his "City of God." He held annual meetings at that site and the meetings still take place there twice a year. Being on the West Coast, we had not always participated in these meetings. However, in the late seventies or early eighties we began taking a large group of people to the campground in an effort to help heal some of the past divisions in the original movement. Brother Mears felt a calling to see the Body restored.

Brother Mears was a candidate for trustee of the campground that year, which made it an especially important meeting for him personally. Our church owned a bus and it was typically full of people who wanted to travel from California to Kentucky for this gathering. The bus would be filled to capacity if Brother Mears asked people to go. I was afraid that my mom was going to die after half the church, including several of my closest friends, went away. Brother Mears' daughter, Becky, told me not to worry about it; that it probably would not happen that way.

As the camp meeting loomed closer, people were preparing to leave. Sister Mears got up in church one night and said that if we could just get Jane to the campground, God would heal her. I knew we could not get Jane to Kentucky. Moreover, I did not believe there was something so special about the campground that God would require my mother to be carried there on her deathbed. None of this made sense to me. Some people said that if everyone went to the meeting, proving to God that His work came first in our church, He would then be obligated to heal my mom. There were a lot of such theories about how to get God to follow through and heal her. I remember thinking to myself, *But I thought He already* said *it was* His will. *Why do we have to do something to inspire Him or obligate Him to keep His word?* I believe other people in the church were confused too. One person said in a testimony that my mom had not been healed because the women were not obeying the church standards on dress, hair, and make-up. It was sad to witness the frustration and conflicting emotions. In spite of it all I never doubted that all these people were well intentioned.

By this point my mom was on morphine, and Hospice was making regular visits, helping us to prepare for what was ahead since we planned on caring for her at home right up to the end. Mom was to receive two teaspoons of morphine per dose. My grandma told me she would use a tablespoon, because she had always substituted a tablespoon for two teaspoons in her recipes. She was completely unaware that there were *three* teaspoons in a tablespoon. Needless to say, we had a long, serious discussion of the proper dosage because my grandma was going to sleep with my mom and give her a dose in the middle of the night. I remember telling my grandma very emphatically, "Grandma, please listen. We are not baking a cake. This medicine is very potent and can kill her if she gets too much. If you give her a tablespoon, you will overdose her. Please, for me, measure it out in two teaspoons even if you think I'm wrong." She said, "Okay, okay, I will. I promise." Well, I did not realize that my grandma was still confused. I must have spent so much time emphasizing that one tablespoon was actually three teaspoons instead of two, that she forgot the dosage was supposed to be only two teaspoons. She did measure out the dose in teaspoons like I asked, but she measured out *three teaspoons*, thinking the dose was a tablespoon and doing exactly what I had tried to avoid.

The following day was one of the worst for me. My mom was in a zombie-like condition from the morphine. She had been lucid the day before, but now she was barely cognizant. That day there was a huge argument downstairs between my husband and my father. It was a misunderstanding that was blown way out of proportion.

As her condition worsened, my mom asked my grandmother and me to promise that one of us would always stay with her. We tried to honor her request without making it obvious or hurting anyone's feelings. I did not tell anyone in my immediate family that Mom had asked this of me at the time. I was just thankful my mom wanted me near her. I was unaware that my devotion to my mother was being misinterpreted. My brother accused me of not allowing others to help care for Mom and wanting to be in control. To make matters worse, instead of coming to me directly, Todd made the accusations to my father behind my back. My father responded by convicting me of wrong motives and actions without even asking me if this was true. He didn't give me the benefit of the doubt. Instead, he spoke cruel and crushing words about me to my husband in the presence of my young son (who would never forget). It was painful and humiliating. I felt like I was losing both my parents. However, I remember hearing an inner voice in the midst of the chaos, telling me, "This is not about you."

Somehow, I was able to get through those terrible moments. I have long ago forgiven the harsh words. I know that stress sometimes brings out the worst in people, but I cannot seem to stop the memories from occasionally returning when I reflect on my mother's death; those painful experiences remain intertwined. Through it all I learned that pain and loss do not always bring family members closer together; including families who go to church four times a week and profess perfection as their spiritual goal. We are alike in one way; we are all flawed human beings.

My mom overheard the argument that took place downstairs that day. My grandma told me later that Mom looked up at her and asked, "What will happen to this family after I'm gone?"

My mom had to go to the hospital that day. The doctor said she needed to be admitted so he could get her medication regulated. However, she would not come home this time. She slipped into a coma and passed away. For weeks I thought that I would be relieved when this moment came because my mother would no longer be suffering. However, as I looked at my mom's lifeless body and her expressionless face, I felt no relief at all. I just wanted her back. I had a very strong urge to crawl into the bed beside her and just hold onto her. Everything I felt that night was unanticipated. I no longer believe there is any such thing as preparing yourself to lose someone you love.

Just as I feared, half the church was gone when Mom died. My closest friend had chosen not to go because she knew I might need her, and I did. I will never forget her being with me in that hospital room. I do not know what I would have done without her.

When the news of Mom's death reached the campground, several of my close friends immediately returned to California to be with us for the funeral. It meant so much to me. My pastor, however, did not come. My dad refused to ask him to return for the service. When he spoke to Brother Mears on the phone my dad gave him the impression that his presence was not necessary. Brother Mears sent his brother, Paul, to preach my mother's funeral. I was deeply hurt that my pastor and his wife stayed at the campground instead of coming home for my mother's funeral. I felt that my mom deserved better after all the sacrifices she made for the church. Based on later comments my dad made, I believe it mattered as much to him as it did to me for Brother

Mears to be at Mom's funeral. My dad just wanted Brother Mears to come *without having to be asked.*

We buried my mom. When the bus returned, nobody mentioned my mother. It was as if everyone pretended that nothing had happened, which was like adding salt to my wound. The people around me went from one form of denial to another.

It took three years, but in 1990 I finally told Brother Mears he had hurt me. He said that he would have come if my dad had asked him to. He never realized he had let me down or hurt me. He asked me to forgive him and I did. I was glad to be able to let it go. And then I asked him a question I had not planned to: "Do you still believe God told you that He was going to heal Mom? If He did, why do *you* think He didn't heal her?"

He explained to me that he still believed it *had* been God's will for my mother to live. However, there was a "situation" in the church during the time of my mother's illness. He had not known about it then, but had learned of it since. He reminded me of the story of Achan in Joshua 7 in which the Israelites were defeated because of the sin of Achan. He proceeded to tell me that he believed my mother was not healed, despite it being God's will, because of "sin in the camp." It was abundantly clear that he was satisfied with the answer. I remember feeling sorry for him as he told me this. His explanation made no sense whatsoever. My first thought was that if an absence of sin were the prerequisite for a physical healing, there would never have been *any* healings. There has always been sin in the camp. Because I had not received the truth of the Gospel, nor did I understand what was accomplished on the cross, it did not occur to me to ask the most obvious question: *"So the blood of Jesus was not sufficient to cover those sins? My mother's blood was required?"* I know that is not true. God did not take my mother's life as a penalty for the sins of another. Anyone who believes the Gospel could never accept that explanation, let alone offer it. I now know that the blood of Jesus was and is sufficient to cover all sin.

Sadly, that question did not dawn on me during our conversation. I was still operating within the context of my former beliefs. What I do vividly remember is the overwhelming sense of awareness that I was not supposed to challenge Brother Mears but was just supposed to hear his explanation and take note.

It was a very long time until I understood why I was supposed to pay special attention to Brother Mears' explanation. I now see that my journey out of that place began with that conversation. It was the first time I absolutely knew beyond any doubt that I had been given false information about God.

I remained a part of the church for another thirteen years. During that time, my eyes were opened, but it was not an instantaneous deliverance; it was a process. I don't know why God kept me in that environment for so many years, but I don't doubt for one minute that He had a plan for my life and those years were a part of His plan.

The story of Joseph comes to my mind whenever I share my testimony. Not because I am some great leader, but because I serve the same God Joseph served. I have been in despair. I have been lonely. I have experienced the sting of false accusation and rejection. My life could have gone in a multitude of directions had it not been for the mercy and deliverance of God. What could have harmed me or even destroyed me, God used for my good. God's redemptive purposes have always prevailed in my life. Many times I have had unanswered questions. I live with unanswered questions today. But I believe those unanswered questions are simply a part of trusting Him.

I'm sure that Joseph did not completely understand why he spent so many years in prison before God liberated him either. None of us can fully understand God's timing. We don't need to have all the answers to our questions. We simply need to trust God through each experience we do not understand.

7

Priorities

My dad waited nearly three years to start dating. But then he dated someone for only three months and eloped. I couldn't believe that he married so quickly. I had reservations about the union because I was protective of my dad. I was very concerned that he *could* be making a mistake. However, he was a grown man; it was his life to live, so I intentionally refrained from expressing my concerns to him.

My dad's new wife, Elvie, tried to befriend me. I wanted to develop a genuine relationship with her. However, I wanted the relationship to evolve naturally on its own and at an unhurried pace. I was nudged by my brother, Todd, to rush the process and to show affection to Elvie for the benefit of the church people, in order to encourage *their* acceptance of my dad's bride to be. The reasoning behind the request was if everyone at church believed the whole family was happy about the marriage, they would be quicker to accept it. In such a tight-knit community, peer acceptance makes life much easier.

Pretending to have affection I didn't yet feel seemed wrong to me. Todd knew I had reservations. In a phone conversation with Todd, I tried to explain my aversion to doing anything that wasn't honest and from my heart. I also pointed out that my dad had never put on a show of approval for me. That didn't go over well with certain members of my family, my dad in particular. He was angry with me. He gave my mother's most precious possessions to others, conspicuously overlooking me. It felt like punishment. My dad believed I had wronged him. I felt that he had wronged me. And we just stopped speaking, but we continued to go to church together several times a week.

My dad was active in the church. He was respected by most of the people, a pillar in the church. He was an excellent speaker. He knew a lot about history and was gifted at tying his thoughts together. When he spoke, he did not wander all over the place. He had a point and a train of thought, which he followed from beginning to end. Then he sat down. As a result of the freedom to speak extemporaneously, many people who spoke in our services rambled on and on incessantly, sometimes never having a train of thought at all.

One night my dad addressed the congregation. He always spoke from the pulpit because he played in the band and was already on the platform. He talked about how we were to treat people in a loving and God-honoring way. What he said was in direct contrast to how he was treating me. He was using himself as a living example, elaborating on how he treated others. And it was simply not true. It was all I could do to sit still in my seat. I wanted to get up and walk out in a very public way. Here I was, his own daughter, sitting right in his direct field of vision as he offered sage advice on showing love to others; yet he was simultaneously ignoring and punishing me for what he perceived as my disloyalty to him.

In another service, around this same time, I had gone to the altar and cried. A few weeks later I was told that while I was there, my pastor's wife pleaded with my dad to go to me and patch things up. The conversation was overheard by some and observed visibly by others. He emphatically shook his head no. He said I had wronged his wife, and he wasn't about to have a relationship with me until I apologized to her. But I didn't know what I had done wrong. And I didn't know he was expecting me to go to either of them. I just felt shut out and rejected. Not long after this, I went to counsel with my pastor. I sat in his living room and cried. I wanted him to understand why I could not always make myself go to church, why it was so painful. My husband didn't go to church with me. My father laughed and joked with other family members before and after service but ignored me; I felt like an outcast. On top of all that, we were singing songs about perfection and overcoming sin in practically every service. To me, we were making a mockery of Christianity (myself included) and the whole thing felt like an absolute sham.

After this long session, pouring my heart out to my pastor, I really believed he understood my struggle. I thought he cared. He showed compassion in his demeanor. I remember daring to hope he might even try to talk to my dad; helping him to see that this was not the behavior of someone who was trying to live for God or overcome sin. I desperately wanted to be reconciled with my dad. But I did not know how to accomplish that. And, in all honesty, it wasn't just my dad who had withdrawn. I had withdrawn from him as well.

Trying to rise above my own heartache, I went to church the night following my counseling session with Brother Mears. When I saw him, he looked at me with disdain and said, "You need to take that lipstick off." Not even a hello; just harsh disapproval and criticism. I was shocked at the apparent indifference toward my broken heart. It was as if we had never had that heart-wrenching conversation just one day earlier. I cannot put into words the disappointment and disillusionment I felt as I confronted the reality of my lipstick violation ranking above and beyond my heart in this man's priorities.

I never had a desire to counsel with him again.

My dad and I finally spoke a year and a half later. The situation had become unbearable for me spiritually. I knew I had to do something, especially since it seemed that nobody else would. I had prayed about it and felt convicted that God wanted me to be the one to choose humility. So one afternoon I dropped by unannounced. When my dad and his wife came to the door I said, "I just wanted to come by and ask you to forgive me for hurting you and for everything I have done to contribute to our estrangement." I had rehearsed it in my mind on the way over. I was intentional in not saying "*if* I have done anything to hurt you." I was not going to make excuses. I was not going to justify my feelings or actions. I was not going to attempt to be understood. I was simply going to choose humility and repentance. And then I planned to leave. I had no expectation that my gesture would be received in a favorable way, but I would know I had pleased God. And that was more important to me than anything.

To my joy, and surprise, my dad and his wife responded in love and kindness. They looked shocked when they opened the door. I know I caught them completely off guard. But they invited me in and asked that I also forgive them. We proceeded to talk for several hours. I asked my dad to tell me everything I had done that I might need to repent for specifically. I found out my dad had *assumed* many things, which had never actually happened. For instance, he believed I had contacted specific friends of his and repeated uncomplimentary things about his wife. He was surprised when I told him that I had never even thought of doing such a thing. Another violation involved a story that had been told to him. It was completely fabricated and I was stunned when I heard the false allegation.

In all that time, my dad had mistakenly believed certain things about me, but never came to me for clarification. I was never totally in favor of my dad's marriage, but I did not try to sabotage it either. And I was never unkind to his wife. Many of the perceived wrongs were imagined, but I understand from experience what it's like to get things stuck in your mind. Forgiveness was not hard for me. I was so thankful our relationship had been restored. Our interaction improved for a long while after that. I also established a loving relationship with my stepmother. We got along fine from that point forward.

My dad was not the perfect father, and I was not the perfect daughter. *I have not always chosen humility.* We have certainly not enjoyed an ideal relationship, just as many other fathers and daughters have not. I am not always able to understand him and I often feel misunderstood myself. However, I genuinely and dearly love my dad. Neither one of us would have been able to reconcile if it weren't for God's grace. It was His love and power that healed my heart and brought us together.

Our circumstances were not ideal for healing and transformation to occur. However, suffering can be an important part of the process. It's all about our priorities. God rewards those who diligently seek Him. I made an effort to set my own feelings aside and do what I believed would be pleasing to Him, and He graciously blessed my effort. But regardless of the outcome, the process was fruitful to me. Through the experience, I learned valuable life lessons. I learned to trust God with every aspect of my life. I learned not to judge His actions by how well they mirror my own desires. I learned to trust Him when I understand and when I do not, when I am overflowing with joy and when I am struggling to cope with life's challenges. I still have fears and anxieties that at times threaten to overwhelm me. Life does not always unfold according to my plan. These disappointments are like waves threatening my faith. Just as Peter temporarily began to sink when he took his eyes off of Jesus, I am pulled under the waves whenever I focus on my losses instead of my Redeemer.

After growing up in an extremely legalistic and performance-oriented environment, I have to remind myself continually that it is not through my flawless performance that I please God. It is the faith as of a little child that pleases Him. Child*ish* faith demands its own way. It is immature and selfish. But child*like* faith is humble, willingly dependent, and completely trusting in the *love* of the Father. We often attribute to God the traits of our earthly fathers. Therefore it is harder to embrace the unconditional love of our heavenly Father when our earthly fathers are manipulative and their love is conditional. In my case, I was taught also to view my pastor as a spiritual father, but this spiritual father did not seem to care much about my heart or my pain. He was difficult to please. It is no wonder that I viewed God as continually disappointed in me or as someone I could never please. But now I know that it is not anything I do but the work He has done in me that brings Him glory. It is my deep conviction that if God allows me to suffer, there is a greater purpose in my suffering. I am convinced that He is a just and merciful God because of His work on the cross where He was both the judge and the justifier, where He paid our penalty for sin.

8

Go Ye Into White House

On January 31, 1993, an article was published on the front page of the *Tennessean*. The article, "Go ye into White House," was about our church's move from California to Tennessee. It explained that the members of the Christian Gospel Temple were "tired of bad air, crime, recession—so tired that they boarded a bus and hit the road in search of a new life." Although I realized we simply wanted the community to accept us, these comments struck a nerve in me. It was true that the move was sold to us in a variety of ways, but bad air, crime, and recession were not the reasons we moved to Tennessee, and everyone knew it. I wondered why we didn't seem to have a problem with shading the truth to make ourselves look better to the community, and I shared in that lack of integrity.

The article described the congregation as "unusually close-knit," believing "there's nothing strange about their mass exodus," and citing that "their church—not their jobs or social contacts—is the center of their emotional and social life." My grandfather, Robert Morrell, articulated our priorities well when he stated, "If people say they really are serving God, then church should be one of the most important things in their lives." The piece went on to explain that "the move was set in motion last fall, when church members, based in Chino, California, in suburban Los Angeles, voted to approve Mears' proposal to relocate here." It said that for two years we had taken trips through Washington State, Indiana, parts of the Midwest, southern and Middle Tennessee, finally finding what *we* were looking for in Goodlettsville, Tennessee. However, I took exception to the assertion that *we* found what we were looking for in Goodlettsville. I believe a more accurate statement was that Brother Mears found what *he* was looking for. We were all waiting for *him* to make the decision. And everyone knew there had not been an actual *vote*. There were a few private whispers and raised eyebrows concerning this whitewashed version of the truth. Yet, to my knowledge, nobody openly objected to the article; including me.

⚭

I was present in the meeting where Brother Mears proposed the move. I remember it well. I was in real estate sales at the time. In an attempt to be a comedian, I decided to wear my Century 21 gold blazer to the meeting and hand out business cards. After all, people would need to list their houses and I was an agent. It was so blatant; it would bring a few laughs. One of my coping mechanisms has always been to find the humor in stressful situations.

The reasons offered for moving to the Nashville area were predominantly spiritual in nature. Brother Mears believed God had told him to leave California and establish a church in the Nashville area. He informed us that God wanted him to take the whole church with him; this was not something God was calling him to do on his own. He then predicted that God's judgment was soon to come upon the state of California, and he pointed out the need for us to leave before that took place. My perception was that Brother Mears was attempting to inspire our compliance through words of warning. But the real reason for our move was that Brother Mears believed he would be used by God to bring the different factions of the Sowders movement back into a restored fellowship. For many years, he longed for what he described as "the healing of the Body." Not only did Brother Mears talk about it, his wife and others testified about the role he would play in the latter day restoration of the church. Sister Mears had cited Zechariah 4 in several church services, becoming emotionally stirred as she quoted Zechariah 4:9: "The hands of Zerubbabel have laid the foundation of this house; his hands shall also finish it; and thou shalt know that the LORD of hosts hath sent me unto you" (KJV). She inferred that William Sowders' original revelation of the Body was the foundation, and Brother Mears would be the one to oversee his vision of restoration to completion. She reminded us repeatedly that Brother Mears was one of the few men who had not compromised on any of William Sowders' original teachings. I remember her pointing to Brother Mears and speaking in tongues as she quoted Zechariah 4:9, clearly referring to Brother Mears as our spiritual or modern day Zerubbabel.

Several people asked questions about the proposed move. At some point in the meeting, one brave person dared to pose the most obvious, but yet unspoken question: "Brother Mears, what if we pray, and we don't feel like God is telling us to move with you?" Silence permeated the room. I was shocked that anyone had the guts to *suggest* such a thing publicly. Brother Mears' response was equally astonishing to me. I certainly didn't expect him to validate this possibility or make room for personal answers from God. However, his answer was beyond anything I could have anticipated. His face looked down into the crowd sternly and disapprovingly as he replied without hesitation, "Then I would fear for your soul."

Was he truly suggesting we could not be saved apart from his personal ministry? Was he claiming God would never speak to us except through him? I remember thinking *that is quite possibly the most arrogant statement I have ever heard in my life.* He was promoting the concept that our souls would be in jeopardy if we believed God was telling us something that contradicted *him.*

So why did I move? It certainly wasn't so that I could be saved by Brother Mears. The one compelling factor motivating me to move to Tennessee was the people. They were much more than members of my church; they were family to me. Many of them had known me since birth, and I had known those younger than me from their births. I would be miserable without them. I wanted to move simply because I wanted to hang onto these precious relationships.

Following his lengthy presentation for moving, Brother Mears asked how many would be willing to go with him to Tennessee. He did not ask us to *vote* on whether or not we *wanted* to move (out of the smog or away from the crime). He asked for a public demonstration of support for doing the will of God. The implied options were to do the will of God, remain in fellowship with the Body, and move to Tennessee or rebel against Brother Mears, stay in California, and lose your soul. In no way, shape or form could this honestly be construed as an opportunity to vote on a proposition.

The majority of the congregation was sold out to the belief that God expected us to support this man's ministry in any way we were asked. We were not a bunch of stupid people being led around by the nose. We were a group of people deeply committed to our belief that we were uniquely called to restore New Testament truths, worship, and unity to the church in the last days. God was going to have a church without spot, wrinkle, or blemish and through the revelations of Brother William Sowders, we were *called* to be that restored church.

Once the move was official, the experiences and testimonies began in chorus. Every dream anyone had now seemed to be focused on spiritual confirmation of the move being God's will for our congregation. It was reminiscent of the way people spiritualized every little thing while my mom was dying. This time around, I viewed much of what I heard as propaganda. I grew weary of the frequent comparisons to Moses and the children of Israel. Brother Mears seemed to take on several spiritual identities; a modern day apostle, a Zerubbabel, *and* a Moses. It seemed contrived to me.

My husband was very upset about being backed into this corner. I pressed him to move. I believed it was in our son's best interest to remain in the church and be close to his friends. This created a great deal of tension and stress in our home and we even fought about it. I didn't want to move, but I did not want to become embittered by this experience. I took the hype with a grain of salt, but I still made a conscious effort to view everything in the best possible light. I questioned many things, but I was trying to have a good attitude. The simple reality was that the people in my life were far more important to me than the state in which I lived. Although I seriously doubted that God was literally requiring this move, enough reverence for Brother Mears had been cultivated in me throughout my life that I also doubted my own thoughts and convictions. What if Brother Mears was right and I was wrong? The safest position seemed to be a willingness to go along with the program.

The reason why I was taken aback by the portrayal of this monumental turning point in our lives as simply *a vote*, is because a vote signifies freedom. Yes, we were asked to stand up in support of the move if we were *willing* to go. Brother Mears may have even used words that *implied* having a choice, like asking everyone "in favor" of following him to stand. But when there is coercion and pressure in the form of spiritual manipulation, there is no freedom of choice. Subtle mind control and implied messages are often the most oppressive. In all the years I spent there, I refused to believe that I was controlled; yet I *never* knew genuine freedom.

‿

The article's description of us was accurate in other ways. The writer noted that the church was known for "a modest dress code—women in longish skirts and hair pulled up." There were even some brief comments from a former neighbor of the church in California: "For being Christian people, I didn't think they were friendly because they stayed in their own group so much." Some in the church dismissed this woman as having an unfair bias against us, but her words were true.

On the night of our last service in the church on Pipeline Avenue there was a sudden power outage during the service. All the lights went out unexpectedly and we found ourselves shuffling around in the dark. I will never forget hearing people all around me saying that this was a sign of the lights going out on California (spiritually). It was not said in jest. It was as if some people literally believed we were the only true Christians God had in the whole state and, once we left, He could shut off the lights. I remember noting how arrogant we were.

ॐ

Around the fall of 1992, many families were well on their way to Tennessee. Some of us, however, had not sold our homes yet and still needed a place to meet while attempting to tie up loose ends. Brother Mears rented a temporary location in which to hold services but expected everyone to relocate. We had to regularly check in with him and provide updates on our individual moving progress. During the transition, Brother Mears divided his time between the two locations.

In Tennessee, services were held in what we believed would also be a temporary location on Dickerson Road in Nashville. We purchased a church that was previously owned by Hank Snow. Many famous Nashville artists had supposedly been to the church. The stories may have been folklore, but they added their own level of excitement and novelty to the adventure.

We had been promised a new building following the move and the people were excited about it. Brother Mears had already purchased a home on 14.6 acres near White House. That was to be our building site as well. We were therefore encouraged to buy homes in the White House area in order to be close to the church once it was finished, which is what the majority of the people did. Nobody imagined that we would continue to meet on Dickerson Road for the next ten years. Brother Mears never did build a church in White House.

In December of 1992, my husband, son, and I went to Nashville to look at property. During that trip, we bought a home in the unincorporated area of Hendersonville, just outside White House. After going home to California to pack up everything I owned, I returned to Tennessee to oversee some cosmetic improvements to the new house, and check out schools for my teenage son. The moving truck arrived on March 13, 1993, in the middle of a snowstorm. If I were tempted to spiritualize, I might view that storm as prophetic symbolism.

◦◦

While I never believed my soul was in danger if I did not move, other fears had been instilled in me. If anyone dared express dissatisfaction, it was considered the equivalent of the Israelites murmuring against Moses. I was afraid to say or do anything that could have been interpreted by others as rebellion or "a bad spirit." I was taught that to submit to the authority of the man of God was to submit to God. This type of submission can easily be exploited.

My paternal grandmother, Nanny, died of cancer when she was forty-nine. I was ten years old when Brother Mears came to pray for Nanny's healing toward the end of her life. She told him that God had reminded her of a time when she had spoken against Brother Mears, and because of that she knew she was not going to get well. My mom told me that story during my mid-twenties to caution me about listening to the complaints of specific friends and sympathizing with them. I didn't fully believe that Nanny died of cancer because she had said something negative about Brother Mears, but seeds of fear *were* planted in my heart nevertheless.

There was another story that instilled fear in me as a child. One time an angry man came to the church with the intent to harm Brother Mears. The man confronted him in a fit of rage and drew back his fist to strike Brother Mears. However, just as he did, there was an earthquake. When Brother Mears would get to that part of the story, he would chuckle about how God sent an earthquake that day to deal with someone who had ill will toward him. How could one escape the moral of *that* story? The message was clear. You don't mess with the man of God.

We were programmed to submit to Brother Mears' wishes even if it meant moving to Tennessee. At the time I never believed I was motivated by fear. It was only after I left the church that I realized my deep-rooted, underlying fears. David refused to harm Saul because Saul was God's anointed. Likewise, we believed it displeased God for us to say anything negative about Brother Mears as a man of God (even if he had done wrong). The ministers of this group were held in such high esteem that they were accountable to no one. This philosophy of elitism encouraged abuses of power that left many atrocities in its wake. Still many remain unwaveringly conditioned by the fear of "speaking against" or even questioning these "men of God." Although it is a warped and twisted view of the Scriptures, people with honest hearts are often vulnerable to manipulation after many years of this conditioning.

9

Garden of Gethsemane

As I was unpacking boxes, the Waco standoff was playing out on television. I was glued to the coverage and could not believe the timing. The community of White House had reservations about a church group of approximately three hundred people moving into their neighborhoods. Who could blame them? The word *cult* had been used. And I wondered what the people in this small town were thinking as they watched the news coverage.

Shortly after arriving in Tennessee I decided to avoid identifying myself with the church unless absolutely necessary. Living just outside the city of White House made that a little easier. I did all of my shopping in the nearby towns of Goodlettsville and Hendersonville. My son went to school in Madison. I avoided White House as much as possible. I didn't deny coming here with the church if I was specifically asked, but when people wanted to know what had brought me to Tennessee, I simply told them that I had friends and family here and wanted to live near them.

Coming from California, I was not accustomed to being asked so many questions by strangers. Living in a large metropolitan area, there is a bit more anonymity. Californians moved around more. Many of the Tennesseans I met had never lived anywhere else. They were wary of "outsiders."

It was a difficult transition for many in the church. There were a few who actually bettered themselves financially in the move, but the majority struggled. A number of men couldn't find satisfactory employment in Tennessee, so they continued to work in California, making frequent trips back and forth to be with their families as often as possible. Although the majority of the congregation had moved, those who had not managed to leave California right away seemed less and less motivated to relocate. Many people were having a hard time adjusting. One of the leading proponents of moving out of California developed an almost immediate dislike for Tennessee. He started talking about wanting to go back to California right away, even though he had been dissatisfied with California, too. There were others who failed to find the life they thought was awaiting them in the new surroundings, but not everyone was in a position financially to move back.

No one in my family had ever *wanted* to move anywhere. In fact, my dad remained in California for several years after the rest of the family had relocated before joining us in Tennessee. I will never forget two things he said to me after the move was announced. First, he told me that anyone who imagined their life would be so much better as a result of moving didn't realize that you take your problems with you wherever you go. There is no magic place where your problems all become solved. The second thing he offered was a humorous analogy between our move and the children of Israel. In Numbers 11 the Israelites complained about not having any meat to eat, so God gave them enough meat to eat until it came out their nostrils. My dad said that Brother Mears had been determined to move our church somewhere for so many years perhaps God just relented and gave him a big, choking dose of what he'd asked for. He said it as a joke. My dad turned everything into a joke. However, I thought this analogy fit better than any others I had heard.

There were a number of things that did not go as planned after we got to Tennessee. That some people had a hard time finding suitable work was one reason. Other reasons weren't disclosed to the congregation, but because of reasons known only to Brother Mears he kept postponing and procrastinating the promised church building. Rumors began to circulate that he was vacillating because he was convinced that God wanted us to go *back* to California. He stated publicly that although he still believed we were supposed to move to Tennessee in the first place; we were not supposed to stay.

In 1996 Brother Mears held a meeting to promote his plan to move the church back to California. I remember someone asking about the possibility that, in hindsight, maybe God had not wanted us to move after all. It was in response to this question that he informed us of his belief that it was God's will for us to move and also God's will to move back. That made absolutely no sense to me and was extremely distressing. The Bible says that God is not the author of confusion (1 Cor. 14:33). I could only interpret his comments one way. He realized he had made a mistake, but he could not admit that. It reminded me of my mother's death, when he had said that he still believed God had told him it was His will to heal my mother, but then things happened that prevented God's will from coming to fruition. He had not been wrong; God had changed His mind. And like the situation with my mother, Brother Mears asserted that we, the church, were to blame for the move not working out according to God's plan. He talked about how many of us had not "lived right" after moving to Tennessee. Apparently, God had not blessed us because of this. I could not believe my ears.

His remarks sparked anger, which is rare for me. Hadn't we all uprooted our lives and moved across the country to show our support for this man, and now he was blaming *us* for everything falling apart? It was highly offensive and a ridiculous conclusion in my mind. Looking back, I see the absence of the redemptive work of the cross in every scenario (including his explanation for my mother's death). What is very sad to me today is the realization that I did not even make that connection then.

In hindsight, I believe Brother Mears must have felt that people would lose confidence in him if he admitted he was capable of making a mistake. But for me it was the opposite. I viewed this as a serious lack of humility. He needed to be able to own up to his own humanity and imperfection in order to have credibility with me. His explanations for God's will not being fulfilled in our lives always felt like a cop out and greatly diminished my confidence in him. However, God ultimately used my broken and disillusioned heart to draw me to the cross and the Gospel of Jesus Christ.

The congregation did not respond favorably to the suggestion of another move. Moving again would have been impossible for many because a lot of people were living on the proceeds from the sale of their previous homes until they found suitable employment. Many had lost their savings and were barely getting by. Property was far more expensive in California than Tennessee and real estate values had only increased since we'd moved away. Many families would not have been able to afford a home equivalent to what they'd left behind. It was a depressing thought.

I remember leaving the meeting that night and saying to friends, "I'm done with this. I'm not moving again. This is absurd." I think more than a few others had the same reaction because the idea eventually fizzled. It wasn't that Brother Mears dropped all attempts to make this happen. He continued to travel to California and look at property for some time. There was a second meeting in '98 where he again attempted to convince everyone to move. But it never materialized and the idea was eventually dropped.

In a letter written by Brother Mears' son, (sent to the majority of the congregation years later), Terry explained it this way:

"[A]fter my father moved the church here, he learned of things that shocked him and totally reversed his thinking towards the purpose in being here. Although he never shared them with the assembly, he knew in his heart it was not God's will to stay here. He was so beside himself, he didn't know what to do. . . . He felt the only thing he could do was return us to California, (and he was willing to spend everything the church had accumulated to help each person return). Obviously, Bro. Mears being the man of logic he was, felt that returning was the lesser of the two evils . . . but virtually no one supported him. Bro. Mears often referred to this as his, *'Garden of Gethsemane Experience.'* The dilemma he faced was this: Either he reveals all the troubling information or faces the humiliation that he had made a bad decision. (Of course, he being a man of character chose to bare [*sic*] the burden himself, and not reveal the awful things that now haunted him). . . . He often asked me to pray with him and help him to pull everyone together to return to California, but because I believed it would tear the church apart, I stood against him."

Brother Mears' own son states that *his father moved the church here* and *his thinking* was reversed by the shocking things *he learned* after coming here. Based on this account, it is obvious that the pastor had made all the decisions for the congregation up to this point. If Brother Mears agonized as Jesus did in the Garden of Gethsemane, as ridiculous a notion as that is, over our move, then it is clear that he felt responsible for the decision in the first place. And if our reasons for moving to Tennessee were, as the newspaper article had reported, to get away from crime and poor air quality, what kind of shocking revelations reversed Brother Mears' thinking regarding our "purpose" for being here? What *was* our thwarted purpose?

I cannot answer these questions with certainty as Brother Mears never revealed them to us, although it seems like he did tell his son. My speculation is that when Brother Mears found out about T. M. Jolly's molestation charges, he knew that healing would not and should not occur. I am convinced that the biggest factor in our moving to this area had to do with Brother Mears' longing to see the original Sowders movement reunited with him being the leader. When this didn't happen according to his plan, I believe that is why he wanted to return to California. The agony was just too great for him.

10

Put it on the Shelf

We were often told to "put it on the shelf" if we disagreed with or didn't understand something. I remember making an honest attempt to shelve many questions over the years. What I never anticipated was that eventually my shelves would crack under the sheer weight of all the unanswered questions and inconsistencies. After moving to Tennessee, I was discouraged many times. Some were minor disappointments, while others were bombshells.

In 1996, a man who had been part of the church in California was arrested, as I was told, in the rural South for attempted murder. Apparently he had beaten someone nearly to death and had left his victim to die. Some men in our church who were friends with the accused told Brother Mears about how badly this man was being treated by the authorities while incarcerated and pleaded with Brother Mears to intervene. No one ever suggested that the man was innocent or had denied the crime occurred. The concern was for his suffering at the hands of cruel authorities. Brother Mears authorized the church to pay a large sum of money, between forty and fifty thousand dollars, to set the man free. After this money was paid, I was told he returned to California a free man. There were never any reports of a trial. If that is true, the church may have enabled a guilty man to escape justice through highly questionable and unethical means.

Our pastor acknowledged the bailout to the congregation publicly *after the fact*. He did not, however, disclose information or seek approval from the congregation prior to his decision. Although there were whispers of indignation, there was no public outcry.

There were conflicting reports about where the money came from. Some claimed the pastor used our tithes and offerings. Others said the money came from Brother and Sister Mears personally, although there would have been no reason to inform the congregation of the gift if it had been from his own account. Brother Mears' youngest son, however, confirmed years later that although his parents donated additional offerings for several months, the majority of the money was paid by the church. There was no such thing as public disclosure of church funds or assets, and we never questioned *any* financial decision Brother Mears made. Asking for accountability would have implied distrust.

I remember more than once hearing Brother Mears say from the pulpit, "If you trust me with your soul, can you not trust me with your money?" The implied message was that we should entrust to him both without question. Without our trust and consent Brother Mears could not have enjoyed this level of authority and control over our lives. The tone of his voice conveyed that he would be personally offended at any insinuation of bad judgment concerning church finances. He prided himself on being a good steward. Few of us would ever have risked implying a lack of trust in Brother Mears or his decisions. If others had financial worries, I never did. The least of my concerns regarding Brother Mears' judgment were financial. I trusted him completely. There are things I do hold him accountable for, but selectively judging him or his wife for financial decisions that we as a congregation empowered them both to make for more than fifty years seems hypocritical to me. The financial injustice of the bailout, as far as I was concerned, was by far the lesser evil. I was not nearly as concerned about the wrong done to *me* in the mishandling of my tithes and offerings as I was *morally outraged* by the greater injustice that was done to others. In my opinion, the decision to rescue that man from the jail, to keep him from facing judgment was *spiritually and morally bankrupt*. It was enabling wickedness and added insult to injury for *at least* one church family because it was not the first time the man had been protected from judgment by the church.

Years earlier, Katie, a little girl of five or six years old, accused the man, a teenager at the time, of repeatedly raping her. She said that he threatened to kill her if she told anyone. She did not tell anyone immediately because she was afraid of her dad's reaction. She remembers feeling dirty as though she had done something wrong. However, when it continued she decided to confide in her mother, who then informed her dad. Her father was more protective of the family image than in protecting his family. Such an emphasis was placed on purity that he was more afraid of his little girl being seen as "used goods," than on bringing the boy to justice. (He has since repented of this and has suffered much pain over his reaction.) Her mother, on the other hand, wanted to protect her daughter and wanted justice. She went to Brother Mears for guidance. His only advice to her was that she should inform the boy's mother. However, when she did that, she got a cold and indifferent, "Boys will be boys." Alone in her outrage she took no further action.

In hindsight, both parents are quick to acknowledge their complicity in dropping the ball. Even today they grapple with guilt and shame for failing to go to the police. They have asked their daughter to forgive them for such gross negligence of their responsibility to her, and she has. I have been a trusted friend of the family for many years and we have had numerous conversations about this unfortunate event. The girl's mother told me that part of the reason she and her husband didn't more strongly pursue justice was because they had a vital need to keep up that perfect image. She noted, "Who could be real? Who could deal with real issues? It was all covered up so we could appear to be progressing down that road to perfection. We were trained up with hundreds, maybe thousands, of implied messages. The image of the pedestal families, and the church on a pedestal, was paramount above any individual." Since leaving CGT, it is profoundly difficult for any of us to understand or explain why we all so willingly yielded control of our personal choices to our pastor. We shared a collective belief that it was God's governmental order for our lives. That is what we were taught again and again from the pulpit. We were not only instructed to seek our pastor's direction, we were taught that he would hear from God on our behalf. If we believed God had told us something that conflicted with what our pastor told us, we were told that it must not have been from God. Therefore, we questioned our own judgment at every turn.

This event was by far not an isolated incident. There were many examples of abuses of this type that were covered up. When abuses were exposed, the parents always counseled with Brother Mears, looking only to him for guidance in how to handle the matter. When Brother Mears (more than once) responded to an inappropriate relationship between an adult and minor as mutual consent rather than sexual abuse, virtually no one challenged his authority or wisdom to adjudicate. We all looked to him for direction, in serious as well as trivial matters. In most cases, the parents were good people who would never have intentionally inflicted pain or shame on their children. Their primary mistake was in placing too much trust and confidence in a man. The fathers seemed to be incapacitated by the possibility of their daughters' suffering a tarnished reputation, even in situations that were clearly *sexual abuse*. I am only aware of one incident in which a single mother courageously broke with tradition, reported an abuse to the authorities and prosecuted her daughter's abuser. The perpetrator spent approximately one year in jail (later rejoining us in Tennessee). However, the congregation as a whole was uninformed.

Over the last twenty-five years, *numerous* adults have confided their abuse to me. A close friend of mine told me years ago that she was molested as a child by an adult relative. As a young adult, she wanted to report the incident for the protection of others. However, before she followed through, she consulted Brother Mears who told her it was simply unacceptable for her to expose this man and bring shame and embarrassment on his family members (who still attended CGT). One woman recently shared with me an incident of sexual abuse that happened to her as a child. She never told anyone because she was in denial it had actually happened and didn't want to cause the man or his family pain and embarrassment. Furthermore, she didn't, and still doesn't, want her friends in the church to feel differently toward her. She believes that people would be upset with *her* if she revealed the abuse today. This does not surprise me because we were taught to cover problems rather than talk about them, and to put what we didn't understand "on the shelf."

Our emotional "shelves" were not intended to carry this kind of weight. Being taught to put it on the shelf rather than deal with our pain sends a horrible message, which inflicts an additional emotional burden on every victim. It makes the victim responsible for the emotions and discomfort of everyone around him or her. Victims of abuse should never carry the weight of hurting or embarrassing their abusers, their abusers' families, their church, or even *their own families*, but they do. Sometimes they carry that weight for the rest of their lives. In some cases, they are encouraged to do so by well-meaning people. Instead the message should be: "None of this is your fault."

Every situation of abuse I am aware of within CGT, whether well known or a well-kept secret, has shared a common thread. The victim has either been shamed for needing to talk, encouraged not to talk, or has *never* talked because he or she fears a negative reaction from family and lifelong friends. Image has always been an important priority in CGT. The image keeping of the church is something I have always wrestled with. And the image keeping at the expense of the protection and justice of these victims is something that infuriates me. Although I am uncomfortable with my own anger, I do recognize that *there is an appropriate time for anger*. And where there is injustice, the absence of anger is merely the evidence of indifference.

There were many abusers in CGT who enjoyed the protection of silence. Brother Mears' motive may have been to preserve marriages and keep families intact, but enabling sinners by shielding them from justice oftentimes led to more abuse.

I once refused to believe that preferential treatment was shown to men by my former pastor, although I would occasionally hear someone suggest it privately. I was in complete denial that women were disrespected by our leadership. In hindsight, I have to admit that women truly did have less value than men. It seems undeniable to me at this point.

Going back to the story of the bailout, our pastor had clearly not made Katie a priority in the way he responded to her rape, and—if he even remembered the violation—sadly, her feelings were not considered in the decision to rescue her abuser from jail. She had stopped attending CGT by the time of the bailout. However, she was present the night it was announced. I remember how deeply injured she was by this announcement.

I do not remember genuine or observable care ever demonstrated for victims. Every instance I am aware of was covered up. I have witnessed countless apathetic observers insist that victims just "have to forgive," even in the absence of repentance. I have seen victims absolutely vilified simply because they needed to talk about what happened to them. And I believe those who remain fearfully silent today choose to suffer privately, at least in part, because they have witnessed the vilification of others who have dared to talk.

Katie told me recently that Brother Mears apparently heard that the bailout had offended her. Therefore, he sent a message through his grandson that if she had something to say to him, he was "willing to hear her out." He made no attempt to contact her himself. There was no compassion demonstrated and no apology offered. He simply wanted her to know that *he would be willing to listen.* This was just adding insult to injury. She declined the invitation and explained to me, "I had *nothing* to say to him."

≫

Over the next ten years, I would learn of even more shocking cases of sexual abuse that had been covered up throughout my lifetime. The most shocking and disillusioning revelation of all came when our pastor's brother, Paul, who served as our assistant pastor for years, was accused by *multiple* female relatives of sexual abuse. The first reported case of pedophilia had allegedly occurred more than forty years earlier and had been kept a closely guarded secret for all those years.

11

By Their Fruit You Will Know Them

"A healthy tree cannot bear bad fruit, nor can a diseased tree bear good fruit" (Matthew 7:18).

The root of false doctrine and spiritual deception produced a diseased tree that brought forth evil fruit; not in an isolated moment but over a *period of production.* "To judge a tree's fruit, we don't look at one particular moment but at a period of production. The product of the life reflects the heart. The product of our discipleship reflects our inner character, what Jesus calls the treasure of the heart. The value of our speech and actions is determined by the quality of the soul that produces them. In other words, works are a snapshot of the heart" (IVP New Testament Commentaries).

The tree of the "Gospel Assembly" churches has deeply twisted roots and is loaded with weighty branches.

William Sowders ordained a man named T. M. Jolly to the ministry. Jolly was appointed to carry on the vision of the Body after Sowders' death. It was only after our move to Tennessee that I would fully discover what a corrupt and an evil man "Brother Jolly" was. He did not simply indulge in consensual affairs; he was a pedophile.

Back in the sixties, my pastor had been among a group of ministers who broke fellowship with T. M. Jolly after his sexual immorality was exposed. A group of men confronted him, asking if he would be willing to "step down." Jolly refused to take a posture of humility. As a result, these men believed they had no choice but to separate from him. Still others refused to believe in his guilt and remained loyal to him. This confrontation produced a major division within the "Body of Christ" movement, originally united under the distinctive leadership of William Sowders. This was the wound Brother Mears had always hoped to see healed. He had a deep and abiding longing to see the restoration of the Body of Christ back to its original fellowship.

The way I found out about Jolly's sin was when a family friend, Margie, was visiting my parents from out of town. I overhead a conversation between Margie and my parents in which Jolly's name came up. Margie defended Jolly, saying something about him having needs and never being married. She suggested we should not be so hard on him. However, I was clueless as to his offenses and still a pretty naive young girl. One of my parents pointed out that Jolly certainly could have gotten married; he'd had opportunities. They were not feeling Margie's sympathy for his *needs*.

It was shortly after this conversation that I asked my mother for the first time what Jolly had actually done. She told me a vague story of his moral indiscretions and refusal to step down. An affair with his piano player was the only specific allegation I recall. At the time, the split felt like ancient history to me; something that had happened way back in the sixties. However, only about a decade or so had actually passed.

Sometime in the late seventies or early eighties, I went on a bus trip to the Midwest with my church. Our trip included other church visits, but our ultimate destination was a fellowship meeting in Paducah, Kentucky. A couple of friends and I had an opportunity to visit my grandma in Mt. Carmel, Illinois, and then catch a ride to Paducah, reconnecting with the bus for the trip back to California. My mother's cousin offered to take us, since he lived in Mt. Carmel and was also planning to attend the meeting. Traveling in the car from Mt. Carmel to Paducah, we drove through the town of Eldorado, Illinois.

T. M. Jolly had a church in Eldorado. I had never been there. Bob drove us through the parking lot, identified it as Brother Jolly's church, and made a dramatic and perplexing statement. In an ominous tone, he told us, "I drove through this parking lot one night looking to kill a man." I thought to myself,

"Did he just say he wanted to *kill* a man? What is he talking about?" But I didn't ask any questions. It was clear enough that he was referring to a very traumatic event in his life; an event I knew nothing about.

When I got home from that bus trip, I told my mom what Bob had said. "Mom," I asked, "what in the world was he talking about? Why did he want to kill somebody?" In hindsight, I am surprised my mom told me. She could have feigned ignorance. Bob was a colorful character. He was known for getting into brawls in his youth. It would have been so easy to dismiss his remark as typical drama. But she did not choose to do that. She knew exactly who Bob wanted to kill, and why. Apparently, Jolly had harmed someone in our own extended family.

As Jolly would come through Mt. Carmel, on his way back to Eldorado from various local meetings, my mother explained that he'd be tired and would ask for a certain young female, my mother's cousin, to drive him the rest of the way. The father trusted Jolly completely and allowed his daughter to go along with him. What he didn't know was that Jolly seduced his young daughter on the trips. Jolly told her that what they were doing was not wrong in the sight of God and that one day he would make her "Sister Jolly." At the time, that was the equivalent of being made a queen, according to my mother.

One day Jolly called this young female and one of her siblings intuitively picked up the phone to listen in on the conversation. The conversation made it clear that something inappropriate was going on. So her sibling went to their father and informed him. Initially, he would not believe the allegation. His confidence in Jolly's moral integrity was unwavering. However, in the end, the truth came out. This would be one of the events leading up to Jolly's exposure.

I remember my great uncle fondly to this day. I was just shy of being eight years old when he died in April of 1967, but I have vivid memories of him. He died of a heart attack not long after these events. Everyone said he died of a broken heart. I had assumed his broken heart was linked to the disappointment of having to disfellowship his beloved Brother Jolly, who was once a dear friend. Until my mother told me this story, though, I had no idea how deep the betrayal was or how personally his heart had been broken.

ം

Before his death in May of 1994, Jolly's rampant pedophilia became fully exposed. Although criminally convicted, he escaped jail time due to his advanced age and poor health. It became apparent that he had used his position as a man of God to abuse children over a period of many years.

At this point, there was no benefit of the doubt to be given. This was an evil man. Shortly after his death, my pastor spoke affectionately about this man who had once been his friend and his contemporary in the ministry. Don't misunderstand me. He did not condone any of the wrongdoings, but he got choked up as he remembered the early years and his fondness for the man who was once a great teacher and friend. That nostalgia might have been acceptable within the privacy of his home. However, in my opinion, it was entirely inappropriate in a sanctuary full of people, some of whom were victims of sexual abuse. It turned my stomach to observe this display of palpable warmth for a man who had destroyed so many lives under the guise of minister. He was not a shepherd. He was a wolf. There were suicides as a result of his conduct, according to many. I just couldn't understand the public nostalgia and I remember feeling troubled by it. Once again, the insensitivity to those victims astounded and sickened me. I believe a diseased tree produced evil and corrupt fruit. Any fear of saying this aloud is gone. I simply cannot override the admonition of Scripture that the fruit will bear witness of the tree.

ം

After revisiting this memory, I remembered specific notes written in the back of my King James Bible many years ago. Brother Mears had given us several "earmarks" of the Body of Christ and had us to write them down. I have not thought about this list in quite some time, but it came to my mind after I finished writing about T. M. Jolly.

I have these eight things written in my Bible:

- Love one another (John 13:35),
- Spirit-filled (Romans 5:5),
- Poor people; rich in faith,
- Not necessarily the greatest in size (Deuteronomy 7:7),
- Having the gifts of the ministry (Ephesians 4:11-12),
- Not one member, but many (1 Corinthians 12:14),
- Knowledge of the truth; wise and understanding,
- The right government prevailing (Hebrews 13:7).

"Right government prevailing" jumped out at me and I looked up Hebrews 13:7. The King James Version says: "Remember them which have the rule over you, who have spoken unto you the word of God: whose faith follow, considering the end of their conversation." The NIV says: "Remember your leaders, who spoke the word of God to you. Consider the outcome of their way of life and imitate their faith."

It was the first part of this verse that was always emphasized in "right government." However, we are admonished here and throughout Scripture to be discerning and wise. As you read this book, I urge you to consider the fruit that is produced by those you are following. Consider the outcome of their way of life. Consider the end of their conversation.

12

Sin in the Garden

I was taught that Adam and Eve's sin in the garden was sex. It was explained that even though God told them to be fruitful and multiply, they had engaged in *premarital* sex ahead of God's timing. This was always confusing to me. *If God created them male and female for the purpose of companionship, physical love, and procreation, why would He forbid this union and punish them for it?* It seemed illogical.

I have often wondered if all the sexual sin in the history of the "Body" was rooted somehow in the emphasis placed on sexual temptation or if the emphasis on resisting sexual temptation was because that was the predominant sin of some of the leaders. In the early days of the Sowders movement, I have read that William Sowders went as far as forbidding women to wear red dresses and open-toed shoes. In the book *Yoke of Bondage*, Wayne Hamburger (GAC member from the thirties and forties) wrote that "Sowders wanted women to dress as plainly and homely as possible. He was concerned that their sexuality would distract the men or interfere with the Spirit of God. He insisted that the females wear long dresses and long sleeves. They were to wear no jewelry and no cosmetics. . . . He preached that when women wore dresses that didn't reach to the ankle, they were the cause of men backsliding. According to him, the sight of women's skin was too tempting for men, which would interfere with the worship of God."

Although I never knew William Sowders, when I read Hamburger's book I could clearly recognize his influence on Brother Mears' ministry. The temptation of women must have been extremely persistent for Sowders. I remember it was implied that women caused men to sin. That was part of the Adam and Eve story, which for us revolved around sex. As a young woman,

I can remember rejecting the idea of making myself unattractive so that men would not be tempted.

I remember thinking *Are these same men not going out into the workplace and encountering attractive women?* If all the women in the church made themselves as plain as possible, might their own husbands then not be attracted to them? Could this not lead to temptation as well? How could we protect them from temptation everywhere they went? It was ludicrous. This is a sexist and chauvinistic mindset. It was also inconsistent with the doctrine of perfection. If the men were so weak that women needed to keep themselves as plain as possible and cover every inch of skin to keep them from sinning, how in the world could any of them attain perfection?

Linked with the doctrine of perfection was the belief that we had to overcome sex within marriage. We were taught that in order to reach perfection, we would have to overcome sexual desire (lust) for our spouses. In order to overcome sin, we would have to love everyone equally, with the same pure brother-sisterly love. Our love for our spouses could be no exception. I think this belief had to do with the philosophy that sex was a product of the flesh and our carnal natures. Instead of focusing on the beauty of what God intended sex to be within marriage, the focus was only on sinful lust. I don't remember sex ever being spoken of as something God created and ordained to be enjoyed by a husband and wife. Everyone I ever talked to about that subject accepted that an "overcomer" would not continue having sex with their spouse. The confusion for me was simply this: if sex within the bounds of marriage was not wrong or sinful, why then would we ever need to overcome it?

Perhaps Brother Mears had his own form of peer pressure. Ministers in the Body were self-pressured to live an "overcoming" life because they preached about "living above sin." I remember hearing that in the late fifties, Brother Mears had tried to prove to himself that he could live this overcoming lifestyle. Apparently, many in the church believed he *was* living an overcoming life. Then Sister Mears became pregnant with their youngest son, Terry. I heard that one woman nearly had a nervous breakdown when confronted with the reality that Brother and Sister Mears were still intimate as husband and wife. Brother and Sister Mears were in their *thirties* at that time. It confirms what I have long believed about Brother Mears. He was a deceived man, and out of his own deception he deceived me.

A friend of mine, about ten years older than me, described how *dirty* she felt when Sister Mears confronted her after she had conceived her third child. Pregnancy was considered the product of sinful lust. However, this friend grew up in a large family and wanted a large family of her own. She told me how Sister Mears one day after hearing about her pregnancy came into the nursery, and announced to all the women: "We don't need you mothers having any more babies and being stuck here in the nursery. We need you out in service working for the Lord!" When I was a young mother, I remember Sister Mears making no secret of her conviction that time was too short for all of us to keep bringing babies into the world. I remember a specific occasion when I witnessed Sister Mears make her feelings quite clear.

A young woman in the church had become pregnant with her second child. Early in her pregnancy, there was concern that she might miscarry. Her mother and I were talking in a group of women as Sister Mears walked past us before the service. The young woman's mother told Sister Mears sadly that her daughter was afraid she might miscarry and Sister Mears' reaction was to smile and clap her hands with glee, as if that would be the best thing that could possibly happen. It caught me by surprise and I thought it was insensitive. However, it reflected her true feelings: this mother did not need to be having another baby.

༄

In spite of the legalism, our church had as many problems with sexual sin as any other group of people. We had strict dress standards, but they didn't seem to deter everyone from temptation. As more and more sin came to light during the nineties, I became more comfortable expressing my opinions. Wearing skirts and dresses was less imposing in the Southern California climate. However, it made no sense to me that we had to put on a dress in freezing temperatures when pants would have kept our legs warmer. By the time we had moved to Tennessee I wasn't concerned about fitting in with peers; I was more concerned with comfort and wearing weather-appropriate clothes. I was feeling brave and willing to test the boundaries.

Around this time, at the age of thirty-five, I decided to have my ears pierced. While on a trip to California to visit my dad and stepmom, I went to the mall and had my ears pierced as a way of celebrating my birthday. As amazing as it might sound, getting my ears pierced felt so liberating. My stepmother went along with me and supported me in my decision (although *she* had stopped wearing earrings in order to fit in with the other churchwomen when she married my dad).

I laugh at myself as I reflect on this. This was an empowering event in my life at the time. I was going to be a big girl and make my own decisions. Yet, in all my boldness, I was still apprehensive around my dad and pulled my hair toward my face whenever he was in the room. Over time, I became less self-conscious and even wore earrings to church. I began to openly question the church standards. One night my pastor's daughter, Becky, stood to her feet in a church service and addressed this "rebellion" in a testimony. She talked about those of us who were questioning the standards, wondering if they really were so important. She characterized this type of questioning as the spirit of Eve. She was attempting to shame people like me for posing such questions. This testimony offended me. She was judging every heart that dared to *question* the importance of our man-made standards. She equated questioning a man with questioning God and God's authority. I remember thinking that judging other people's hearts was far worse than questioning—

or even ignoring—a dress code. And I remember recognizing the blatant attempt at control through manipulation and intimidation.

໑

It would not be long before the first signs of Brother Mears' dementia appeared. The signs were subtle at first, but even after his mental decline became obvious, he remained in the official capacity of pastor. No one close to him felt free to tell him he was failing, and he certainly did not recognize it himself. His family would not even insist that he stop driving long after he was an obvious danger to others. They said he would get mad at them if they tried to tell him the truth or take his keys. Nobody was willing to risk making Brother Mears mad, even in his diminished capacity.

In the beginning, Brother Mears started to talk about the same things over and over. He began telling the "little Moses" prophecy more often. One afternoon, my son mentioned this to a friend, suggesting the possibility that something was wrong with Brother Mears. His friend was offended and reprimanded Danny for even suggesting such a thing. Before long, others would begin to see the same signs and quietly acknowledge it to their closest friends.

This went on for a period of years. It was one of the many elephants in the room we all avoided confronting. I guess it goes back to that "touch not mine anointed" thinking that you do not dare to suggest a man of God is not at the top of his game. Respecting and honoring Brother Mears was more important than anything. It bothered me that honoring Brother Mears took precedent over the welfare of the church. Once again, the main concern was image. Telling Brother Mears the truth was considered to be the equivalent of robbing him of the honor and dignity that was rightfully due him.

Brother Mears' son-in-law, Steve Farmer, was performing in the capacity of unofficial pastor while we carried out the charade of Brother Mears still being the real pastor. Pretty much everyone knew Brother Mears was not mentally capable of fulfilling that role any longer, but we played along. During this time, I remember hearing that Steve's granddaughter referred to her grandpa as the "pretend pastor." So, even children recognized what was going on. Steve may have been guiding the services, but he had no actual authority.

There was a degree of restlessness growing within the church. While large sums of money sat in bank accounts and accumulated interest, we did not even have adequate facilities for our babies on Dickerson Road. Many in the church were still longing for a permanent church building. As Brother Mears declined, he also became more and more suspicious of the motives of others. He did not trust people within his own family, making it even harder to reason with him when it came to important decisions, like the building. However, there was one person who seemed to have a great deal of influence with Brother Mears during this time; his son, Terry.

Terry became aggressively involved in trying to secure property and a new building for members. He became the advocate of the people, in a sense, trying to save the church and his dad's legacy by giving the people something to get excited about and possibly distracting them from other issues as well. Beginning in 1998, sexual abuse allegations against Paul Mears, Brother Mears' biological brother, were circulating and people were upset that Paul was participating in our services. Brother Mears—despite his mental impairment—was still officially at the helm of the ship and making the decisions. Brother Mears had not removed Paul from the platform, which was disturbing to many. We could not buy property or start a building project without a signature of approval from Brother Mears. And there was a great deal of "strategy" involved in getting that signature, but Terry was ultimately successful in breaking ground.

ഇ

Paul Mears had been the pastor of a church in Phoenix for many years. According to Cornelius Mears, Paul stayed in contact with him regarding church matters on a regular basis. My understanding, based on many public statements, was that Paul and the church in Phoenix operated under the direct supervision of Cornelius Mears. Therefore, Paul was obligated to "check in" with him regularly.

According to a CGT timeline, made public in 2008, Paul was in Phoenix from 1984 to 1998. In late 1997, his youngest granddaughter, Lynette, accused him of having sexually abused her during many of those years. After moving with her mother to California, she reported the abuse to a school counselor, then to her mother and her maternal grandfather. The abuse was reported to the authorities in California and it was demanded by the family that Paul resign from pastoral leadership or he would be prosecuted. I knew some of the details because Cheryl, Lynette's cousin, became my sister-in-law in 1990. During the late nineties we worked out together several mornings a week and I walked with her every step of the way as she experienced her grandfather's removal and then his presence in our church. We had many conversations about her grandpa and Brother Mears, as well as the things that were being said to her privately by Becky and Steve.

According to their official timeline, CGT states that Paul resigned and sold the church. With a large portion of the proceeds, Paul moved to Clarksville, Tennessee, and attempted to start another church, bringing twenty former members with him from Phoenix. None of the former members were informed, however, of the reasons for his resignation and relocation. While he was in Clarksville, he also frequently attended our services in Nashville. And he always sat on the platform. *The platform* was a place of prominence to us. It was an elevated position reserved for ministers and men who were *invited* to sit there. It was considered an honor to sit on the platform.

Initially, very few people knew the reason for Paul's relocation. Ultimately, his efforts to have his own church failed and he joined our congregation under his brother's leadership. When he did so, he was shown the continued respect of having a seat on the platform in spite of the alleged abuse and his refusal to address it. When he spoke, he took the pulpit. This unimaginable scenario went on for quite some time. Every time I went to church, I felt disheartened that Paul was still sitting on the platform.

Brother Mears had to have known the alleged abuse was likely to have occurred. Even if Brother Mears didn't remember, Steve knew about it and did nothing. Steve would later say his hands were "tied." He said he could not do the right thing because it might split the church if he openly challenged Brother Mears. By 2001, Steve was preaching hot and heavy against sexual sin, including pedophilia and incest. It was obvious to everyone that he was directing these sermons at Paul, but I wondered; *why did the congregation have to endure these chastisements?* All the time spent on trying to convict Paul's heart by preaching at him became laborious and Paul was just resisting, digging his heels in deeper and deeper. I think Steve has always believed in his heart that Paul was guilty. He admitted to some allegations and denied others. Yet he refused to repent. Even though others had been asked not to attend church in the past for less, for reasons that remain unclear, Steve never felt that he could ask Paul to stay away. Paul would brazenly walk up to people and thrust forth his hand, putting others in the awkward position of choosing between showing kindness and showing conviction. Most would allow him to intimidate them into a handshake. I could not understand why so many people in CGT were accepting this situation. As Cheryl and I both lost confidence in the leadership, we went to church less and less.

Brother Mears had banned me from a close friend's wedding because I had been inconsistent in church attendance. Brother Mears would not approve my youngest brother (Cheryl's husband) giving his cousin away in the wedding I gave for her in my own home because my brother, Chris, was not coming to church at the time. Brother Mears had publicly forbidden us from attending the weddings of those who married outside the church (causing a great deal of pain for family members in the church). Brother Mears controlled how many attendants couples could have in their wedding and what kind of dresses brides could buy. On multiple occasions, he made phone calls in an aggressive effort to prevent anyone from going to a professional sporting event. Brother Mears told us who could have wedding and baby showers, and who could not. He approved the guest lists. There are many other examples of control. Yet Paul's situation went unaddressed.

Cheryl encountered her grandmother in the church restroom in the middle of all this. She asked her grandmother about the alleged sexual abuse of the past and her grandmother responded indignantly, "I knew about that. It wasn't that bad." Her grandmother maintained that the real wrong was that this was brought up these many years after Cheryl's grandfather had "apologized." Cheryl was mortified and never again trusted her grandmother.

At one point, Steve and Becky asked if they could meet with Cheryl and my brother. Cheryl said they wanted to get her to come back to church, but also to get Brother Mears off the hook. One of the first questions they asked was, "You don't *blame* Brother Mears, do you?" referring to the alleged abuse. Cheryl responded that nobody was to blame for the actual abuse other than the perpetrator. However, she did blame Brother Mears for not exposing the sin for the protection of others.

They asked, "Well, what can we *do* for you? What will make you *happy?*" She said she just sat there in disbelief at the questions. Instead of wanting to do the *right* thing, they just wanted to make *her* happy in order to "brush it under the rug." Cheryl believed they simply needed to have integrity before God in this matter. Steve did not feel that he had the authority to act independently of Brother Mears, who was obviously still calling the shots. He claimed he could not make this decision according to his own conscience without possibly splitting the church in half. Instead he and Becky asked Cheryl if she would be willing to go talk to Brother Mears personally and ask him to tell her grandfather not to come to church *for her sake*. It was as if Steve and Becky were afraid of approaching Brother Mears themselves, so they attempted to put this off on Cheryl. Cheryl refused the request. By this time, she was becoming wise to the manipulation. It was not about her. It was about right and wrong. Steve tried another tactic. He said that he was going to challenge Paul publicly in an upcoming service, but he needed Cheryl to be present so that she could back him up on the allegations. Although she felt uncomfortable, perceiving this as possibly another form of manipulation, she complied with his request by going to church on several successive occasions, giving Steve the opportunity to confront her grandfather publicly. He never did.

I struggled to reconcile the discrepancy between the types of issues that were handled aggressively and those that were not handled at all. Every instance of sexual abuse I knew of had been swept under the rug. Yet for minor infractions, such as trimmed hair or wearing lipstick, people were shamed publicly. I had always believed Steve represented change in the CGT. Yet his impotent approach to these matters left me heartsick. I thought I knew this man. I believed he had integrity and would take a stand. I had deep respect and admiration for him as a Christian. However, he was becoming someone I did not recognize.

Steve constantly vacillated and made excuses. At one point, with regard to alleged abuse, he said, "Sister Cheryl, you can believe whatever you *want* to believe." In relating that conversation to me, Cheryl asked with intensity, "What the heck is THAT supposed to mean? Truth is irrelevant?" I began to wonder if Steve had changed or if I simply had never truly known him.

13

Coming to Terms with Our True Selves

The Gospel Assembly Church is very patriarchal. The women served the men at our church gatherings. When people went forward for prayer during the service the men would go to one side of the church and the women would go to the other. Unmarried males and females were forbidden from sitting next to one another in church services. Nothing about any of these practices was extraordinary, and none of them bothered me much. There was a church tradition, though, that did bother me when I got older and began questioning things. During conventions, a certain protocol was observed as the afternoon service was dismissed. Our pastor would request that all the congregants (or "the little people," as some of us liked to tease) remain in their pews until all the ministers and their wives had filed into the dining room to be served first. They didn't just go ahead of everyone else; they had their own partitioned room and specially designated servers. Just as the platform was a place of honor, so was the minister's dining room. It was a privilege to be asked to *serve* in the minister's dining room as opposed to the regular dining room. Personally, I did not want to go near that room because I felt intimidated by those men and their wives, and was afraid I might accidentally pour tea or coffee all over a minister's lap.

What I remember most about the ministry was how the ministers and their families were treated like royalty. It was as though they were the dignitaries and we were the common folk. I can see how people could become addicted to this attention or aspire to the ministry for the wrong reasons as a result of it. At some point, I realized that for all the talk of being like Jesus this behavior was very unlike Him. Jesus never would have looked for a special dining room or a seat of prominence. He said that the greatest among us would be the servant of all. I never thought of the ministers as servants. They were much more like kings to me. And I felt as though we served as the *subjects* of Brother Mears.

For most of my life, this was an unspoken kind of thing. However, some time after the move to Tennessee, my pastor's daughter actually verbalized it. This was another one of those red-letter days in my life that I have reflected on many times. Some friends and I had gone to lunch in Green Hills, a suburb of Nashville, and we ran into Becky and her party. As we were leaving, we stopped and chatted at their table for a few minutes. Somehow, we got on the topic of Princess Diana. Becky compared Diana's rebelliousness toward the Queen and her attempts to change the protocol of the royal family with the young people in our church who challenged her dad and the way things had always been done at our church. The blatant identification with royalty took all of us by surprise. The minute my friends and I got in the car to leave, we stared at each other with raised eyebrows and gaping mouths. We were all thinking the exact same thing and we knew it. I can't remember who spoke first, but we laughed as we shared our reactions to those remarks. "Can you believe she *said* that? She was comparing her dad to the Queen of England! And she doesn't like Diana because Diana won't bow to the Queen and royal protocol!" This conversation has *always* made me laugh. After all we had been through, moving to Tennessee, having so many disappointments, Brother Mears trying to move us back to California, we were becoming harder to manipulate. Brother Mears' power over us was ever so slightly diminished, but he was still greatly revered.

We were *taught* to please people; principally our pastor. Therefore, we quite naturally placed Brother Mears on a pedestal. He did not warn against it or refuse worship. He was between God and us in many ways. My personal relationship with God was stunted by the way I was taught to view my pastor. Many people who have left in recent years have told me they were unable to have a personal relationship with God in all the years they were there. One of the struggles after leaving is learning how to have a personal relationship with God. Many of us continually looked to Brother Mears instead of looking directly to God. All of this man-worship was instilled in us through many direct and indirect messages; including the songs we sang. Brother Mears demanded an elevated place in our lives (i.e., suggesting our souls were in danger if we did not follow him). Then as the house of cards began to tumble, several family members began to claim that *the people* made him a god. It wasn't that *he* wanted that; we did it *to* him. Those claims are false. This behavior could have been easily discouraged. Instead, people earned brownie points through their allegiance and compliance. There were plenty of church politics constantly in play.

Over the years there were many young people whose violations were overlooked. However, certain people's sins were exposed, and they were made examples of. I say *certain people* because it depended upon who you and your family were. Not everyone was treated the same. In some situations, there was mercy. In others, breaking a rule would lead to public consequences.

Not long before I left CGT, Steve, the acting pastor at the time, denied permission for a baby shower because of a moral infraction. Becky explained *their* position to my sister-in-law, Cheryl. She said that getting to have a shower was a "perk" for doing right. In this case, a shower was undeserved. Certainly, we would never want to be guilty of minimizing disobedience or ignoring God's boundaries for our lives; however, putting our choices into the context of doing the right thing in order to get "perks" is wrong. The motive for doing the right thing should be pleasing and honoring God, not getting perks and rewards from the church or other people. However, this was another example of the way our system operated. In my view, it was all about having the seal of approval from other people, especially those in a position of authority. This way of thinking led to façades and pretenses; not confession and repentance.

As you might imagine, there was a lot of depression in our church, which was not a condition Brother Mears understood. He said from the pulpit that mental hospitals were full of people with "evil spirits and guilty consciences." He left the impression that there was always an underlying spiritual cause. If one relied more on God, they would feel better. Further compounding the problem was that we were taught to avoid outside help for emotional issues. Psychiatrists, psychologists, counselors, and mental health professionals of any kind, and certainly medication, were frowned upon. This kind of health care was considered worldly. We were taught instead to get help only through God and the church. However, Brother Mears was no trained counselor. Any time I ever went to him, he would simply ask questions like: "Have you been reading your Bible? Have you been praying? Do you have the victory?" I never came away from a session with him feeling like he had given me any tools to help me deal with a problem. I just felt *more* inadequate (since I usually had not been praying or reading my Bible enough). And I never once felt as if Brother Mears could relate to me. I was so far beneath him, I thought. He didn't seem to live in the real world.

The answer to every problem was simply that you needed to be "in church." Whenever there was a wedding, my dad would video tape the ceremony and reception as a gift to the newlyweds. He would walk up to people with the camera running and ask if they had any marital advice for the new couple. Repeatedly, people would say the same thing: "Stay in church." It was as if attending all the services would ensure a happy marriage. It was an over-simplification and a very unrealistic view of what it takes to have a happy marriage. A recipe for disaster, you might even say. I came to learn that very few people had any concept of how to have a healthy marriage, including me.

From 1997 through 1999, my husband at the time was suffering from clinical depression. Brother Mears was beginning to decline and every time he was involved in any type of counseling, he made matters worse. I did not want to go to him for counseling. I had learned that lesson years earlier, even before his decline. However, my then-husband wanted to hear certain things directly from Brother Mears, and I was trying to be a supportive spouse. It was a mistake. In one particular session, he said that depression was often the result of God giving someone over to a reprobate mind. We began seeing a Christian counselor unconnected to CGT at this time. Even after my husband's depression subsided, I continued in counseling for my own emotional and spiritual growth. It was therapeutic, beneficial, and rewarding to receive actual assistance in learning how to pinpoint the underlying reasons for my unhealthy behavior and responses to others. It completely changed the way I viewed myself, as well as my relationship with God. One major personal revelation to come out of counseling for me was learning the true motives of my heart. I discovered how easy it is to convince myself that my motives are noble and pure when they are actually selfish and self-preserving. For many years, I had unconsciously operated out of a false belief that as long as I *did* the right thing, it didn't really matter *why* I did the right thing. I can see now why I assumed that. God is not a respecter of persons, but my church leaders were. So many things were purely political. I can see why the leadership of my former church felt threatened by such personal growth. I ultimately became strong enough to break free from all the oppression in my life; including CGT.

You cannot follow Christ and protect your old nature. Following Christ is about dying to self and putting to death your old nature. It was painful for me to confront how much my people-pleasing was driven by selfish motives. We often think of people-pleasers as being focused on others; but the truth is, people-pleasers have an unquenchable thirst for being loved and affirmed. Rather than being noble and good, my actions were selfish. Once I saw my true motives and the selfish heart that was driving me, I knew I *had* to change. It's one thing to be sick and not know you're sick. I could endure a lot of unhealthy behavior in other people as long as I viewed myself as being healthy. However, once my eyes were opened to my condition and I saw myself, I wanted to change and become healthy. Above all else, I wanted to become spiritually healthy.

There was nothing more painful for me than confronting my self-centered heart or self-serving motives. I was so good at deceiving myself. I did not even realize I was self-centered, that my motives were all about keeping myself comfortable and safe. So, on many occasions since, I have asked God to reveal the hidden motives of my heart and make me more aware of them—in small doses, of course. (If He showed me everything He sees, it might be more than I could handle all at once.) In the words of Philip Yancey, "God already knows who we are: *we* are the ones who must find a way to come to terms with our true selves."

14

Deception

On December 8, 1998, I had been sitting in my office at home when the phone rang. It was my lifelong friend, Janette. She called me from her doctor's office to tell me the exciting news that she was carrying twins! She was so overjoyed. She had just had an ultrasound and learned that her twins were little girls. I was so excited for her. In the middle of our brief conversation, she whispered into the phone, "Oh, the doctor's back. I need to go. I'll call you on my way home!"

Some time later, the phone rang again. It was Janette. This time she was crying. Just minutes after learning she was carrying two babies, Janette was advised to terminate her pregnancy. She was informed that her little girls had a condition of the placenta called Twin-to-Twin Transfusion Syndrome, or TTTS. In early pregnancy, TTTS can cause both babies to die. It can also cause severe disabilities. In Janette's case, the doctor offered not a shred of hope for a positive outcome and recommended an abortion as soon as possible. Janette refused.

Janette explained that, as their mother, she simply could not even entertain the thought of ending these two lives herself. If God wanted them to die, then He would have to be the One to terminate their lives. Although it would be difficult emotionally, she was going to carry her babies for as long as they remained alive. There was no way she would be able to *take* their lives. She totally rejected abortion as an option. She went home and researched TTTS for herself. Her exhaustive research efforts led her to a doctor in Florida who was doing an experimental surgery for TTTS with a pretty good success rate. She contacted his office and made an appointment for a consultation. She had been on an emotional rollercoaster for days, and now she was on her way back up. She had been given a ray of hope.

Less than two weeks after being given this grim prognosis, she was accepted as a patient and went to Tampa for surgery, knowing there was a chance the doctor might not be able to save either of her babies. Following the procedure, she could immediately lose one or even both of them. However, I remember Janette telling me that no matter what the outcome; at least she would know that she had fought to save her babies' lives.

Watching their small beating hearts repeatedly in the ultrasounds caused Janette to bond intensely with her daughters that she fought so diligently to save. She wanted to give them names prior to surgery. One baby was visibly stronger than the other. Breyanna had been the first name she had picked out, so it seemed natural to give that name to the stronger baby; the one she thought had the best chance at survival.

The doctor performed the surgery on December 20; then Janette began the process of waiting to find out whether her twins would thrive or decline. The outcome was bittersweet. She did lose one of the twins almost immediately. However, instead of losing the more fragile twin, it was Breyanna who rapidly declined following surgery.

Janette carried her living child and her lost child to term, delivering them both together on April 29, 1999. As you can imagine, this pregnancy was emotionally draining from that first ultrasound all the way to delivery. At its conclusion, there was both joy and sadness. For the rest of her life, Janette will see the exact representation of the daughter she lost at every age and every stage of life. She was profoundly thankful for Baylee's healthy birth and at the same time profoundly grief-stricken over Breyanna's loss. Breyanna was and always will be her child; not merely an impersonal *fetus*.

This fight for the life of her unborn children forever changed my friend. She told me later that as she continued to sit through services at CGT while pregnant, light bulbs were going on in her mind. The Psalmist tells us that God knows the unborn and that He knits us together in our mother's womb.

But we were being told something different. She began to focus on the teaching that unborn babies had no souls. She contemplated being in a church where ending the life of your own unborn child was not considered wrong. She said to me recently, "I had surgery on my placenta, lost the twin, and had an epiphany. I seriously began to consider whether or not I was in the right church during December of 1998. The abortion issue was the catalyst for getting me out of there. The gravity of using the Bible to justify taking a life was not lost on me and single-handedly gave me permission to seek my freedom from that place."

Because of our close friendship, I witnessed Janette's anguish in a very personal way. I remember listening intently as she expressed her inner turmoil. However, at that time, I wasn't sure what I believed about her lost, unborn baby. I had always believed that unborn babies did not have souls. I had experienced two miscarriages earlier in my life and had not really *grieved* either loss. I had taken both miscarriages in stride and simply thought of the life inside me as a *fetus*, not yet a human. On the other hand, I was quite aware that Janette's experience was far different from my miscarriages. Janette not only knew the sex of her lost baby, she knew that baby's identical twin sister. Her loss was more tangible than mine. I realized I would not have much to offer in the way of wisdom or insight. I knew my role was primarily to listen and comfort my dear friend.

Janette later told me that although there were many conflicting emotions involved in leaving CGT, their denial of life beginning at conception became intolerable, and she could no longer remain in a place where everyone denied that her lost child was now in the loving arms of Jesus. I did not try to talk her out of leaving the church even though I thought she was making a wrong decision. I remained brainwashed by a lifetime of indoctrination. I was fearful of displeasing God. Although I did not know it then I made most of my decisions based on my fears, fear of disappointing my friends, fear of displeasing the leaders, and even the fear of the unknown. At the time, I cannot say that I fully understood her convictions, but I did feel her pain and her struggle.

Baylee was born in April and Janette found a new church by October of 1999. After leaving CGT and becoming a part of Christ Church in Nashville, Janette experienced a spiritual transformation before my eyes. She was hearing the message of the cross; that eternal life was hers through faith in Christ alone, not as a result of her own moral perfection. After believing herself to be a Christian her whole life, she was hearing these Gospel truths and experiencing the *grace* of God for the first time. However, I was not. I questioned many things, but the doctrine of perfection and the passages repeatedly quoted to support it were etched on my brain. I could not simply get rid of them. While Janette was experiencing the freedom given to her through the shed blood of Christ, I remained captive in spiritual bondage.

Most people in CGT pulled away from Janette and her family because of their leaving. However, I was determined that our friendship would not fall by the wayside because Janette and her family were attending a different church. While I could understand and empathize with my friends' reasons for leaving the church, I also feared that they might be making a mistake. And one of the many reasons I was so determined to preserve our friendship and our closeness was that I viewed myself as quite possibly their bridge back one day, should they ever regret their decision to leave. This may sound strange, but our pastor used to say that if we were not for him, we were against him. People did not leave the church to go to a different church. It was even a rare thing for anyone to leave Brother Mears' church for another Body church. We felt so privileged to be under his ministry. We asked his permission to *visit* other churches within our fellowship. And that permission was often not granted. On a few occasions, I remember that he did not want us to visit certain churches for our own protection. He knew things he did not share openly with the congregation.

Churches outside "the Body" were designated the false religious world or Babylon. It was stated that we would be better off in a backslidden condition, not even serving God, than *thinking* we were serving God in Babylon; it was the equivalent of selling the precious "truths" that God had privileged us to receive. Believing that Jesus "paid it all" was said to be taking the easy way, the way of deception, the broad way that led to destruction. This deception was deeply lodged in my thought processes. On the one hand, I was confronted with the inconsistencies and evidence that we could not be who we thought we were. On the other hand, because of my fear of God being upset with me, I could never completely get away from questions such as: *What if they are right? What if I am deceived? What if this is the true church and I leave? Will God be mad at me for leaving? Will I be cut off from God?*

One night Janette and I met for dinner at Outback. She was absolutely bubbling over with joy. This was the joy I had longed for as a child but had never found in "the Body." She went on and on about the Gospel and God's grace and how wrong our teachings had been. She said, "Shari, my eyes have been opened. I love you, and I want you to experience the joy and the freedom I've found. It makes me sad to think of you staying there."

I explained to her that I was happy for her, but I did not feel a conviction to leave. I believed I was where God wanted me. I believed that healthy change could come to CGT and I could possibly be a part of that change. I remember saying, "Janette, if everyone who recognizes the need for change leaves, how will change ever come about? I choose to stay because I think I can help bring about change." Janette responded, "I think you're staying because you're trapped and you just don't realize it."

Her remarks were insulting to me, but I didn't let on. I tried to respond without showing the emotion I was feeling as I gently pointed out that I disagreed with her assessment. I told her that I did not feel trapped there, and I could leave any time, if that was what I wanted to do. I denied my fearfulness (because I was denying it even to myself). And I told her that although I realized she meant well, I felt like she was suggesting that I was not intelligent enough to know whether or not I was trapped.

Janette's concern for me was out of genuine love, but I did not trust her motives in spite of the fact that she was my friend of many years. In my heart, I thought she wanted to control me. If I joined her in leaving, I would validate her. I didn't love her any less. I just wasn't going to let her control me. Now that she was outside "the Body," whenever she spoke against the church or whenever there was an issue in the church, I felt the need to defend and protect the church. Like in a family, you are permitted to have objections and opinions, but heaven forbid an outsider have something negative to say.

Whenever I feel frustrated with people who remain ever vigilant in their loyalty to CGT today, I remind myself of how I felt when Janette first left. I understand why they cannot trust or understand my heart or comprehend my love for them. I understand their thought processes because I was at one time just like them. I understand the need to defend and protect the church and its image. And just as I misjudged the motive of one of my closest friends, I have been misjudged and misunderstood by people whose friendship I desperately did not want to lose. I must always remember that I have been where they are, but they are not where I am. I must look at their behavior and choices through eyes of compassion even as I contend for the truth.

Years later, after I had found the true Gospel and my freedom in Christ, I would come to understand that Janette's motive had been sincere and unselfish. I remember the first time I confessed to her that she had really ticked me off that night. I had rejected virtually everything she said and attributed selfish motives to her desire to get me out of CGT. I admitted this to her and asked forgiveness for misjudging her heart. I now understood that she had simply wanted me to have the joy and freedom she had found. I knew it was because she loved me and not because she was trying to control me. We laugh about it now, but I believe God gave me that experience for a specific purpose.

15

My Eyes Were Being Opened

In 2000 my husband found his dream job. He had always been self-employed in real estate investing. But now he had an exciting opportunity in the lending industry. The position was lucrative and offered benefits. He had battled depression for a long time and this job opportunity seemed to be the catalyst for his reengagement with life. While he was on the upswing, I began to feel down. I was thankful he was finally happy, but I was still feeling the after effects of the previous years. My counselor had explained to me that I had been under severe stress for so long; it had taken a cumulative toll on me physically. I remember him saying that I hadn't given myself permission to be a person in years because I always felt responsible for the emotions of others. He warned me about suddenly hitting a wall. I thought I would be fine, but he was right.

I recognized the symptoms because I was familiar with depression by this time. I was not myself. I had no interest in life, no physical or emotional energy. I went to the doctor right away. He knew what the last few years had been like for me. He said my emotional reserves—and probably my serotonin levels as well—were depleted. He suggested that I take a low dose anti-depressant to help my body through this difficult time. I am normally a passionate person who gets teary-eyed at the drop of a hat. While on the anti-depressant I hardly felt any emotion at all. I must say that I *enjoyed* the brief vacation from emotion. However, I knew that a vacation was not the proper use of medication. Therefore, my emotional hiatus ended within nine months.

One Sunday, I was listening to my husband talk excitedly about his new job, what it would mean for him financially and emotionally. I shared his enthusiasm over the new job opportunity. Our son had recently graduated from college and was embarking upon the beginning of his career in education. This made me think about the opportunities I had missed, and I casually mentioned that I wished I had gone to college. His response surprised me. He said, "What's stopping you now?" I just looked at him and asked, "Would it really be okay with you if I went back to school?" Without hesitation, he replied, "It's the perfect time. Not only would it be okay with me, I would be *proud* of you." He had just said the magic words.

You see, we were young when we married and he had convinced me to drop out of high school. A few years later I finished my GED, but I'd never had a graduation ceremony or a high school reunion. I always regretted that. He was known for his caustic sense of humor, and he would often poke fun at me by asking when I was having my reunion with the GED-ers. I laughed and pretended it didn't bother me, but it stung.

I obtained my real estate license at the age of eighteen. I enjoyed some success at that. I worked as a secretary and an assistant escrow officer in California. However, it always seemed that when I received the praise of others for my efforts and abilities, it was a threat to my marriage. I was pressured to quit jobs because my working interfered with family time, but I was belittled for not having ambition when I did not work. I was quite content to be a stay-at-home mom, but the criticism and jokes made me feel inadequate and inferior. I later learned in one of my college courses that I had been in a predicament called a "double-bind." I could not please my spouse regardless of what I did. I turned forty in 1999 and the frustration was catching up with me. I was taking stock of my life and evaluating the sacrifices I had made. Feeling deeply inspired by the opportunity to grow as a person *and* make someone proud of me, I went to the local community college and registered in the fall of 2000. I took my entrance exams, selected my first semester classes and completed enrollment requirements within two weeks. I remember how intimidated I felt as I walked onto the campus. I had not been in a campus setting in twenty-five years.

I took several honors courses while attending Volunteer State, and I became absorbed in my studies. Once again, the validation I received became a threat to my marriage. Where I had originally been encouraged by the dangling carrot of making someone proud of me, I was now experiencing a great deal of resistance. I felt guilty. My enthusiasm was met with contempt. I was asked not to bring up the subject of school because it was so laborious to my spouse. I was asked, "Why do you want to do this? It's so much work. Why don't you just enjoy how great your life is: going shopping and out to lunch with your friends?" It was turning out much differently than I had anticipated. I certainly never set out to make anyone miserable. I thought I was doing something *pleasing*.

I was beginning to feel resentment because it seemed to me like I had earned this opportunity. I had provided love and support for many years. I was determined to succeed, to overcome the high school dropout jokes. This opportunity had been *offered*. I would not allow it to be taken away. I knew from experience that if I yielded to the pressure to quit, it would later be used against me. I would be mocked for being a quitter and never finishing what I had started. At times, I wondered if I had been set up to fail, but I was determined not to let that happen.

It was at this same time that I began to grow spiritually. I was recognizing just how oppressive my life was on different levels. I was discovering things about myself through counseling and education. I had sacrificed so much in an effort to gain love and acceptance and to please others in my church as well as in my marriage. Yet I was never good enough. These realizations were the first steps in the process of becoming my own person. I concluded that I had to take responsibility for my own growth; both emotionally and spiritually. I became focused on the absence of true worship in so many of our songs. I began to take mental note of how many testimonies honored the church, the ministry, the group we were a part of more than Jesus. I began to listen for the name of Jesus and how often He was spoken of in contrast with how much emphasis was given to who *we* were. I began to notice that everyone spoke about when they found "the Body" instead of when they found Jesus. For some reason, all these characteristics were growing increasingly apparent. I also was even more clearly aware of the injustice of honoring a man who was an unrepentant child molester. I was breaking free from the chains of influence the church had on me.

At a Halloween party in 2001, my son met his future wife, Rebecca. I remember Danny coming home that night and telling me that he really liked this young woman, but he couldn't see it turning into anything serious. He thought she was too sophisticated for him, and he doubted that she would ever be willing to come to our church. Rebecca was already a dedicated Christian, strong in her faith. She had traveled all over the world doing missionary work. She probably wouldn't fit in at our church. I look back now thinking how sad it is that my son might have forfeited the perfect wife for him because he was willing to choose CGT over a relationship. At the time, though, I believed that if Rebecca was meant for Danny, she would embrace the church as well.

Once they began dating, Danny invited her to church. He had prayed about whether or not God wanted him to stay in CGT for several years. At times, he told me he had pleaded with God to release him because he was miserable there. He had not yet felt the freedom to leave, so he remained. Perhaps God wanted him there for a reason. He shared his concerns openly with Rebecca and told her that he felt like God still wanted him there for some reason, but he was not in denial of the problems.

They fell in love, and she told him that she went to church with him only because he was so honest with her about the things he saw that were wrong.

Because he did not try to convince her that these problems did not exist, she trusted that God was already convicting his heart, and she would support him as he followed God's leading. My daughter-in-law was wise, and she trusted God.

Two memories from that time stand out in my mind. One service, a man spoke from the pulpit about how thankful he was to be in "the Body." As he did so, he made a statement about other Christians outside our fellowship. He said, "These poor Christians who *think* they have a relationship with God." His remarks were dripping with pity for the whole Christian community who did not believe our "truths." It repulsed me. My future daughter-in-law looked at me and said, "He's talking about people like me." The three of us got up and left shortly thereafter.

One night after church, Steve summoned Danny to the front. Rebecca had been wearing pants and pantsuits to church. She was so lacking in self-focus that she had not even noticed she was the only woman in pants. Steve and Danny were close friends at the time. Steve implored Danny to ask Rebecca to stop wearing pants to church because it might adversely affect others. Danny simply responded that if there was a Scripture he could give Rebecca backing up the request, then he would ask her. However, he did not think it was a biblical request, so he wasn't willing to impose that on her. Steve said, "It could make a difference in you having *a position* in the church one day." Danny told him that he wasn't interested in a position.

I couldn't believe that Steve was applying pressure in such a minor matter but was unwilling to ask an alleged pedophile not to attend services because he did not have the unanimous support of the people.

How could I deny the reality that despite Steve's knowledge of similar allegations as early as 1967, he was making decisions based on anticipating *people's reactions* instead of what was right and just before God? I try not to judge the hearts of others. However, this was one struggle I could not put on the shelf.

16

Breaking Out of the Box

My goal during the two years in college was a 4.0 GPA, but I also wanted to balance school with my family responsibilities. I quickly became immersed in learning and found school to be invigorating, but I was not abounding in self-confidence. It was beyond my comfort zone. I feared failure.

The first few days on campus were intimidating. I was a non-traditional student. I was closer in age to my professors than to the other students. Therefore, I did not expect to make many friends. I subconsciously anticipated being somewhat of a misfit. However, to my surprise, I made friends quickly and effortlessly. I connected with professors and students alike.

I remember the first time it dawned on me, "I *can* do this and I *am* a likable person." It was so positive and liberating. No wonder school felt so good. Not only was I allowed the freedom to share my thoughts and opinions, my insight was *welcomed* and other people seemed genuinely *interested* in hearing what I had to say. I was forty years old and felt like a caterpillar becoming a butterfly as I began to emerge from my cocoon.

I was thankful for the people in my life who continually allowed me to express my enthusiasm for school and offered loving encouragement. I have fond memories of conversations with my youngest brother, Chris, who was pulling for me to succeed. He seemed to enjoy my accomplishments and urged me to persevere and not let anything or anyone stand in my way. His reassurance helped me counter the unwarranted guilt I carried. He encouraged me not to let the pressure deter me. I knew he believed in me, and it meant so much more than he probably ever realized.

Another avenue of encouragement came from my counseling. I looked forward to my appointments because I could talk freely about my ongoing process of self-discovery and learning. I learned how to identify and confront the motives of self-protection and self-preservation that were hiding behind my actions. I learned how to evaluate my response to others, whether I was responding in a healthy way or was conditioning them to treat me badly by enabling them. I began to recognize manipulation and intimidation tactics and resist the attempts of others to control me. I understood how ungodly manipulation is and my obligation as a Christian to resist ungodly behavior.

Counseling is a waste of time if you are unwilling to discover painful things about yourself and change. Counseling will make you feel pretty uncomfortable at times. It's not a place to go if you simply want to feel good about yourself and be assured that someone else is the problem. Unfortunately, we are all part of the problem.

One time my counselor, Floyd Dawson, asked me this question: "When Jesus said the words, 'Get thee behind Me, Satan,' do you believe He loved Peter?" I agreed that He did. Floyd then pointed out that to say anything other than that to Peter would have been *unloving*. Jesus loved Peter enough to tell him the truth.

For the first time, I contemplated how unloving my enabling responses had been. I learned that when you enable someone's ungodly behavior, you are only thinking of yourself. If you truly love someone, you will tell them the truth instead of what they want to hear. For the most part, I usually tried my best not to rock the boat. I had convinced myself that that was a good thing. Floyd made me see that it was selfish. My underlying motive in not rocking the boat was that I did not want to suffer unpleasant consequences. I had an insatiable need to be loved by others.

The two areas of my life where I felt the most oppressed were in my marriage and CGT. I was committed to both, and I wanted to be a part of positive change. I did not fully comprehend at the time that I had a role in my oppression, but my desire for change was strong. I was willing to do anything. I wanted to learn *how* to become healthier and better equipped to respond as God would have me respond in *all* areas of my life. I wanted to grow as a person both emotionally and spiritually. However, I did not grasp the major changes this growth would bring to my life.

For me, the turning point in my outlook was discovering how self-absorbed I was and that I, too, was an unhealthy dysfunctional mess. I had played a key role in many of my circumstances because of the way I responded to the behavior of others. Floyd showed me how I had made an idol out of other people's opinions of me. I will never forget the illustration he used to get this across to me, and I will always be thankful that God allowed my heart to be completely open to this insight.

In one of my sessions, Floyd asked me to tell him what the three most important priorities in my life were. I said, "God, being a good person, and other people thinking of me as a good person." He said, "You're in trouble." I remember feeling puzzled. Those seemed like good priorities to me at the time. What could be wrong with any of those desires? I naively asked, "Why am I in trouble?" Floyd responded, "Do you think everyone thought Jesus was a good person?"

Shari: "Uh, well, no, of course not."

Floyd: "Do you think Jesus *cared?*"

Shari: "Um, well, probably not."

Floyd: "No, He absolutely did not. And the reason He didn't was because He knew who He was and He never would have compromised His purpose in order to gain someone's validation or approval. He looked only to the Father for that. Any time other people's opinions and validation mean so much to you that they make your 'top three' list, you are in serious trouble. At some point, you will compromise what is right in order to be considered a good person by others."

It was as though my whole life had shattered before my eyes. I had always *wanted* to do things for the right reasons and had convinced myself that all my motives were good. However, at that moment I realized that I didn't even know how to identify right motives from wrong motives and apparently I had been taught wrong motives my entire life. Floyd's question had revealed the true desire of my heart. There, fully exposed in my top three priorities, was my desperate need to be viewed as a good person by everyone around me. I wish I could tell you that today I do everything out of right motives. That would be a lie, of course, but I *have* made progress.

From that day forward, I consciously began to evaluate my motives more carefully. The way I make critical decisions now is by asking myself the question Floyd used to ask me in counseling. "Who is that about?" In recent years, I have been faced with some big decisions, including how I was going to respond to the abuses that were covered up in my former church. My decisions have been agonizingly painful at times. I do not enjoy criticism, and I fear rejection. Nevertheless, I have taken some bold stands in the midst of my worst fears, suffering harsh criticism and rejection. My ability to do that goes back to the insight I gained from those early counseling sessions. When faced with difficult decisions, I now know how to evaluate my motives for acting vs. not acting (or vice versa). If the choice is between my own comfort and doing what is right despite criticism or rejection, I now can easily identify the wrong decision *by exposing the wrong motive*. Instead of making it about me, I do not seek my own comfort but I attempt do what is right at any personal cost.

As selfish creatures we often justify our inaction so we don't feel bad not doing something hard, not taking an uncomfortable stand. Additionally, I have learned that when we can convince ourselves that our motives are noble and pure instead of self-preserving, it becomes much easier to justify saying or doing nothing.

Because of Christian counseling, I now have a barometer for evaluating the pressure on my heart in these situations. If my overriding concerns are how something is going to affect *me* and how *I* can avoid unpleasant consequences, then my decisions will be dictated by self-protection and self-preservation. It cannot be a combination of that *and* the selfless, sacrificial love of Christ.

Today I try not to tolerate my self-preserving instincts *because I know that God has not called me to serve myself.* Anytime I am focusing on my pain instead of the pain of others, I recognize that I am in danger of making the wrong decision. Because of this heart-exposure, I now find it increasingly difficult to *choose* self-preservation. I do not want to cultivate this in my heart. I am well aware that I have made errors in judgment. In some cases, I probably believed I was required to say or do something that God may have not required of me. However, even though I will make mistakes, I now endeavor to choose the painful and unwanted consequences over failing to take the stand I believe God requires of me. The path I am consciously endeavoring to avoid these days is the path of least resistance. That path leads to regret and the cultivation of a selfish heart.

While still attending Volunteer State, I learned of an academic scholarship awarded annually by Lipscomb University to one non-traditional student transferring from a community college. I had to apply for it and write an essay. I had to have completed a minimum number of hours while maintaining a high grade point average. I more than qualified academically since I had taken multiple honors courses and maintained a 4.0 in my two years at Vol State. I applied for and received this scholarship, which covered two-thirds of my tuition. It was quite satisfying, as I did not want my education to be a financial burden on our family. My hard work had paid off.

Many good things were happening. It seemed to me like we should have been happier. Our son, Danny, was engaged to be married in August. We were building our dream home. My then-husband was making a lot of money. However, there was this constant underlying strain in my marriage that I could never seem to anticipate or manage. I had no idea how close my marriage was to ending. I had made up my mind long ago to make the best of my life and focus on my blessings rather than my problems. I sincerely wanted the marriage to survive. In spite of that, it seemed like things were going south quickly.

My attempts to respond in a more healthy way to the conflict at home seemed to make matters worse. Floyd told me that any change in my defined role (as enabler) was probably going to be unwelcome and that I should expect tremendous resistance to my efforts. When two people want to change, things can greatly improve. However, if any or all change is unwelcome and unacceptable to one of the parties, the heat might go up dramatically. My marriage was heading toward a rapid "crash and burn" situation based on my desire to change. However, I was deeply committed to change and willing to take this risk.

Once I had seen the ways in which my own unhealthy behavior had been an essential element in the toxicity, I simply could not remain in that role knowingly. It was not an option for me. I was committed to becoming a healthier person and a healthier Christian. Although I hoped my personal growth would not result in rejection, I was willing to live with that consequence if it happened.

Danny and Rebecca were married on August 3, 2002. I filed for divorce on August 27, a day after moving out of our brand-new home. A big, fancy house is no substitute for a healthy relationship. In fact, it can be quite empty and hollow. I discovered the house meant absolutely nothing to me. I had spent an entire year overseeing the building process, putting my personal touches everywhere. It was to be my dream home, the home I intended to live in for the rest of my life. But giving up my dream home was the easiest part of leaving.

I asked my dad if I could move in with him so that I could continue going to school full time. I couldn't keep my scholarship if I wasn't a full time student with a high GPA. He welcomed me. I moved from 4500 square feet into a small bedroom in my dad's home. As a few of my possessions were being loaded onto a truck, I looked around the house and knew in my heart that it was the end of the road. There would be no reconciliation this time. I was forty-three, and my life seemed to be collapsing around me.

I moved on Sunday and began a new semester in a completely new environment on Tuesday. The timing was rotten. I had worked so hard to earn that scholarship, and instead of this being a time of celebration and joy, I was emotionally devastated. Day after day, I walked the Lipscomb campus feeling intense pain. My nerves were shattered. The anxiety was constant. Tears were continually in my eyes or ready to form in my eyes. As I walked from one class to the next, I remember asking God, "*How* can this be happening? I tried so hard. You know I didn't want this. I just don't understand."

I never blamed God for the unfortunate things that happened, but I didn't understand why my life was in shambles just when it seemed to me that it should have been getting better. I came to believe with all my heart that if God allowed me to suffer, He had a purpose. I knew God saw me. I knew He saw my broken heart and the tears in my eyes. I knew there were things He could teach me during this painful time and I wanted to open my heart to His will for my life. He could have prevented this outcome, but He did not. Maybe His purpose was simply equipping me to help another hurting person someday. Even if there was nothing beyond that, it was enough for me. So I made every effort to accept my circumstances and move forward, putting myself completely in His hands.

Lipscomb was an ideal environment for me during these difficult weeks and months. I looked forward to chapel every day. There were days that it seemed as if God was speaking directly to me through the songs. I felt His presence. I was thankful for the privilege of attending a Christian university and the blessing of my scholarship. I recognized God's provisions for me and realized that He began a process of redemption in me long before my current circumstances. God had worked out all the details of my life so far, and I knew that He could see the future, He could see *beyond* my present pain. He would certainly continue to take care of me in the days ahead.

God knew the future He had in store for me would surpass my grandest hopes and dreams. His abundant provision was so much closer than I could have ever anticipated. I love to reflect on the anxiety of those days and the questions I was asking Him. In the depths of my despair, after so many years of disappointment, I had resigned myself to a long wait before something positive happened. However, God had other plans, *amazing plans*, for my life.

17

The Letter

During the fall of 2002 my anxiety was so intense it was affecting me physically. I had lost ten pounds. Now I understand how an eating disorder might develop for some women out of this kind of stress. My life felt out of control and one thing that gave me a sense of satisfaction was stepping on the scale each morning. In spite of the fact that everyone was telling me I looked emaciated, seeing that number made me feel good—like I was controlling *something*.

One of the reasons I had resigned myself to the divorce was that I did not feel I could continue living in such extreme stress. It was taking a toll on me physically, and I noticed myself becoming emotionally detached and passive. My ex-husband thought that I was indifferent. I wasn't indifferent or apathetic about the marriage; I had just developed a new coping mechanism. I left thinking that at least being apart would bring peace, but it did not. The divorce became bitter and hostile.

There wasn't a marriage or even a friendship to salvage. In so many words, I was told to hit the road. However, in my mind, since I had moved out and filed the paperwork, I was the one who ended the marriage. In our church, there had always been great emphasis placed on who left and who filed. In most situations, the implication was that the person who left was the person in the wrong. I was struggling with the persistent fear that God was mad at me for being the one to leave.

The fear of God's wrath was the greatest contributing factor to my constant anxiety. Everyone was telling me that God knew and understood— even people I never expected to say that. It just wasn't enough to put my mind at ease. The tapes in my head played on. One day, I broke down sobbing in my car. I had held in tears all day and I just couldn't hold them back any longer. I had a conversation with God that was different in tone from any I have had before or since. I told Him flat out, "I cannot live like this. I can't concentrate. I can't eat. All I do is cry. I am living in constant fear that you are angry with me. If I have displeased you, I will do whatever you tell me to do to make it right even if it's not what I want to do. But if you want me to go back to my marriage, you have to make it glaringly obvious to me. And if that is *not* your will and you are *not* displeased with me, *you've got to take away this anxiety!* The only way I will know that you are not mad at me is if you remove this constant fear. If you take it from me, I will know that only you could have taken it."

I had never prayed in a demanding tone, but I was desperate to hear from God. The minute I finished that prayer, a sense of calm settled over me. My whole body relaxed. I felt peace. No more tears. The anxiety dissipated. The next morning, I woke up a different person. My fear and anxiety never returned. Because He answered my prayer in such a remarkable way, I was able to rest in His assurance that I was not out of His will. From that point on, I just got stronger and stronger.

My second semester at Lipscomb was much better. Once again, I made new friends and became comfortable in my new environment. My mind was at peace regarding my failed marriage. However, I felt self-conscious about the fact that I was getting divorced. I had to fight my neurotic inclination to explain my circumstances to people I barely knew (God forbid anyone *think* that I had not taken my vows seriously.) It was nobody's business and no one ever made me feel judged; it was just my compulsive need to have others view me as a good person.

It was refreshing to be on a Christian campus. I decided to major in family relations. I loved focusing on the family dynamic, and I gained new insight into my past through these studies. Since I always seemed to choose electives in either psychology or communications, I wound up with two minors. I had inspirational professors who loved God. There were fewer non-traditional students at Lipscomb than there had been at Volunteer State, but I really didn't have a hard time fitting in. Even though I was old enough to be everyone's mom, I never felt out of place.

As I was gaining a new acceptance of my personal circumstances, I was continuing to struggle with the issues in CGT. I hardly attended services at this point and began visiting other churches, but I had not made a real break. Danny and Rebecca were on the verge of leaving by now. Cheryl had stopped going to CGT as well.

I spent most of my free time with Cheryl. We had been as close as sisters for many years. She and Chris lived right around the corner from my dad, and their home was my favorite place to hang out. I loved having dinner with their family. Dinner conversation with their three kids was always a riot. Laughter is great medicine. I lived at my dad's, but Chris and Cheryl's house was *home*.

A new church was finally built in Cross Plains, Tennessee. Everyone was excited about the new building. I was not. I was realizing that I had not felt a part of this church for a very long time. I was held by indoctrination, a deep sense of loyalty, and many lifelong friendships. Yet while I was going through my divorce, I felt the emotional absence from those friends. It wasn't that they didn't care about me; I knew they did. I chalked it up to everyone having their own set of problems, but I felt the distance. I realized I needed to find a new church home, but I felt it would be wrong of me simply to disappear. After all, I had spent my entire life in CGT. Prior to his mental decline, Brother Mears was my only pastor. Becky had known me since I was born. Steve had known me since 1966. I had moved from California to Tennessee to stay closely connected to this group of people. They were my life. Steve was now my pastor. I wanted to leave in a respectful manner. I did not want him to have to speculate or make assumptions. Since there had been so much controversy, I wanted them both to know that I loved them and was not leaving because I was angry or offended. I didn't agree with the way Steve had chosen to handle certain situations, but I was not leaving in protest.

It has always been easier for me to express myself in writing, so I chose to write. I poured my heart out in a letter. With the exception of a few personal remarks (removed out of respect for the privacy of another), this is the letter I wrote in 2003:

April 18, 2003

Dear Steve & Becky,

I am writing this letter because I am considering leaving our church and, while I feel strongly that you deserve to know why, I feel more comfortable conveying my thoughts in writing. I believe that the view of most people in Body of Christ Churches is that there is no other place one can go; we alone have the truth and are God's special people. So, when I tell you that I am leaning heavily toward making another church my home at this time, my expectation is that you will view me as someone who is lost, or at the very least, someone who has "lost their vision." And that could cause *me* to respond defensively. So I decided a letter was best.

I want you to hear directly from me why I feel the need to go elsewhere. I don't want you to have to rely on speculation. I want you to know the truth. Not only do I feel I owe you that; but it is my sincere desire that you would not misunderstand my motives or feel bad toward me. My friendships at CGT will always be important to me. I don't want to remove the church or the people from my life. I'm not leaving because I have anything against anyone, because I don't think it matters how I live or because I'm looking for an easier way. I just want to grow spiritually and I haven't been able to do that at CGT for a long time. (I would be the first to say that I am responsible for my growth or lack of growth, which is another reason for this decision.) On the other hand, I want to make it clear that I'm not saying this is a decision for all time or that I will never come back. It's not that kind of decision. And I will always endeavor to remain open to God's will.

I have spent almost 44 years in our assembly and, because of the emphasis on perfection, I can't remember a time in my life when I truly believed (for more than a few minutes during a spiritual high) that I would get to go to heaven or see Jesus. Part of the reason I felt in a rush to get married at such a young age was because of the end times teaching and the references to 1989 possibly being the beginning of the last hour. I felt like I barely had enough time to have a family before the battle of Armageddon. When Danny was born, I wondered if he would even make it to the age of accountability. I have always felt doomed and just grateful that I didn't believe in a burning hell. However, in spite of my defeated outlook, I haven't had a struggle with still wanting to live my life as a Christian; even without the hope of eternal life, I wanted to please God because I love Him. And as far as I'm concerned, if I love God, live a good life and still die, I can accept that. But there is something very wrong and sad about that outlook.

At this point, it feels like I'm getting older by the minute. The (equally yoked) marriage I have invested 27 years of my life in and fought so hard to preserve has collapsed. . . . Because of being taught I have to be perfect since I was a child, I feel no hope of eternal life. And I see *this* life slipping by. I am desperate to experience the hope and the joy that I see in the lives of other Christians (who do not come to our church). I have frequently heard people in our church say that Christians in other churches don't even think it matters how you live (because they don't believe they can be perfect). But this is so untrue! I have not met even one Christian who believes that way. I have crossed paths with wonderful Christians whose lives are dedicated to God and are bearing obvious spiritual fruit. And I keep thinking that even if the perfection doctrine is true and I can't make it somewhere else, I'm not going to make it at CGT either. So I might be able to be more Christ-like and more of a fulfilled Christian in *this* life by being somewhere else. And after forty-four years of expecting to just die, I am longing to experience the anticipation of even *possibly* going to be with Jesus someday. I'm sure you can't understand that because you DO feel like you will make it. But I never have.

Lipscomb has been a haven for me. I know God placed me there at this critical time in my life. When I started there in the fall, my life was freshly torn apart and I couldn't get through a single day without tears and anxiety attacks. The future was so scary and I couldn't understand how this was happening to me when I had become so good at not having any needs and not making any demands in order to hold my marriage together. But every day in chapel, God was right there comforting me and assuring me He knew what I'd been through and He would take care of me. Over and over, He demonstrated His love in obvious ways. He has used students and faculty at Lipscomb to speak to me. I would pray about something and He would answer my prayer immediately. . . . I knew I was free. . . . I asked God to take the inner turmoil . . . and He immediately took the anxiety away from me—that very day. I never struggled with my decision after that because God gave me such a complete peace. I knew He answered my prayer because I could not have done that for myself. . . . I felt that God had shown me this was His will for my life and to accept it. So I did. But I have to tell you, I didn't feel like you or Bro. Mears (if he were still the pastor) would have accepted what God had given me [because] . . . I remember Bro. Mears saying from the pulpit that we should not pray that God would show US, we should pray that God would show HIM.

I have always believed God loved me. But I've never believed the details of my life mattered much to Him. I've always felt insignificant and worthless in His eyes. But that has changed this year. And it's changed as a result of being at Lipscomb and going to several other non-denominational churches regularly— experiencing the God who loves me so much He will relentlessly pursue me—instead of the God who is ready to cut me off or shake me out if I step out of line. I've begun to believe that I'm *not* insignificant to God and He has a plan for my life. I feel accepted by Him, in spite of my weakness. But my spiritual growth has come through people and places I once would never have imagined. I've believed all my life that I might as well give up trying to be a Christian unless I was in our church. And I've watched a lot of other people grow up, feel like a failure and completely give up on God because they couldn't do what was expected of them and "measure up" in the eyes of other people. That just feels so wrong to me. I don't want to make one group of people so special in my mind that I unintentionally limit God and the vastness of His plan—or even worse, elevate myself to a level that is not pleasing to Him. You may not understand how I can feel this way, but there are so many times when I have felt (for years) that we worship the Body of Christ more than we worship Jesus – especially in our songs. When I worship in other churches, I feel like the emphasis is more on God and less on self and who the people are. I'm not telling you this to be critical. I am doing this because I think it's important for you to know how I came to this decision. I'm just sorry I am so long-winded. But I want you to know my heart.

I don't want to make this a list of grievances. All churches have problems. But I do want to tell you something specific that has been very discouraging to me; especially in light of some of the major problems we've ignored or failed to appropriately respond to. I sincerely don't understand making rules, which cannot be backed up by the Scriptures, for the purpose of our being more accepted by Bro. Jolly's followers. That just seems inherently wrong to me and not at all about God. I don't believe people should be required to conform to a rule that is not only un-scriptural, but is done to obtain acceptance from other people, in order to qualify for participation in our services (i.e., having to wear a white shirt to play in the band). That is making a rule more important than a person. Isn't that the sin of the Pharisees? Things like that are deeply troubling to me. I have done things all my life that I did not believe God required of me because I had such a strong need to be accepted and approved of by the other people in our church. But that isn't serving God. It's serving my own need to be loved! In that environment, seeking God's approval is transformed into gaining social acceptance and status within the church. I'm not saying that is the case for everyone. I know there are people who are convinced God requires those things of them and are doing them for the right reasons. But there are many who are doing it for the sake of conformity. Because when you stop conforming, people view you differently—as though you're lost or you're disobedient to God (because you aren't convinced every rule came directly from God.) I believe that what God wants from me is pure motives. And if I am motivated to do things that make me *look* "good" or "right" to others, then that is my reward. I can't conform anymore to things I don't believe God even cares about in order to be approved of by people. It feels insincere.

But that creates another problem for someone like me. I removed myself from all areas of participation a long time ago because I don't conform to all the church rules. I wear pants. I wear earrings. I don't always cover my knees or elbows. My hair isn't long. But the thing I fear being more than anything is a hypocrite or a fraud. So I don't do things based on where I am going or who I might see any longer. God sees me at all times. However, if I do not conform in a "visible" way, there are many who would not consider me a proper representative of the church in the community—no matter how well I treat others or how sincerely I am trying to live as a Christian. The fact is, I have lived with those types of superficial judgments (and even been guilty of them) my whole life. And that causes me to be reluctant to be active in our church in any capacity (not that I feel my involvement is even desired).

I have struggled with whether or not I should help in the kitchen. I did not sign up for a team. And only when I was approached, I said I would be happy to help out with the gravy. But I feel conflicted about having any kind of job in the church when I do not embrace all of the outward appearance standards, which are regarded as so important and such an indicator of spirituality. So what do I do? Does God want me to be in a church where I cannot put my whole heart into His service? What kind of a Christian life is it when you feel constrained by the choices of either doing something you don't believe, in order to gain people's acceptance, or being a spectator in the church? I can't thrive spiritually by approaching my church life this way. I want to be a part of a church I can put my whole heart into; not only through worshiping, but by being actively involved and helping others. But in our church, those who do not conform are not taken seriously as Christians; they are dismissed as rebellious or worldly and have no credibility. Maybe this has changed somewhat, but that has been my experience over the greater part of my life. And I am wounded when I sense these attitudes toward me -- or anyone else, for that matter.

I feel like an outsider in the church I grew up in. I have felt that way for many years. I felt so alone when [my husband] was in that two-year-long depression. And the church has not been a haven for me during the last eight months. The focus in our churches is more on the shepherds than the sheep. Sometimes it seems like the ministry is considered more as royalty than as servants. Our church is not even able to function under a true, recognizable leadership because of the emphasis that has been placed on one man and his inability to recognize that he can no longer lead. I mean no disrespect. I love Bro. Mears. But for years now, it just seems like it's far more important to maintain Bro. Mears' status and dignity than to have a properly functioning assembly. It's like the people in the church just don't matter as much as the minister does. I am probably going way out on a limb to be this honest about my feelings. But I think God expects me to tell you these things, no matter how it affects your feelings toward me. God knows I do not want to offend or hurt either of you. Please forgive me if I have. I am speaking directly from my heart. And I am saying these things in love. I love both of you and I love the church.

I probably don't need to say any more. I hope I haven't said too much. I want to make this shorter, but I don't know what I would take out. It's important to me that you know I am not leaving God and I am not an enemy of the church. I just feel like I am not growing spiritually there and yet I am in other settings. Steve, I've heard you say many times that if we are not convinced we are where God wants us, we should find wherever that is. That's what I'm sincerely trying to do.

There was no response to my letter.

18

Self-Disclosure

The only thing holding up the finalization of my divorce was a financial settlement. My ex-husband had openly begun a relationship with someone immediately after I left. Different people felt compelled to tell me they had seen him out and about with another woman. At first, I thought he could be simply hanging out with a friend. However, when I finally connected the dots, I realized this attraction had begun before I left. I knew the person casually and was aware that a friendship existed, but I was never suspicious. At this point, I *wondered* if the friendship might have contributed to the demise of the marriage, but it didn't really matter. The marriage would have ended anyway. His relationship provided a further sense of release. Because he had moved on with his life so quickly; I felt freer to move on with mine. After being separated for seven months and knowing my ex had officially moved on, I discovered the world of Match.com.

Being single was unfamiliar and a bit scary. I didn't know *how* to be alone. I had been married for the majority of my life. It wasn't that I was lonely per se, but I did have a fear of being alone. In hindsight, I realize I was more vulnerable than I realized. However, at the time, I believed I was ready to start dating. I felt conflicted about dating prior to my divorce being final, but finally decided to purchase a subscription to Match.com, telling myself I was just going to make some new friends. I did not expect to meet someone online with whom I would have a serious relationship. It was supposed to be a fun diversion until I met the *right* person in *real life*.

Looking at the online profiles was reassuring. More than anything else, I think Match.com represented concrete evidence that there were lots of people *of all ages* looking for companionship. I wasn't alone.

I wanted to be able to email someone if I liked their profile, so I bought a year's subscription for $99.00. However, I was uncomfortable with the idea of a public profile. I did not want to be seen by anyone other than someone I might *choose* to contact. At first, I simply enjoyed reading profiles. I created a profile of my own, but kept it hidden. I could share it privately if I chose to.

Over the next few months I developed email friendships, talked on the phone, and went out on a few dates. In that process I learned that I had many deep-rooted and unfulfilled emotional needs. I am thankful my first friend was a professional psychologist with an honest heart. Despite the fact that we were hardly compatible, I immediately became emotionally attached and quickly opened up, sharing many details of my life with him. He recognized my vulnerability and told me early on that we should not continue to see each other. He said that it would never work because our personalities were so different, and he did *not* want to be another person in my life who had hurt or exploited me. It wasn't what I wanted to hear at the time—I wanted someone to date—but I knew God's mercy was in play. This proved to be a valuable learning experience for me. I could have made some terrible mistakes during that time, and even briefly entertained some harmful ways of thinking. I was thankful that God protected me from myself. As you might imagine, my son and daughter-in-law were concerned for my safety and emotional well-being. They knew that I was vulnerable. One time Rebecca told me that Danny could not sleep and had been on his knees praying for me in the middle of the night. I think it's supposed to be the other way around. In a way, I was reverting to a time of life that I had skipped over and never lived. I felt bad about worrying my son, but I wanted to do things my way for once. As I continued to go on dates, it dawned on me that it wasn't that bad being single. I didn't need to be in a relationship. I was enjoying my freedom, and I began to feel confident that I *would* be in a healthy relationship eventually. So, until that time came, I was going to make the most of being unattached.

I remember a pivotal conversation I had with my friend, Dee Dee, about the uncertainty of my future. She told me I should pray for my future husband. She said, "I don't mean you should pray that God will *bring* you a husband. I think it's *a given* that you will get remarried. I mean you should start praying *for* him. You don't know him yet, but God does. Pray specifically that God will accomplish what needs to be accomplished in his life, as well as yours; that you would both be whole and healed from your wounds before you find each other. He has probably been through his own share of pain, you know." This wise advice made an impression on me.

Shortly thereafter, I did pray *for* my future husband, whose identity was known only to God. While praying for him, I began thinking about the *kind* of man that I would want to marry. As I did, I thought about the kind of *woman* he deserved. As I prayed for him, he became tangible. It may sound strange, but I knew I wanted to be true to him before I even met him. From that time forward, I could no longer entertain certain thoughts or possible choices. In hindsight, I am amazed at all God was doing in my heart and mind despite my double-mindedness.

On one hand, I had a sincere desire to grow toward *God*. On the other, I simply wanted to please and indulge *myself*. I had been attempting to justify and excuse temptations toward ungodly choices at exactly the same time I was expressing my need to leave CGT in order to grow spiritually. Then it occurred to me how this is the struggle we *all* contend with over the course of our entire lives. Though we outgrow some selfish desires and battle others, the drive to please ourselves is always present on some level. Yet our desire for God keeps us engaged in the struggle to resist those selfish impulses.

Toward the end of May, I discovered a profile I had never seen. I looked at his picture, his religious preference. I looked to see if he was a non-smoker. I read his comments. I liked everything I read, but the sentence that sparked my interest was, "I think anger is an ugly emotion." Kindness and a non-combative temperament were high priorities for me in a relationship. This was how I described my ideal person:

> "The essential traits I'm looking for are strong character, sincerity, warmth, kindness, emotional stability, balance, optimism, intelligence and the ability to communicate (which means being able to express emotion and hear/care what another person feels/thinks). I like people who can laugh at themselves and not take life (or themselves) too seriously. Life is too short to get bent out of shape over little things. I'd like to find someone I could have fun with, laugh and be silly with, spoil with attention and affection, and share my deepest thoughts with. It would be nice if you also like to work out and take care of yourself physically. I'd love a regular work out partner. I'm not a complicated, demanding or high-maintenance woman. So an uncomplicated guy with the ability to appreciate me for my strengths and laugh with me about my shortcomings would be ideal. I promise to offer the same. Also, I realize conflict is an unavoidable part of intimacy. However, I don't enjoy it; so if you're mellow and easygoing – that is a BIG plus for me. And being a Christian is a must."

Although I didn't know it yet, those words described John Howerton to a tee. A friend had talked him into posting a profile, but he was ambivalent about dating. After all he had been through, he wasn't sure he would ever want to be in a relationship again. However, he thought it would be nice to find a friend whose company he enjoyed.

After studying John's profile, I sent him an email inviting him to view my profile. I emailed him on Thursday, and he replied right away. He said he wasn't interested in most emails he received, but he felt something different about me right away. He *wanted* to respond. The night following our initial contact, we spoke on the phone. After talking for a while, he said, "I guess we should meet in person some time." I said, "Sure!" He asked when I would like to get together, expecting me to put him off a bit. However, I responded enthusiastically, "What are you doing tomorrow?"

We made plans to meet for dinner at Famous Dave's. He worked six days a week and Saturday had been a particularly exhausting day. I was there waiting when he called to let me know he was running a little late. Then he said, "I thought about canceling." I laughed and said, "Well, it's a good thing you didn't stand me up. I'm glad I won't have to hunt you down and kill you." As the words left my mouth, I thought, "Why did I say *that?*" I was in a playful mood, and it's not uncommon for me to blurt things out unexpectedly. Later in our relationship he told me that he perked up about our date after that comment. He said he thought to himself, "Hmmm. She's got a personality. I like that."

When he walked in the restaurant and approached me, I nervously extended my hand. He gave me a hug instead of a handshake. I will never forget John's eyes as we talked over dinner. He was completely engaged in our conversation. We sat there for hours. He maintained constant eye contact. He never glanced at his watch. He wanted to know all about me and spoke very little about himself unless I asked a specific question. When I shared some of the pain of my past, he was so compassionate. However, throughout this first dinner, I didn't feel any romantic chemistry. When we got up to leave, John went into his comic mode. He did a little spin and dance. He made me laugh. He impressed me as the kind of person I would want in my life. We got in our cars and waved good-bye as we each drove off in separate directions. I remember thinking that I had just made a dear friend but nothing more.

The next morning I had an email from him. It melted my heart. We started emailing and talking on the phone every day. I learned that John loved music, and the Eagles came up in conversation. He had just seen them in Nashville and had tickets for their upcoming show in Memphis the following weekend, although he had not decided if he was going to go. I told him the Eagles were my all time favorite group. He invited me to go with him but was not pushy or presumptuous. I felt safe with him and said I would love to go. I mentioned how much Chris and Cheryl would love to see the Eagles. He suggested inviting them along and bought four new tickets on ebay (close to the stage), so we could all sit together.

We talked on the phone and emailed daily. He was such a neat person; I was feeling kind of disappointed there had been no chemistry on that first date. However, when he came to pick me up to go to the concert, I experienced a completely different feeling than I had on our first date. I took one look at him and thought, *Chemistry is not going to be a problem.* I was immediately attracted to him. Although he is very handsome, I had not felt physically attracted on our first date, and I have always been glad; because it was his *heart* that I was first attracted to. Halfway through the concert in Memphis, I was smitten. I told Cheryl at intermission that, although it was much too soon to know for sure, I believed John was the one for me. She said he felt like family to *her* within ten minutes of being introduced to him.

John got each of us our own rooms and took us to brunch the next morning at The Peabody Hotel. It was a magical, but strictly platonic weekend. The following weekend when we saw each other, I laughed and told him that my dad asked if he had kissed me. John looked surprised and said, "I never would have kissed you. For one thing, even though your divorce is almost final, you are still legally married. Also, I didn't want you to think I had an ulterior motive for taking you to Memphis because I didn't." I was impressed. My first thought was that a guy this old fashioned would be very loyal in a relationship. We agreed to remain strictly friends until I was legally free. My divorce became final twenty days later on June 19, 2003.

Long after that night, I told John that I had driven away from our first date thinking, "I have just made a dear *friend* for life." He said, "You did; I am your *dearest* friend, and I always will be." I felt like I had won the lottery. There was just one thing I had to get out in the open before we became any closer. I had a terrible failure in my past that I felt compelled to disclose. I didn't think he would reject me for it, but it was possible. We had known each other less than a month. However, if we were to share a future, I wanted no secrets between us. I wrote a long email revealing the worst thing I had ever done.

క్ల

When I was twenty-two years old, I found myself on a selfish path that resulted in a serious sin; the sin of adultery. Having married so young, we were immature and had an unhealthy relationship. I was vulnerable, and a flattering remark was all it took to lure me down a deceptive and destructive road. Although I never intended to commit this sin, I quickly found myself addicted to kind, flattering words. It was not about a person; it was about filling an emotional void. Instead of repeating the sin, I came to my senses immediately and repented. However, I suffered for years over the pain I had inflicted on others. Twenty-eight years later, it remains the single biggest regret of my life.

When I revealed this to John, I wanted him to understand that this was an isolated incident of weakness, not a character trait. I knew I did not have to share this with him, since it had happened more than two decades before I met him. I simply wanted a relationship built on complete honesty and integrity. He responded to my self-disclosure with compassion and sensitivity. It was never an issue between us.

19

Brittany

By the end of July, John and I set a wedding date of January 4, 2004. We would have set the date earlier, but we realized that Brittany, John's eighteen-year-old daughter, needed more time. Our relationship had progressed quickly and we wanted to be sensitive to her. God put a love in my heart for Brittany the night I met John; before I knew he would be anything more than my friend. I can't explain it, but when he talked about her and the things she had gone through—including the loss of her mother at such a young age to alcoholism—I wanted to be a friend to her so badly. At the same time, I did not want to push myself on her. I wanted her to have time to get to know me and learn that she could trust me. I wanted her to know that the one thing I would never do was come between her and her dad. A father's love is vitally important in a daughter's life and I wanted to nurture the bond between them. I wanted to be instrumental in the two of them having a closer relationship and never be her rival. She responded to my affection more quickly than I expected, even initiating some heart-to-heart talks. One afternoon she said, "I can tell you love my dad just the way he is, even his goofy side. You don't want to change him. And I like that about you." I assured her that I *adored* her dad the way he was, and the last thing I would ever want to do was change him. I thought it was sweet that she was evaluating me based on how I interacted with *him*. She didn't make it about herself. This let me know just how much her dad's happiness meant to her.

In a relatively short time, I gained Brittany's trust and we developed a genuine friendship. I had no idea how little time we had and how brief our relationship would be. I am so grateful that I didn't give her more space. Being the extrovert that I am, I threw caution to the wind and just loved her as much as she would allow. I wanted to help Brittany through the remainder of her teenage years, encouraging her to give her life fully to God. I wanted to be the right kind of example to Brittany. I was always painfully honest. I allowed her to question me. I acknowledged my own sinfulness and selfishness. I wanted to be real with her. There is no doubt in my mind today that Brittany knew I loved her. Several of her close friends would later come to me and tell me privately, "Brittany really loved you and she told me how happy she was that her dad was going to marry you." Those friends will possibly never comprehend how much it meant to me to know those conversations had occurred.

Brittany graduated in August after completing summer school. We bought her a pair of diamond stud earrings and surprised her with them that evening. She had recently been in a minor car accident and had broken her ankle, which had not healed properly. So Monday morning she was to have outpatient surgery on that ankle. She was going to need help while recuperating and, since I was between semesters, I offered to stay with her as much as she wanted me to. She said she would like that. I stayed that Sunday night, planning to go to the hospital with them early the next morning.

Around 4:00 a.m., Brittany called for her dad over the intercom. She had battled severe asthma since she was a baby and John had been through many a middle of the night crisis before. Once again, she was struggling to breathe. He practically flew up the stairs. She was standing when he entered her room. He carried her over to the bed and set her down.

I had no clue how serious the situation was until I heard John scream Brittany's name in a way that spoke loudly and clearly to me; *he was losing her.* She went into cardiac arrest. From another room, I called 911. I stood outside her bedroom door and prayed as medical personnel worked aggressively to revive her, but they could not bring her back to us.

Just as the ambulance was pulling into the emergency room entrance, the paramedics succeeded in restarting her heart. However, by this time, her brain had been without oxygen for close to forty minutes. We think the doctors knew what the outcome would be, but they kept her on a respirator for forty-eight hours as they thoroughly tested and observed her. While we waited in uncertainty, I told John that whatever happened I was as committed to him as if we were already married, and I would never abandon him. If Brittany came home and needed care around the clock, I would quit school and care for her. I assured him I wasn't going anywhere. I would *never* leave him.

John and I slept in recliners at the hospital, wanting to be close to Brittany in case there was any change in her condition. There was no brain function or any involuntary responses to stimulus whatsoever. Ultimately, her doctor took us into a private room and broke the news that she had suffered irreversible brain death. The only thing keeping her alive was the respirator. It was time to say good-bye. I stood in the doorway as John went to his daughter this one last time. This was the one and only time I would ever see him break down in sobs of anguish. My heart ached for him as he touched her face and whispered parting words of love to his precious little girl.

Sunday night we had celebrated her high school graduation by giving her diamond earrings. Friday we were burying her. Life felt cruel and unfair. However, John's faith sustained him. He told me he believed with all his heart that if it had been God's will for Brittany to live another day, she would not have died. He said the timing made it more difficult. "She was about to have what she had always longed for. We would have been a real family, and you would have been the mom she had always longed for," he told me. "But she belongs to God, and He loves her even more than I do. I *accept* God's will even though I will never *understand* it in this lifetime."

John had no idea how inspiring his strong faith was to me. I knew this was the hardest thing he had ever faced. We had only been together two and a half months. I could not imagine his pain, and I wondered if he would sink into depression or emotionally withdraw from me because of his grief. I knew this could potentially change John and therefore change our relationship. There was just no way for me to predict how he would respond to this kind of devastation. However, I was determined to be by his side no matter what. To my surprise, he never withdrew emotionally or shut me out of his pain. He leaned on me. He shared his grief. He embraced me as the comforting presence in his life that I longed to be.

I had just completed a course called Death and Dying at Lipscomb. Although I had been through my own grieving processes, through this course I became educated in healthy grieving and in how to be a resource and support to someone else as they grieved. Some might think of that as a fortunate coincidence. I believe it was the mercy and provision of God. In every way He was equipping me to be what John needed. *Had I not prayed that He would do that for both of us before I even knew John's name?* I knew that John was a gift from God in my life. I would soon realize that I was also a gift from God to John at a very crucial time in his life.

We give God all the credit for the life He has given us.

Friends and family came to the house after we left the cemetery. When everyone other than our closest family members had gone home, John whispered that he wanted to show me something. He led me into another room and privately handed me a beautiful wooden box. He knelt down on one knee, took my hand and said, "I never could have made it through this week without you. I love you so much. Will you marry me?" I said, "Yes, you *know* I will."

In that box was the largest diamond I had ever seen. I remember saying, "This is a movie star's ring, not a regular person's ring." He responded, "It's the ring you deserve." I reminded him that he had not known me long enough for me to deserve that ring. I told him the ring was gorgeous and stunning; I loved it, but I would have been just as thrilled to marry him if he had given me a ring out of a Cracker Jack box. With feigned disappointment, he said, "Now you tell me."

August 15 will always be a bittersweet anniversary. I cannot think about John's proposal without also thinking of Brittany and the pain of losing her just as we were about to become a family. However, I will be eternally grateful that God brought John and me together before her tragic loss. Although I can never fill the void of her absence, I know that my love and support helped John through the worst moments of his life.

Although I grieve Brittany's loss and the loss of many hopes and dreams for our future relationship, I have accepted this outcome—along with meeting and marrying John—as God's will. I know I would not have been the perfect stepmom, but I loved her. I take comfort in knowing that God ordained the number of her days and He loves her more than we ever could have. One thing we are certain of is that Brittany would not want to come back. Because of her faith in Christ, she has gained a family relationship that surpasses anything we could have provided for her.

John and I were legally married on January 4, 2004 as planned. In our hearts, however, we married months earlier. He told me that in the middle of our hospital vigil, right after I assured him I would never leave, he had gone to the chapel and vowed to God that from that day forward he would be committed to me as a husband for the rest of our lives. Going through one of the most excruciating experiences a couple can ever face made us even closer. Our commitment rapidly grew deeper and stronger. It felt as if we had known and loved each other all our lives. With the exception of losing Brittany, our life together is like a fairytale. We have enjoyed the most loving, tranquil relationship I could have ever imagined.

Strike that. It's been better than I could have imagined.

20

Gone but Not Free

Breaking away from CGT was hard. I had grown up there. All of my closest friends were a part of the church. I had always worshiped (four times a week) alongside my biological family as well. All my closest relationships were under this one umbrella. I had moved clear across the country in order to avoid separation from these people. That is how vitally important they were to me. Needless to say, leaving was extremely difficult.

Only those who share this unique history and the painful journey of leaving can fully understand or appreciate just how difficult this process is. That is why those who leave naturally gravitate to one another. Around the time I left there were other people—families and individuals—who felt the same calling to leave. We did not all wind up in the same church, but we would get together and share our understanding of where we had been and what we were learning in our spiritual journey.

Some of us were labeled as enemies of the church. Although I had been so very careful to leave in a loving and respectful way, it was said that I had left angry and bitter. Those kinds of remarks were hurtful and untrue. I did have family and friends who wished me well and assured me they did not believe I was lost, but our relationships still changed. I realize now that this was simply unavoidable. Although I did not want to lose any of my close friends, we no longer had the common bond of CGT. I knew from personal experience that they would view me as an outsider. They would be defensive and protective about the church. I knew this because I did the same thing to close friends who left before me. As a direct result of suffering the painful losses of so many lifelong friends in CGT, some of us who left made a concerted effort not to lose each other. Although we were viewed by many in

CGT as ex-members who got together to bash our old church; the truth is we really *needed* each other for support in what amounted to a scary and painful transition for us.

Only after I made the decision to leave did I come face to face with many of my deepest fears, one of them being the fear of losing my friends. That fear motivated me to move to Tennessee. However, there were other fears I had never confronted.

One of the first fears I had never confronted was the fear of having to participate in communion: the Lord's Supper. I was taught that all of Christendom had misunderstood what Jesus intended communion to be. We were told that Jesus did not intend communion to be observed through the eating of bread and drinking of wine or juice. The bread was symbolic of the Word of God, which we were to consume daily. The wine was the Spirit, which we were to drink in fully. The observance of communion accepted by most Christians was believed in CGT to be an empty, meaningless ritual. We never received communion in this way. Since I had never visited churches where communion was served, I had never been confronted with a decision regarding participation in this "meaningless ritual." When I began to visit churches outside CGT, I had to decide whether or not to partake of the bread and the cup. I had to make this decision on the spot because I had not thought about it in advance.

I remember well the first time I faced this decision. I felt palpable anxiety as I contemplated whether God would be displeased with me for receiving communion. There were several phrases in my head as the bread and the cup were served: "Meaningless ritual," "not what Jesus intended," and "the beast." Because I did not want to draw attention to myself and have people possibly misunderstand my abstaining, I received the bread and the cup. In one of the churches I regularly visited, the Lord's Supper was observed every Sunday, so I had many opportunities to confront my fear. However, it took me a long time to become completely comfortable with the observance of communion.

Today, I love the observance of communion. It is not a meaningless ritual to me. It is deeply personal and a reminder of what Jesus did for me on the cross. It is a time of meditating on Christ's body that was broken for me and the shedding of His blood on my behalf. One of my favorite Christmas traditions is attending the Candlelight Christmas Eve service at the church John and I attend. We serve communion in this service together. John serves the bread and I hold the chalice of juice. As each believer dips a piece of broken bread into the cup, I look into their eyes and say, "The Lord's blood, shed for you." It always moves me to tears to consider how Christ personally died for each of us. The blood of Christ shed for you . . . shed for you . . . shed for you. I can hardly fathom that I once dismissed the observance of communion as an empty ritual.

When I first met John, he invited me to visit the church he had been attending for several years, World Outreach Church in Murfreesboro, Tennessee. He was very happy there.

What initially struck me when I first visited WOC was the size of the church. It was almost ten times the size of my former church. I didn't want to be an anonymous face in the crowd.

Another concern I had was regarding the content of the sermons and the depth of the message. One of my preconceived notions was that a church this size must surely be shallow in the Word of God. I was carrying a lot of spiritual baggage. I needed grace in my life. However, I knew I could not agree with a humanistic message intended simply to make me feel good about myself. I needed sound biblical teaching that would challenge me to live a life of obedience.

My fears were allayed when I heard Pastor Allen Jackson preach. I was hearing the uncompromised Word of God at World Outreach. That was a great comfort to me. He taught that we cannot earn our way to heaven through our good works; it is by grace we are saved. But he also challenged us as believers to live lives of obedience, pointing out that obedience is the most dramatic evidence of our faith. (In all the years I have now attended WOC, Pastor Jackson has consistently taught obedience and grace with balance and humility.)

It was Pastor Jackson's humility that made the greatest impression on me in those early months of attending WOC. He put himself right on the same level with every other believer in the congregation. I had never experienced a humble pastor, and this was so refreshing. He frequently emphasized that being a Christian was not about joining the right group; it was about a personal, transforming relationship with Jesus Christ as our Lord and Savior. He never put an emphasis on our specific congregation or himself. The emphasis was consistently on the Kingdom of God and our opportunity to cooperate with God's purposes in the world. He frequently referred to "our time in the arena," urging and inspiring us to live our lives in such a way that we would make a difference in the lives of others, pointing those around us to Christ. I found myself being continually inspired to live a more God-honoring life than ever before.

I immediately felt at home in WOC and was eager to make whatever effort was required to establish relationships. Since the church actively facilitates connecting with others and forming personal relationships, it turned out to be much easier than I imagined. There is a strong sense of community despite the size of the congregation.

୭

Although I had left CGT and embraced God's grace in a fuller way, I was afraid to let go of everything I had been taught. I still did not believe I was going to heaven based on faith in Christ alone. The perfection teaching haunted me. "Saved by grace" was labeled as "taking the easy way" in CGT. Even though I couldn't ever see the good news in learning you had to be perfect, I still held on to that doctrine. I often wondered if I *had* simply opted for the easy way. Certainly the Gospel of grace was good news, but was it too good to be true? After a lifetime of being told I had to reach perfection to *merit* eternal life, it was too big a leap for me to be quickly convinced that Jesus truly paid the price and the work was finished.

ৡ

Another doctrinal belief that posed an extremely difficult challenge for me was the Godhead. I had been raised believing that Jesus was the Father's first creation; He had not existed eternally with the Father. My former pastor mocked the Trinity from the pulpit, laughing at how "absurd it was" he would say, "Who could understand *that?*"

When my son, Danny, was in high school and wanted to become involved in a Christian youth group outside of our church, I encouraged him because I did not want him to embrace the mindset of our group, that we were the only true people of God in the earth. However, I vividly recall giving him a stern warning about embracing the doctrine of the Trinity. We believed in one God, the Father, and His *created* Son (who was *not* God). The Holy Spirit was the power or force that emanated from God, not a member of the Godhead. For some reason, this was the one foundational belief I did not want my son departing from.

After leaving CGT in 2003, I wanted to learn why other Christians believed in a triune God. For the first time, I was not afraid to learn what other Christians believed. I wanted to understand what they believed and why.

ৡ

In my last year at Lipscomb, I participated in a weekend marriage seminar. I was considering the field of marriage and family counseling, so it would be valuable experience for me. There were many different exercises for the couples, and I participated along with everyone else, sharing my personal experiences, conflicts, insecurities, hopes, and fears. After everyone had shared all weekend, there was a concluding exercise. One person at a time would sit quietly while all the others called out words they felt described this person. You couldn't say anything when it was your turn. You just had to listen and take it all in. Someone would write down each word, so that every person could reflect on what was said later. The exercise was intended to help each of us see in ourselves what others saw in us.

I have never thrown away my folder from that weekend. Somewhere I have a long list of all the adjectives used to describe me that day. There was one word, however, that stood out above all the others and made a lasting impression on me. It was electrifying. It was a word I heard frequently in CGT, but it was always used in conjunction with the word perfection. None of the people from the seminar knew me very well and certainly could not have imagined the depth of impact this word would have on me in light of my past spiritual indoctrination. Somewhere in the middle of this stream of words, I heard someone proclaim loudly, "Overcomer!"

The word stunned me. I wondered if God was speaking to my heart that day. The person who chose that word was obviously not suggesting I was perfect. However, they saw me as having *already* overcome many difficult challenges in my life. It was a defining moment. I had never viewed myself that way, but I remember thinking, "I *am* an overcomer." I had overcome many challenges and there could be no doubt that I was still holding onto my faith in God to endure to the end. Perhaps *that* was the definition of overcoming that God wanted me to embrace.

21

Using Wisdom

Growing up in such a tight-knit community leads to lives becoming deeply intertwined. Most marry within the group. This results in a high percentage of members being related in some way. There are endless family connections, which is another reason why it is so hard to leave. Even though I had left, I was still connected. There was a continuous flow of information coming from current members to former members.

Sometime in 2003 I heard that a family was moving from California to Tennessee to join CGT. They looked into buying my former "dream home." I heard this new couple had visited CGT through the invitation of friends. Both husband and wife were professional musicians, and the husband was considering being a part of the music ministry of a CGT member, also a professional musician. After their visit I heard that this couple had "fallen in love with the church" and were moving to Tennessee to be a part of CGT. I wondered how much they knew about the church prior to making this decision. Most certainly they had not been told about the allegations of abuse. I assumed they did not know everything CGT taught doctrinally, either.

In all the years I attended CGT, we did not openly share our distinctive doctrinal beliefs with other Christians right off the bat, especially anyone we were hoping to win to our fellowship. We were taught that this was "using wisdom." God would reveal these deeper "truths" when hearts were ready to receive them. We were cautioned not to get ahead of God in this way. It was considered a waste of time to offer precious truths to someone who was not searching for them, someone who would simply trample those truths under their feet because of their lack of understanding. We tried not to scare anyone away by introducing one of our "truths" prematurely, before God had prepared their heart to receive it.

A friend told me once that if her new husband knew about such and such, he would never come back. So she didn't tell him. This was common. I recall many conversations in which we would ask quietly, "Does he/she know yet that we don't believe in the Trinity?" or "Do they know yet that we don't believe in a literal hell or devil?" The group was typically not forthcoming with all of their beliefs and many wrongs were kept quiet. However, this was simply wise and loving, *not deceptive.*

The practice of withholding anything and everything negative from a prospective new member was considered using wisdom. I remember friends of mine who "protected" family members, potential spouses, and friends outside the church from knowing anything scandalous that had ever happened, even when their own lives had been recently touched by the scandal in a very personal way. It wasn't that they were trying not to gossip; they were hiding big things (including alleged abuse) that would mar the image of the church. It is my belief that CGT members weren't hiding these things out of malice. I'm convinced that they were hiding these truths with good intentions, probably because I always thought I had good intentions when I deceived others.

The couple from California had fallen in love with the people. There are many wonderful, sincere people there. They are unusually close. The majority of them are warm and likable. If I did not genuinely feel this way about them, it would have been much easier to leave. They are friends from my past that I will love and miss until the day I die, regardless of our differences.

I never met the new couple, but my son briefly met the husband, Eric, on one occasion. Danny was occasionally visiting CGT in an attempt to maintain relationships with some of his friends. He told me that he had walked in simultaneously with a group of guys one particular night. Eric was one of them. Danny and Eric had never met. As the group of guys entered the building together, Eric made a comment about the church seeming too good to be true. Danny started to respond with sarcastic humor when one of his buddies quickly shushed him. Danny kept his mouth shut.

I would not hear much more about Eric and his wife, Ann, for a while after that. They were settling in at CGT while I was making a new life with John an hour away.

✺

When John and I returned from our honeymoon in California, I began my last semester at Lipscomb University. I planned to go on to graduate school immediately and get a master's degree in counseling. My goal was to become a Licensed Professional Counselor. That was before I had any idea I would meet and marry John. As I approached graduation, John and I discussed my options. I had poured myself into school fulltime for four years. I was finally experiencing a slight bit of burnout. I was torn between continuing and taking a break.

John assured me that if becoming a professional counselor was something I needed to do to be happy and fulfilled, he would support me one hundred percent. However, he was hoping to be able to slow down in the next few years and work less. He looked forward to spending more time together. He pointed out that I would be starting a new career just as he was attempting to slow down. John appreciated and valued me as a person. Any time I would make a self-deprecating remark about not *contributing an income*, he would remind me that I had given him everything he had always longed for, a nurturing relationship and a loving, tranquil home life. Nothing meant more to him than that.

At risk of making some women gag, I actually loved the idea of devoting myself to my husband and his happiness. The one thing I had always wanted was a happy marriage. Having a successful career of my own was never a major aspiration of mine. I wanted to become a professional counselor because I believed I was going to need to support myself. However, as I contemplated my future with John, I realized that I could use my education and the gifts God had given me to help others even if I *never* got paid for it.

୭

By Easter of 2004, John and I had been together almost a year and many of my old friends had never met him. I was so proud to be married to him. I really wanted my old friends to be able to meet him. So a week or two prior to Easter, I started asking John if he would be willing to go to CGT on Easter Sunday. He reluctantly agreed. (He refers to that Easter Sunday as "John on Parade Day" because of the steady stream of people I introduced him to.) I told Cheryl we were going. She no longer attended CGT either, but she said she would like to go with us just to be together for Easter.

The first part of the service was fairly ordinary as far as I was concerned. John said he felt a little uncomfortable, but that did not surprise me, since he had never been to a church like this. After we finished singing, one of the men on the platform took prayer requests. One of these requests was concerning a child custody case. He explained that if this child's mother were granted custody, the child would be taken out of a "Body" church. I had no idea who this woman was. The congregation was asked to pray that the mother would not be granted custody of her child. No reason was offered for praying against the mother receiving custody *other than keeping the child in the group*. There was a time in my life when I would not have given this request a second thought; however, after being away from CGT for a year, I realized how bizarre this sounded. Cheryl and I exchanged glances. John commented on it after we left.

I was not expecting Steve to touch on any major Body doctrines on Easter Sunday. I just assumed his message would focus on Christ's resurrection. He began to speak about receiving the Holy Ghost. Steve emphasized that day the Body's doctrine of tongues: one's soul remains dead to God prior to receiving the Holy Spirit *and* speaking in tongues. It had always been taught in our church that speaking in tongues was evidence of receiving the Spirit, and *this* experience was the new birth. Additionally, we were taught that no believer gained entrance into the Kingdom of God until they had spoken in tongues and nobody went to heaven who had not spoken in tongues. Such great emphasis was placed on speaking in tongues that it was forbidden to marry until both parties had spoken in tongues in order to be considered "equally yoked." Even though 2 Corinthians 6:14 cautions us not to be unequally yoked together *with unbelievers*, in "the Body" we were expected to postpone marriage indefinitely if one party had not "prayed through" and spoken in tongues.

The Holy Spirit is powerful. I believe the gifts of the Holy Spirit are manifested in believers. However, I do not see scriptural support for the belief that one's soul is not alive to God until he or she speaks in tongues. In fact, that belief stands in direct contradiction to 1 John 5:1. "Everyone who believes that Jesus is the Christ has been born of God, and everyone who loves the Father loves whoever has been born of him."

As Steve repeated the words "dead to God" numerous times throughout his sermon, I could not stop thinking about it being Easter Sunday. I heard a message of death, not life. It was an odd way to celebrate Christ's resurrection. John made it clear to me on the way home that he had no desire to visit CGT again. He thought most of the people he met seemed sweet and sincere. However, he had experienced a bad feeling concerning the men on the platform throughout the service, especially those who had spoken.

I had no desire to go back. After being away from this environment for a year and hearing the true Gospel in other settings, I felt an overwhelming thankfulness that I would not spend the rest of my life under the oppressive teachings of this group. Sitting in the service that day reminded me of the spiritual chains God had broken for me.

If Eric and Ann had still been attending CGT, we would have had an opportunity to meet that Easter Sunday. However, after attending for only a few months, they discovered the Body teachings and stopped attending. Very little was said about their departure. One person had remarked to Cheryl, "Ann convinced Eric that we are a cult because we don't believe in the Trinity." That remark aroused curiosity in both of us. I never imagined that I would one day know Eric and Ann. They were faceless names to me. Only God knew that our paths would eventually cross in His perfect timing.

22

The Message Board

It was the mid to late nineties when someone first told me about the EX-GAC message board on the Internet. I was still attending CGT and was shocked that there was a place where people who had left the Gospel Assembly Churches (GAC) could openly share their negative experiences. Some of the experiences were much worse than my own, but there were similarities. We definitely looked like a destructive cult. I was still in denial that CGT was that bad and feared that readers would lump our church in with these other abusive congregations. Although our church had never gone by the name "Gospel Assembly," we were a part of this fellowship and shared the same founder, William Sowders.

At the top of the message board, there is a welcome along with a description of the website's purpose. It reads:

> "Welcome to the Message Board. The purpose of this board is to give EX-GAC MEMBERS a voice, where many had none before. It is for FORMER members of the Gospel Assembly Churches stemming from William Sowders as well as other ex-members of other abusive groups."

I read countless stories of abuse in other GAC churches on this website. It was here that I downloaded Wayne Hamburger's book *Yoke of Bondage*. So much of the book reflected my own experiences. The person who maintained the website had been a part of Lloyd Goodwin's GAC in Des Moines, Iowa. According to the stories on the message board, Lloyd had done far worse than anything I had ever been exposed to. I believed these testimonies to be true because I remembered that Brother Mears had maintained distance between himself and Lloyd Goodwin. It was rumored that Brother Mears "knew things" that he didn't share openly to protect our assembly from bad influences. Though he was a part of the same movement, I had always been under the impression that Lloyd Goodwin was not someone Brother Mears trusted. When I read the stories, it was like finding a missing piece of a puzzle for me.

In 1992 some ex-members of a church in the Bay area of Northern California had appeared on the *Geraldo Rivera Show*. They exposed their pastor, Lacy Hawkins. Among his many abuses of power, he had urged young couples to get sterilized. I was shocked because I had believed he was a good man prior to this. I had been to a convention at Hawkins' church once. I remembered enjoying the people and the worship and wondering why we didn't fellowship more with Hawkins' church. In 1996, an angry and obviously troubled ex-member of his congregation shot him in the face and neck in the church parking lot. He survived. Although Hawkins' abuses were extreme examples, it became obvious to me that we shared common roots. I could not deny my familiarity with much of what I read concerning the *beliefs* behind these practices. He had simply gone further in his quest for control.

On the one hand, it could be viewed as a positive thing that Brother Mears kept some distance from Hawkins. On the other hand, considering everything I now know about that man, I am baffled as to why we associated with him at all. Brother Mears remained silent and appeared to have a relationship of mutual respect with Hawkins. He attended our conventions and always took a seat on the platform.

Once I discovered the message board, I was unable to stop reading it. I wondered what impact it might have on this group. Initially the mere existence of this website felt threatening and uncomfortable, yet I could not help but wonder if the exposure might eventually serve a higher purpose. The Internet certainly made it much more difficult to keep people silent.

In the GAC world, talking about personal problems or problems you have with the church had been considered one of the worst sins. If you disagreed with anything the leaders said, you were "murmuring and complaining." If you questioned a rule, you had the spirit of Eve or you were defying your pastor. If you challenged the legalism, you were rebellious and had "a bad spirit." If you dared to admit that Brother Mears was failing mentally, you were "dishonoring him." Everything was swept under the rug. We protected the image of the church at all costs. Brother Mears often quoted Proverbs 17:9: "Whoever covers a transgression seeks love, but he who repeats a matter separates close friends." The problem was that this verse addresses gossip yet was being applied as a biblical reason for not dealing with sin like pedophilia and encouraging others to keep such secrets. The Bible clearly tells us to "Take no part in the unfruitful works of darkness, but instead *expose* them" (Ephesians 5:11).

After I left CGT in 2003, I became addicted to the message board. I could only go so many days without checking to see what was being discussed. I began to share my own experiences. I wrote lengthy entries about specific past events and how they had impacted me. I openly shared my confusion and the struggle I was engaged in to overcome the indoctrination. It was a place where I found the understanding and validation that was available nowhere else; everyone had a voice.

My intent was never to hurt anyone. My postings were a way to express myself and be heard, something I had rarely experienced at CGT. The people who posted messages related to me. I wanted to reach out to the people who read this message board out of curiosity. I hoped that as my old friends read what I shared, they might be able to understand my heart better, to know that I was not wanting to hurt them. I just wanted them to understand my frustration and confusion. Regardless of what anyone thought, there was something empowering about finally having a voice.

Around this time, I went back to CGT for a funeral. Every time someone from my past died, I would make every attempt to go to the visitation. I did not enjoy going there. I dreaded it. It was uncomfortable and awkward, but I wanted my old friends to know how much I loved them and that I wanted to be there for them. I felt like this was an opportunity for me to demonstrate my love.

On one such occasion, an old friend approached me warmly. She was a little younger than me, but we had sat next to each other in the band for a number of years when she was a teenager and I was in my twenties. Because of long hours spent in services together, we had formed a bond despite our age difference. As an adult, she married and moved to another state, but she was in Tennessee for this funeral. She walked up to me and hugged me. We talked for a minute or two. Then she said, "I want you to know I have read all your posts on the message board, and they have troubled me." My heart sank. I thought she was about to tell me that she felt betrayed (as others had). After a moment she added, "The thing is, I know the reason I feel troubled is that you are telling the truth. Everything you've talked about, I remember." She assured me that she knew I had never lied or embellished the truth. Her validation meant so much to me.

Most of my old friends have never understood why I felt compelled to post on the message board. Many accused me of betraying lifelong friendships. I have received hostile emails from some people in CGT, condemning me and accusing me of hidden motives and personal agendas. I have been accused of *using* victims—instead of really caring about them—to further my own agenda. I have been called a parasite. However, I have never attempted to conceal my identity. I want the accountability of attaching my name to everything I write. Although I have periodically taken sabbaticals from the message board, I have always returned.

There have been other people who have appreciated my posts and encouraged me to continue sharing my thoughts. Still others have written to me seeking support and encouragement after leaving a Gospel Assembly Church. A few have asked to speak with me on the phone. Most of those who have reached out to me have been abused, either spiritually or sexually. I have tried to be a caring friend to victims of abuse. I have felt convicted to take a strong and visible stand when it comes to the crime of sexual abuse. I have witnessed the damage done to so many lives by this heinous sin and by the mishandling of these sins as well. I have watched otherwise good people vilify a victim because he or she needed to talk about what happened to them, making the victim guilty of the "greater offense" of talking about someone's transgression. This indifference has come from people who are choosing self-protection and self-preservation, all the while proclaiming to be followers of Christ who calls us to lay down our lives for others.

The message board has been maligned as a harmful place full of people's bitterness and hatred. The truth is; there *have* been hateful posts. I don't agree with every view expressed there. We all deal with our past wounds differently, and some are struggling with bitterness. I may disagree with someone's tone or conclusions, but I still feel their pain.

There probably will come a day when I no longer read or post on the message board. However, I believe God has used that website for a greater good, in spite of whatever negativity may have come from it. I hope that something I have contributed there has made a positive difference in someone else's life; that many victims of spiritual, emotional, and sexual abuse at least know how much I care. And that far outweighs any criticism I endure.

23

The Meeting

July 1, 2004, is a date I will always remember. I went to spend the day with my sister-in-law, Cheryl. She was freshly home from the hospital after giving birth to her fourth child earlier in the week. I thought she could probably use a little help, and we enjoyed spending time together.

Since I had moved to Murfreesboro, I missed our spontaneous visits. When we lived around the corner from each other, we could call on a moment's notice to have lunch, run errands, or go to the gym together. Once I moved an hour away, we had to plan to get together. The only thing I missed after moving to the other side of Nashville was time with Cheryl, Chris and their kids. That first year, I made the drive about once a week to see them.

Cheryl and I were (and still are) like sisters. Both of our lives had been eventful in recent years, and we had leaned on each other. We bounced our thoughts off of one another. She knew my pain, and I knew hers. We had fun together. I will never forget having my first glass of wine with Cheryl, sitting at her kitchen table. I was forty-three and she was thirty-one. We called ourselves "Church girls gone wild." (Our definition of wild was mild.) In light of our strict upbringing, we considered having a glass of wine to be daring—something we had never permitted ourselves to do.

As we sat in Cheryl's kitchen that July day, we discussed the implications of a special meeting that had been announced to address sexual abuse within CGT. This meeting was precipitated by much controversy, including the circulating allegations against Paul Mears and posts on the EX-GAC message board.

∽

Although she no longer attended CGT, my friend, Janette, had continued to leave her little girl in the care of a CGT member who also cared for other children from CGT. The caregiver had once been Janette's Sunday school teacher and was like a grandma to the children. Janette never questioned her daughter's safety.

For several weeks in the spring of 2002 her daughter began exhibiting unusual behavior; including a sudden fear of closed doors and being abnormally clingy to Janette. She also developed vaginal irritation during this time. Not connecting any of this with the babysitting environment, Janette continued to take her daughter to this babysitter once or twice a week. Even when her daughter had said a couple of times that she didn't really want to go back to the babysitter's house, Janette didn't think much about it. Since her daughter had been so clingy, she assumed her daughter was just going through a stage of wanting to be with *her* more than usual.

One afternoon when Janette picked her daughter up, there was an adolescent boy in the house *helping* the caregiver, by her own admission, as she had to periodically go upstairs to check on her elderly mother who was in poor health. Janette had not anticipated her child being left in the care of someone else at any time, certainly not an adolescent boy. On the way home this same afternoon, her little girl repeated that she didn't want to go back to the babysitter's house anymore. Janette was baffled, since her daughter had always *loved* to go there. Later that evening, her daughter mentioned not wanting to go back again and Janette asked, "Why don't you want to go back, Sweetie?" Her little girl proceeded to tell her, in detail, what had happened to her. She pointed graphically to the area that had been touched and told her mommy who had taken her behind a closed door and touched her. She was far too young to have made up the scenario she described. Janette became very alarmed, but tried not to show any emotion that might further traumatize her child.

Janette called the caregiver the next day and explained what her daughter had told her. At first, the caregiver responded with remorse. She assured Janette that she had felt something "wasn't right" and the boy would not be coming back. She was so sorry. She would make sure that there was never an opportunity for such a thing to happen again. This phone conversation occurred on a Friday. Janette so trusted this woman that she took her daughter back on Monday or Tuesday of the following week. However, when she picked her daughter up that afternoon, the older boy was there again. Janette became visibly upset and a confrontation ensued. This time the caregiver's response was hostile and uncaring.

Janette reminded the caregiver that she had *promised* her this boy would never be present again. The caregiver said that she had questioned the boy, and he said it never happened. She now believed that Janette's daughter must have made it all up. Janette was accused of wanting to hurt *the church* with the allegation since she no longer attended CGT. Someone even alleged that Janette's daughter had been abused at home and was transferring blame to an innocent party.

Janette was in stunned disbelief. She reported the abuse to the police, and they attempted to investigate the allegation. The investigation ultimately went nowhere. Nobody would willingly talk or cooperate. The wagons were circled. The caregiver was viewed by church members as Janette's victim. Even the pastor showed no compassion for Janette's daughter after she personally contacted him to explain the situation in detail.

Janette was advised by law enforcement that a lawsuit would force people to give depositions. After months of careful consideration Janette decided she did not want to inflict further emotional distress on her daughter *or* go to war with her former church. However, she felt so betrayed by her old friends and could not process how she could have become so disposable to them, so evil in their eyes that they would rather assume her a liar than try to find out what had actually happened.

After the passing of many months and much frustration, Janette's hurt feelings turned into anger. She heard a rumor that the same boy had molested another child, and she began to feel a responsibility to do something she had never considered doing—going public. For a number of weeks in the spring of 2004, she posted about sexual abuse—and the mishandling of sexual abuse—on the EX-GAC message board anonymously. Eventually, she was challenged to substantiate her allegations. Around that same time, she heard that during a church service Steve had publicly challenged anyone who was posting derogatory information on the Internet to "Bring it on! Let's get the skeletons out of the closet!"

His words were antagonistic and mocking. Steve had known Janette since her birth and here he was openly taunting and provoking her. The way in which he chose to respond to the situation had deeply and repeatedly wounded her.

Adding insult to injury, Steve's wife had told a story about what happened to Janette's little girl. The story was repeated to Cheryl, who asked Janette if it was true. Janette was shocked at hearing this story because she had spoken to Steve personally about the specific details of what her daughter had reported. He *knew* the truth, his wife *knew* the truth, and the story she spread did not even *resemble* the truth.

Janette and, in a separate phone meeting, Cheryl both confronted Steve about the fabricated story. Instead of trying to get to the truth, Steve became defensive and angry. It was extremely heartbreaking to watch how this played out over these many months. For all the talk of change and new leadership, this situation was being handled worse, by far, than many past situations.

The accumulation of stress took an enormous toll on Janette. Ultimately, one night in June of 2004 when she could not sleep because of her raw and ragged nerves, she posted on the message board at 4:00 a.m., using her real name. She wanted to set the record straight publicly. She revealed details and names. She allowed the challenge of "Bring it on!" to trigger her emotions.

However, in her exhausted state she posted sensitive information about other past incidents that were not entirely accurate, opening herself up to criticism.

≫

Shortly after the postings, on that July 1 afternoon, Cheryl and I were sitting at her kitchen table. We heard about the meeting scheduled at CGT that night. She looked at me and said that the meeting was supposed to be about abuse, but she thought it was going to be about damage control. She knew some of the things that were going to be said because Becky had made certain statements to Cheryl privately. Cheryl recalled previous conversations in which Becky had tried to convince her that her grandfather, Paul Mears, had never been "sent" by Becky's father, Cornelius Mears, to pastor the church in Phoenix; he just hadn't stopped him from going. Cheryl knew this wasn't true because she knew her grandfather answered directly to Brother Mears the whole time he was the pastor of the Phoenix church. She knew that Brother Mears had provided financial support for his ministry. Cheryl believed that in addition to discrediting Janette at the meeting, there would be an attempt to rewrite history in such a way as to put distance between Brother Mears and Paul. Cheryl believed Becky was determined to deny her father's responsibility because, in a prior conversation, Becky had stated adamantly to Cheryl, "I will do anything to protect my dad's dignity."

Cheryl had been close to both Steve and Becky in the past. Steve is her mother's uncle and Becky is her father's first cousin. She had lived in their home at times as a teenager. She knew them privately as well as publicly. She felt that Becky had an expectation of unconditional loyalty from her. However, Cheryl had sought counseling from a professional who specialized in abuse. She was not in denial of the truth. After explaining the background of the family and the church to the psychologist, he told her that she was in an incestuous church whose family's problems had infected the entire congregation. He told her that while she may never go public with everything that's happened, someday someone would. The secrets were not going to remain secret forever.

Cheryl wanted to be there in order to personally challenge the false claims she was almost certain would be made by Steve, but she had given birth just four days earlier. There was no way she would be able to go. The possibility occurred to both of us, almost simultaneously, of my going in her place and speaking for her. I remember her saying, "I wouldn't want to *ask* you to do this. I don't want you to feel obligated. I know it would be awkward." It's not that I *wanted* to do it, but I was more than *willing* to.

We held on to some hope that the meeting might be only about the abuses in the church. There had been recent reports that Steve was repentant and broken when it came to the past abuses and how they had been handled. I wondered if it was possible that he might apologize for his mishandling of recent events. With all my heart, I wanted to believe that perhaps repentance was the purpose of the meeting. Maybe it would be unnecessary for me to speak. Just in case, I memorized what Cheryl had specifically asked me to say in response to certain statements, and I borrowed a skirt from Cheryl. Showing up was awkward enough, since I no longer attended CGT. I had worn pants to Cheryl's that day and even after being gone for over a year, I did not feel comfortable to enter the building in a pair of pants.

I told Danny that a meeting had been called and I was going. He and Rebecca wanted to attend as well and decided to meet me there. As I drove up I-65, I prayed that there would be humility and repentance. I told God how scared I was to have to say anything in this meeting. I had anxiety about walking in the door. I knew some would think it was inappropriate for me to come, since I no longer attended the church. I imagined that people would see me and think, "What is *she* doing here?"

I walked in and took a seat in the back. A few minutes later, Danny and Rebecca arrived and sat down beside me. My insides were shaking. As Steve approached the pulpit to begin the meeting, I silently prayed, "Please, Lord;

let this be a meeting of repentance and restoration. Please don't let Steve say any of the things Cheryl thinks he's going to say." My heart sank as Steve made a carefully worded statement—as though reading from a script—informing the congregation that Brother Mears did not "send" his brother to Phoenix, he simply "did not object." Early in the meeting Steve requested that we refrain from using personal names, but he held up a print out of Janette's post from the message board and pointed out only her mistakes in an obvious attempt to personally discredit her. There was no question that I was going to have to speak. Cheryl was right. There was no repentant Steve with the broken, gentle spirit. He was performing damage control exactly as Cheryl had predicted. At one point, Steve made an analogy between covering up sexual abuse in the past and well-meaning parents putting butter on burns. He explained how years ago people thought that putting butter on a burn was a good thing. Today we know that this is one of the worst things you can do for a burn. He then asked if anyone would be *mad* at their parents for having put butter on a burn.

He implied that no one should be upset about Brother Mears covering up the abuse because he was simply doing what he thought best. Once again the leadership of CGT was being manipulative and inflicting guilt on the victims and anyone wanting to hold Brother Mears accountable for the abuse he had covered up.

It made me sick to my stomach to hear a comparison being drawn between something as evil as sexual abuse and something as benign as a burn. As far as the statement about Brother Mears not "sending" Paul, I believed it was a *blatant* attempt to rewrite history. There had been many services in which Brother Mears told the congregation that Paul was in Phoenix under his authority and leadership. He spoke about Paul calling him on a regular basis to "check in" with him and keep him informed about the services. I remember it well because it always seemed to me that Brother Mears wanted to make it clear that it was really *his* church in Phoenix, like it was purely an ego thing. I knew nothing of Paul's perversions at the time and wondered why he couldn't just let Paul be in charge of his own church.

Another inner conflict I felt was in reference to the second half of the statement; that Brother Mears simply "did not object." This begged the question: Why would he object unless he knew of any reason why he could *not* "send" his brother to pastor a church? If he did know of some wrongdoing, did he not have a moral and spiritual obligation *to* object? Did he have the option of not taking a stand? Why did his family believe that this would take him off the hook? I hoped that others would think this through clearly and rationally.

As Steve continued with his remarks, he completely ignored everything in Janette's post that was true and commented only on specific claims he could refute (concerning what Brother Mears knew or did not know in the past). He made carefully worded, well-defined statements that excluded known abuse he did not want to acknowledge. One of the things that was so offensive was that Steve appeared to be choosing all of his words in such a way that he believed he wasn't technically telling a lie; however, he wasn't telling the complete truth either. Dan Courtney, a former member who attended the meeting, stood to his feet and pointed out that he could name several cases of known abuse. Steve again tried to respond in a way that protected Brother Mears and denied responsibility. It seemed to me that Steve was suggesting no abuser had gone on to abuse others because Brother Mears had failed to respond appropriately. He claimed that Brother Mears had never allowed a known abuser to remain on the platform (or in the band). That wasn't true.

At that point, Jennifer felt compelled to speak.

৯৹

Jennifer was not born in CGT, but she grew up there from a very young age. I will always remember the Sunday afternoon her mom visited CGT in California for the first time. She was a complete stranger. During this first visit, she stood to her feet and chastised the congregation. She was disturbed by all that was going on around her in the service. She observed women looking at magazines and photo albums, carrying on conversations, writing notes, eating candy, etc. It was obvious to her that they were disengaged from the service. She rebuked us.

She could not have known how common this behavior was. The services were long and drawn out, and these distractions were routine conduct. Nobody seemed to think much about it. Although I thought her public rebuke was confrontational at the time, I can certainly understand now why this behavior troubled her. However, she came back that night and has remained at CGT ever since.

When Jennifer was seven or eight, a much older teenage boy in the church molested her. He also allegedly molested several other girls. Jennifer told her mother about the abuse, and she went to Brother Mears. Jennifer's mother was a divorced parent at the time and Brother Mears was like a surrogate head of household. He told her that she could handle it in any way she saw fit, or she could allow him to handle it for her. Jennifer's mother says she felt the freedom to report the situation to the authorities, but she *chose* to have him handle it.

Brother Mears said he would speak to the boy's parents. However, many years later Jennifer discovered that neither of her abuser's parents had ever been informed of the abuse by Brother Mears. The mother learned about the abuse years later when Jennifer called her to talk about the abuse. The boy not only went on to abuse other girls, he openly taunted Jennifer in church services. She remembers him making obscene gestures and gross comments to her whenever she had to walk past him at church. Since she had been instructed not to talk about what had happened to her, she said nothing and endured further abuse.

Jennifer spoke in the July 1, 2004, meeting. It was Jennifer who stood to her feet and publicly reminded Steve that, just a few days earlier, she had told him that the person who molested her *had* in fact molested others because the abuse was not properly handled by Brother Mears. At the time of the meeting, Jennifer was attending CGT. She could not be labeled as an angry ex-member, as others of us had been. She left the church when Brother Mears was the pastor. She never trusted Brother Mears. However, when she learned that Steve was the acting pastor, she came back with great hope for the future. She had developed a relationship of trust with Steve and thought of him as her friend.

Jennifer rose to her feet and openly challenged Steve, reminding him that she had told him personally about *her* abuser and how many other girls he had sexually molested. Steve *knew* that what he had just said was untrue. Steve morphed into lawyer mode and cross-examined her in a gentle, friendly tone in an attempt to manipulate her words. He was very smooth.

Danny was sitting beside me. I had no idea how deeply impacted he was by this scene playing out until he loudly cried out in an emotional plea for victims not to be treated as though they were on trial. It was certainly an emotionally charged event.

Many people spoke that night. I was one of them. When I stood to my feet, I was literally shaking inside. Just before I stood to my feet, I prayed that God would give me the words He wanted me to say. Other than the specific things Cheryl had asked me to say for her (and I had well rehearsed those statements), I didn't know what all I would say. I left that up to God. I stood and waited for the microphone to come to me. The minute I began to speak, an unexpected calm came over me. My whole body relaxed. I don't remember everything I said, but I do remember the main point I made was that Cheryl had asked me to come to be her voice since she was recovering from childbirth. I told the congregation that her uncle had sent her grandpa to Phoenix and was very much the overseer of that church. I explained that Cheryl also felt *exactly* the same as Janette about the way these matters were handled in CGT. Then one thing after another just came to my mind; things I had not even planned to say. One of the ways I knew God was directing me was that I did not linger on any one thought. This is unusual for me. I am wordy and I often tend to say the same thing three different ways. However, I was not wordy that night.

I mentioned hearing that Steve in recent months had asked the congregation during a service to stand if they believed that Brother Mears' church had always been a safe place for children. Many people privately admitted to standing out of peer pressure. I pointed out to him and the congregation that night that if you want to know how someone truly feels on a matter, you ask privately where they will share honestly from the heart. Besides, nobody can make such a claim in truth anyway because there are *no* completely safe places. We are all sinners. Parents and grandparents have abused their own children in some cases. Danger is all around us in this world.

Another point I brought up was that I did not think Brother Mears was ever able to admit he was wrong. When I sat down, it seemed like that was all anybody had heard me say. Person after person corrected me, asserting that was not true. Several even spoke of a specific service in which he had indicated he might have made a mistake. I leaned over to Danny and said, "Is this all anybody heard me say?" Danny replied, "Mom, everyone is talking about the same *one time* he admitted he might have been wrong. They are actually proving your point. Don't worry about it."

The meeting continued with many members sharing that they had been abused in other settings, but received help in CGT. Others publicly acknowledged abuse at the hands of someone in CGT. After the meeting ended, I was surprised when several people thanked me for coming and speaking. Of course there were those who thought that I was abrasive that night, but some people stated openly that I had made them think about things they had not previously considered.

Just before the meeting ended, I remember Steve focused on the danger of being a false witness and warned everyone about false witnesses. It seemed like an odd way to close this meeting. In the context of the meeting on abuse I could only imagine that he was defining a false witness as anyone who would claim abuse who had not been abused. Over the next few days, a number of people suggested he was warning the church about people like Danny and me. Some believed he was calling *us* false witnesses.

One of the things I said in the meeting that night was that CGT taught that you could not find God outside "the Body." I told the people this was not true. I now wondered; *Was Steve trying to undermine my words by planting the thought of a false witness?* The thought of being a false witness produced a degree of anxiety in me.

That weekend, my husband assured me that I was no false witness and encouraged me to pray and ask God to help me overcome my anxiety. After years and years of conditioning, I still let Steve get in my head. I was still not free of it. I still had anxiety and fear and wondered from time to time if God might be mad at me for leaving. That night I fell asleep praying that God would speak to my heart in church the next morning, to assure me that I was not a false witness and to confirm that I was in His will *if I was in His will.*

As I was waking up the next morning, I was in a kind of twilight sleep. I was neither fully asleep nor fully awake. I had a dreamlike vision. I saw an empty room. I couldn't see myself, but I knew I was there. I heard a child's voice say, "Abba?" I knew the voice was mine, and I was looking for Abba. I called out His name as if to ask, "Are you here?" That was it, and then I was fully awake. The experience was very real, yet I had no idea what it could possibly mean. *Abba* was not a term I used for God.

By the time we got to church, the experience had left my mind. Then we began to sing the Hillsong United song "You Are Awesome in This Place." We came to the line that says "You are awesome in this place, Abba Father" and tears began to well up as I sang "Abba Father." I had told John earlier about the experience and my confusion. When we sang this song, however, I knew exactly what the experience meant. With tears in my eyes, I told him, "God was drawing my attention to this song. He knew we were going to sing it today. He is telling me that He is here, and I am exactly where He wants me. I am not a false witness. I am His child."

24

Giving Up Cherished Friends

For the first year or so of my marriage to John, I continued to go back to CGT for funerals and visitations of friends' loved ones. I hoped to preserve a few treasured friendships. It was awkward and inconvenient. (I had to drive an hour each way.) However, it was well worth it to me. I felt like the effort I made demonstrated my genuine love for old friends in a tangible way.

At some point the CGT began holding funerals at night instead of during the day. I was told that it was to make it easier for people who worked during the day to attend a funeral. The change turned funeral services into church services and made my attendance a much greater challenge as I would be driving home alone at night, unless John went with me. He was never comfortable with my going back. I explained to him that I had known these people my whole life, and I wanted to show my love and sympathy to people I care about. If I didn't go, it could be misconstrued that I didn't care. John pointed out that people I had known in CGT would be dying for the rest of my life. He told me that at some point, I had to cut the cord, but I have a difficult time letting go of people. On at least one occasion, John agreed to accompany me so I would not have to go alone. His only request was that we go to the visitation, express our love and sympathy, but not stay for the long service. I agreed. I had heard some people were confused by my presence and considered me two-faced for showing up to the church after expressing my negative feelings. Once I became aware of these scrutinizing comments, I was even more uncomfortable walking through the doors let alone staying for the service. Years later, I learned that at least one person had been hurt by the fact that I had not stayed for the actual funeral service. When I was made aware of it, I apologized to him and explained my reasons for not staying. He didn't buy it. I couldn't win either way. And the troubling thing to me is that I only went back at all out of genuine love and sympathy. It was never easy. I did not look forward to seeing certain people. Walking through those doors was always awkward after leaving that way of life. However, I tried my best to rise above the feelings of discomfort and do what I believed was the right thing to do. If my actions were misunderstood or misjudged, I knew there was nothing I could do about that.

༄

A short time after John and I were married it occurred to me that God had blessed me with a wealth of discretionary time. I could give a tithe of this free time to the Kingdom of God. In August of 2004, I began volunteering regularly in our church's office. I didn't know a lot of people in my new church, but I wanted to be involved. I did not want to be an anonymous spectator. I wanted to contribute something. That would be a very personal contribution and a way of demonstrating my thankfulness for all that God had done for me. In addition, I could establish new relationships within my church family.

I had spent my whole life in one church of a few hundred people. We did not have a church staff. I remember viewing the WOC website and the large staff of people who worked full time for the church. I could not imagine why they would have a need for a volunteer in the office, but I wanted to offer my time anyway. I must have thought I needed to sell myself as a volunteer because I sent a lengthy email that resembled a résumé to people in various ministries.

Kathy Jackson, our pastor's wife, responded to my email. She asked me to come in and talk to her in person. I was nervous. I didn't know her. I didn't know anybody. I wasn't sure they would even want me. I remember going into a small conference room with Kathy and another staff member. Kathy assured me that they needed help in the office. I offered to come in on

Mondays and Thursdays. I didn't care what I did. Wherever I was needed, I would be happy to jump in and help. Before I left, she mentioned to me that she was about to organize a women's study focused on the book *The Excellent Wife*. She asked if I would like to participate, and I enthusiastically accepted her invitation.

CGT had not offered these types of studies for women. I had never been in a home Bible study. This would be my first experience. I didn't know anyone in this group well. I had met only a couple of the women prior to attending the study. However, that did not inhibit me from sharing. This study focused on the attributes of a Proverbs 31 wife. The book set the bar high and addressed many struggles that wives face. Newly married to John after a long, turbulent marriage that had ultimately failed, I had a lot of emotion just beneath the surface. I am an emotional person by nature, and I could not speak about my difficult past or my wonderful present without tears. I cried just about every time I opened my mouth.

Susan, a new friend who was hosting this study, happened to be a longtime friend of Anita, who was my first close friend in Murfreesboro. One night John and I were having dinner with Anita and her husband, Mark. Anita told me she had run into Susan, and Susan had said nice things about me. Then Susan had added, "I know one thing; she sure does love that John! There is no doubt about that!" I laughed.

There is no one who knows me—even casually—who has any doubt about how much I adore my husband. I once shed tears at a cosmetic counter when the girl helping me complimented me on my wedding ring. I was quick to tell her that the only thing more spectacular than my ring was the man who gave it to me, and I was instantly overwhelmed with thankful tears. My mother-in-law was with me. She squeezed me as she smiled at the salesgirl and said, "She *really* loves my son. She cries every time she tells me. But this is the first time she's cried in a department store."

I made some good friends in the study. Not long after it ended, I was invited to participate in an "Excellent Wife" study to be held at the church. Kathy wanted to offer this study to a larger group this time. She asked several of us who had participated in the home study if we would be willing to lead small group discussions and prayer following the lecture portion of the class. I wanted to be a willing helper in the church. However, I had only participated in one women's study and had never led a prayer. At CGT everyone either prayed quietly and collectively or a man led a prayer. The thought of having to lead a prayer intimidated me. I felt inadequate. However, I knew that if I truly wanted to grow and be used in the Kingdom of God, I would have to be willing to be stretched beyond my personal comfort zone. What a better opportunity to be stretched? I thought about something my new pastor said in a sermon: if we *didn't* feel inadequate to be used by God in new ways, there was a problem. He confessed that nearly every time God had put a new opportunity before him, he had felt inadequate. The fact is, we *are* inadequate and God uses us anyway.

My desire to grow in God was greater than the fear of leaving my comfort zone. I would push through my fear of praying audibly in a group setting in order to make myself available to God. The first night of this study, those of us who had volunteered to lead small groups scattered ourselves around the room. When Kathy finished her lecture, she asked all of the leaders to stand. Then she instructed everyone seated around us to form small groups with the group leader who was standing closest to them.

My particular small group remained with me after that first study ended and we eventually moved our meeting place to my home for a less formal atmosphere. Several of us have continued to get together and read inspirational books. We have added to the group over time and each of these women have become my cherished friends. I would have missed out on many blessings had I not been willing to let God stretch me beyond my comfort zone. Those of us who were brought together in that first study have always believed that God crossed our paths for His divine purposes.

Around this time John convinced me to stop going back to CGT for funerals or visitations altogether. As I was feeling the loss of some of my dearest lifelong friends from my childhood, God was filling my life with new treasured friends. He was providing friends who would be there for me in the second half of my life. I remember one day when I was grieving the loss of all of my old friends. I felt that God was telling me to "let them go." It felt like God was urging me to focus on the new life He had given me. One of the people who helped me learn to accept and even embrace my losses was a man I have never met: Tim Keller. He is a pastor at Redeemer Presbyterian Church in New York City. My son, Danny, had subscribed to Keller's sermons online, and he had shared a few of them with me. I learned so much from him that I eventually subscribed to his weekly sermons online. Keller's sermons have been extremely influential in my life. Tim Keller illuminated for me how every story in the Bible points us to Christ. The whole Bible is the story of Jesus.

I have learned the Gospel from my pastor and from Tim Keller. Neither of them, of course, ever knew they were team teaching. They each have their own distinct preaching styles. They complemented one another, and I learned from each of them. I couldn't seem to hear enough sermons or read enough books on the cross. I knew that it was not sufficient to be delivered from the false beliefs of my past. I had to replace the false with the true. I had such a strong desire to know the true Gospel of Jesus Christ. However, I had to be convinced biblically that the good news of the Gospel was not a fairytale or "taking the easy way."

Believing in God's promises was a struggle for me because of my past indoctrination. I continued to be plagued by specific statements I had heard repeatedly throughout my life. While I had always had doubts about the doctrine of perfection, I was not free of the influence it had on my thinking.

I could not shake the teaching that nobody's soul goes to heaven when they die (except those who are perfect).

⚬

As a result of volunteering regularly in the church office, I had the privilege of getting to know many staff members. In those early days at WOC, I was struggling to overcome my indoctrination and the many biases that had been cultivated in me. I had so many questions. I needed so much help.

It was obvious to me that my new pastor worked very hard, invested long hours and had endless responsibilities. I did not want to take up a lot of his time. However, I felt comfortable enough to email him questions now and then. Allen was patient and so kind to me. Several times, he made a point of coming downstairs to the front office to ask if I needed to talk about some of my questions. I never asked for an appointment. I was afraid to be a bother because of my past.

It was often difficult to make an appointment to see my former pastor, yet he was far less engaged in daily "work" of the church than my current pastor is. My former pastor would press you to meet with him after a long church service. He kept unusual hours and was never available in the morning. If you needed to counsel with him about anything, you were asked how much time you needed and encouraged to see him after the service. I always felt like I was a huge imposition on his time. So I didn't want to presume upon my new pastor's time.

I felt self-conscious and I often apologized for my emails, but Allen always put my mind at ease and assured me I was not a bother to him. One thing that had impressed me when I began volunteering was the genuine appreciation I always felt from the entire staff, including Allen, for my time and service. I really didn't feel like I did that much. However, I felt truly appreciated. It was a completely different experience than at CGT.

On several occasions, Allen took time out of his busy day to sit in a conference room and talk to me, trying to alleviate some of my anxieties. In one particular session, I sat in his office and talked to him about not believing I was going to heaven. I had never believed I would go to heaven when I died, and although I was trying to believe it now, I did not feel the assurance or the hope that other Christians seemed to feel. I shared with him what I had been taught about perfection and how those teachings still played over and over in my mind.

He quoted from the book of Galatians:

> "You foolish Galatians! Who has bewitched you? Before your very eyes Jesus Christ was clearly portrayed as crucified. I would like to learn just one thing from you: Did you receive the Spirit by observing the law, or by believing what you heard? Are you so foolish? After beginning with the Spirit, are you now trying to attain your goal by human effort?" (Galatians 3:1–3)

Allen explained that there is only one path to salvation: Christ and Him crucified. Believing in any other way, such as our own works "meriting" the gift of eternal life, is the equivalent of witchcraft according to the apostle Paul. The Galatians had been poisoned by a perversion of the Gospel, which had evoked a strong response from Paul.

I had also been poisoned and enslaved. I did not know how to break the spell of those false teachings. Even though I had left and tried to embrace the truth of the Gospel, the good news, I continued to be in bondage to my past and robbed of my freedom in Christ. Allen suggested that I needed to repent for the things I had believed. Then I needed to go one step further. I needed to *renounce* those beliefs and ask God to help me believe the Gospel. He assured me that I would gain freedom through those prayers, and I would begin to believe God's promises of eternal life through the cross of Jesus Christ. He added, "You may have trouble with this. If you do, come back and see me. I'll help you."

The only person who had ever previously used the word witchcraft in conjunction with my former beliefs was my son. He says things strongly at times; I prefer gentler approaches. I had recoiled from the word. However, when Allen said the very same thing to me, I knew that God was confirming the seriousness of believing in a false gospel. I went home and got on my knees. I did not struggle with repentance for what I had believed. I did struggle with the word *renounce*. I felt fear come over me.

The one thing I knew was that God saw the sincerity of my heart. He had put me in the church where He wanted me. He put Allen Jackson in my life. I told God that I renounced my former beliefs, and my involvement in the group that taught me those beliefs. I did it more than once until I no longer choked on the words. Amazingly, just as Allen had assured me, I began to believe in my heart that I was going to heaven because of Christ's finished work on the cross.

Allen told me that if anyone came to him asking about God's deliverance, he would tell them to talk to me. He reminded me that my life was a story of God's deliverance. I recognized that. I only had one gnawing question: "Why would God deliver me and not others? There are so many good people there who are still being deceived. I do not understand why God would see fit to rescue me and not them."

Allen responded, "Shari, God did not drag you out by your heels. You got up and walked out, so can they. People don't leave places like that because it is too disruptive to their comfort. You didn't care about that. You were *willing* to leave."

25

Open Rejection

Steve Farmer became the official pastor of CGT in July of 2005 and installed new trustees. Another major scandal immediately surfaced. However, this situation was handled more openly and aggressively than any I had ever witnessed. I don't know all the details, but there are a few things I do know. The trustees believed they had discovered an inappropriate allocation of church funds and a business meeting was called to address it. The trustees alleged that Sister Mears had unethically given substantial sums of money to her youngest son, Terry, and his wife, Janelle. The meeting took place in September. The meeting was called while Terry and his family were out of town. Sister Mears had not been invited to the meeting, but she heard about it and went to defend herself. People in CGT said that she incriminated herself.

When I initially heard about this discovery, I *assumed* the Mearses were guilty. In spite of that, I felt compassion for them because of the harsh public inquiry and judgment of CGT. When I saw how quickly and aggressively they were taking care of this problem, I could not help reflecting on Steve saying "My hands are tied" when it came to allegations of sexual abuse against children. I believe it is revealing of what they value most.

In December of 2005, Terry wrote a "Letter of Apology and Response" to CGT members. Since he had been denied the opportunity to address the congregation or respond to the allegations publicly, he apparently decided to defend himself and his parents in a written document. In January, his wife sent me a copy of the letter. We had not had a lot of personal contact, but Janelle had always made it clear that she valued my friendship. She knew she and Terry were being labeled thieves by the church, and she wanted me to hear their side. In his letter, Terry claimed that the word *defraud* was branded into the people's minds throughout the business meeting. Sister Mears was accused of acting independently of Brother Mears in these matters, an allegation she and her son vehemently deny.

Certain statements in Terry's letter rang true with me. Never in the history of CGT were Brother and Sister Mears held accountable to anyone for their financial decisions regarding CGT funds. Although I heard jokes over the years about the financial benefits certain family members enjoyed, nobody ever voiced objections openly as long as Brother Mears was in charge. It would have been unthinkable to insinuate impropriety on his part.

When these allegations were made public, Brother Mears was failing mentally. Therefore, it had been suggested to the people that he was completely innocent of this impropriety, preserving his dignity and his legacy while letting Sister Mears take the fall. To me, this was reprehensible. Sister Mears never acted independently of Brother Mears. Their marriage did not function that way. I never saw a shred of evidence to support such a claim. If she was guilty, so was he, but nobody wanted to blame *Brother* Mears so they attacked *Sister* Mears instead. It was deplorable.

I will be completely honest. I often had a difficult time with Sister Mears. She was not compassionate in my opinion. I often felt her displeasure and disapproval in minor areas. She could be unnecessarily harsh and abrupt with people. In spite of all that, I resented the way she was being treated. I did not enjoy seeing her suffer this way. It bothered me to witness the contempt that was directed at her. After all, I had not seen this level of contempt for pedophiles.

If the rules had changed regarding their autonomy, somebody should have told her. She acted within the boundaries of the wide discretion that had always been afforded her and Brother Mears as guardians of CGT assets. I believe her when she says she viewed the payments to her son as investments that would pay a return or at least be repaid as a debt. The congregation empowered the two of them to control the money without accountability.

Therefore, the harsh way this matter was judged has always felt wrong and hypocritical to me.

I don't agree with everything Terry said in his letter. However, I found several claims to be extremely credible and forthcoming. Among those was this statement:

> "[F]ormer trustees often signed documents without ever questioning what they were for. They often knew of investments the church was making without ever requiring explanations. They always knew there were large investment accounts but never saw the statements; there was a tremendous amount of trust. While these former trustees knew of many loans, financial aid, and compensation, many other times, only my parents knew. On numerous occasions, these monies were never accounted for, and they weren't kept in some kind of accountant's ledger. . . . Why didn't the trustees retroactively judge the large amount of money Bro. Mears generously allocated for the release of a certain young man from jail??? I don't recall Bro. Mears asking for any public approval or public business meetings about that. While my parents did donate additional offerings for several months, the majority of the money was paid by the church. Again, this seems to be a situation where everyone has an opinion but doesn't know all of the details. Why wasn't that included in the resolution to be judged??? I'm sure there were people who opposed that. . . . How can you judge one and not the other??? Is it because the new trustees only want to pick and choose??? Or is there something even bigger here that I haven't told you about???"

Terry stated in his letter that his father set up the church as an unincorporated association and wrote the original by-laws himself. He explained, "It is clear my dad wrote them with virtual autonomy to himself and my mother. While it is not specifically mentioned in the by-laws, it wouldn't be hard to prove that my father never intended for anyone other than my mother to have the same autonomous authority in his absence."

Terry further claimed, "The vast majority of the church's wealth was accumulated through shrewd real estate transactions and clever management of church finances, NOT BY TITHING or FUNDRAISERS."

The accusers insisted that Brother Mears was not intellectually capable of giving his approval on these matters. They suggested a breach of trust had occurred in which Sister Mears had acted independently. Terry effectively pointed out that Brother Mears was being viewed as quite capable in other business matters at the very same time. If he was not, why were others continuing to seek his approval and consent? Some of the matters in question had actually occurred as much as four years prior to this business meeting.

There was a great deal of inconsistency in the selective responses of CGT leadership. I believe that Terry's questions about why certain matters were challenged and others were not are valid. I questioned that myself, and I think he and his family deserved an answer to that question. Instead, they were ostracized and shunned.

For instance, Janelle had been invited to a CGT friend's bridal shower. Steve called to tell the bride that if Janelle showed up at this shower, the women in CGT would get up and leave. Although Janelle had been a friend to the bride, she was subsequently uninvited to avoid an embarrassing scene. Steve had explained that these women should know better, but he could do nothing. (His hands were apparently tied again.) That comment was shared with Janelle as well.

I did not care if Terry had benefited from my offerings. I consciously gave to God and left those details in His hands. What truly shocked me was the way those in CGT treated Sister Mears. All my life, what I had witnessed was the constant preservation of a church image and the pastor's image. Why was Sister Mears now so expendable? Many people said that it was actually a family feud and a power struggle between Becky and Terry. Because of my closeness to certain Mears family members, I think that observation is valid.

There had always been tension behind the scenes. Brother Mears had a soft spot for Terry. As his dementia increased, he demonstrated distrust of Steve while Terry became his close confidante. At one point, the only person who had any real influence with Brother Mears was Terry. Most of us knew that Terry was directly responsible for convincing his dad to buy the property on which the current church in Cross Plains is located. Nobody else had that kind of influence.

While Terry never represented a threat to Steve as far as becoming the next pastor, he did know things that represented a potential threat (which would explain why he had to be discredited). Becky had made comments to Cheryl in the past that after her parents were gone, she would "take care of" Terry. Years earlier, Cheryl was sure a family power struggle was on the horizon. She just never thought it would happen *before* their parents were gone.

Within about two weeks of burying her husband, Sister Mears received a letter from the church trustees informing her that since the former pastor was deceased, all financial support was being terminated immediately. CGT would no longer be responsible for her care. Her income, healthcare, insurances, and other expenses would now become her responsibility.

How could the trustees justify such callous treatment of an elderly widow? They professed literal *perfection* as their goal. How could they reconcile their beliefs with their actions? Sister Mears had been like a queen in our church for over fifty years. Her sacrifices and dedication had been publicly extolled in endless testimonies. She had now become a pariah for doing what she had *always* been empowered to do without scrutiny. I lost whatever shred of respect I may have had for Steve Farmer. After all, this was his mother-in-law of nearly forty years at the time. Even if she had over-stepped her boundaries, there should have been mercy. I don't think the church could have hurt her any more deeply if they had taken her out and publicly stoned her. In fact, I think in some ways *that* might have been easier for her.

When you are rejected by an entire group of people with whom you were devoted for all or most of your life, it is agonizing. The weekend that followed the business meeting my friend, Janette, threw a baby shower in her Brentwood home for my daughter-in-law, Rebecca. She was pregnant with my first grandson, and all of my family members were invited. Cheryl had been unable to come due to a severe migraine. I had spoken to her and knew she was so sick, she could hardly open her eyes or talk. But since I had not heard from anyone else, I was expecting the other members of my family.

The shower was a luncheon and Rebecca's family members were all present, along with several of my friends from Murfreesboro. We had prepared hot food for the guests and were waiting only for my family to arrive before serving lunch. Nobody had called to say they were not coming, and I naively assumed they would be arriving any moment. We waited and waited. Finally, I called one close family member to find out when she thought she would be there, explaining we were holding lunch. She said coldly, "Oh, I'm not coming." That was it. I was hurt and embarrassed.

Not one member of my extended family showed up. Since all the missing guests still attended CGT, I could only assume they chose to skip the shower because it would have been awkward and uncomfortable for them in light of recent CGT events. The family member who told me she wasn't coming, with no apology and no explanation, chose to go shopping with her daughter-in-law that day instead of coming to the shower.

By the time Brother Mears died in July of 2006, I had stopped attending CGT funerals and visitations. However, I knew this visitation was going to be a stressful atmosphere for the shunned family members. I felt a great deal of compassion for Sister Mears because I had also experienced the pain of rejection. For the first time, I saw her as vulnerable.

Terry's wife, Janelle, had suffered agonizing trauma from this ordeal. We had not been especially close, but we had grown up together and I felt drawn to her in these circumstances. Her world had caved in on her and many people she had believed to be her lifelong friends had turned their backs on her.

༄

I cannot help but relate to people who are suffering rejection. Because of the way CGT was collectively treating these family members, I felt compelled to be there for them in any way I could. I went to the visitation, which took place at the funeral home. Most of the people I encountered were friendly. At least one friend walked away rather than greet me. I did not go to the funeral, which was held at CGT. I simply could not sit through that service and Janelle understood why.

Between Brother Mears' passing and his funeral, there had been a lot of controversy surrounding the arrangements. Sister Mears said she would not have his funeral service at CGT. In fact, she had even suggested that she might have the funeral at Christ Church in Nashville and bury her husband there, which was surprising because Brother Mears viewed any church outside "the Body" as part of Babylon. Cheryl and I chuckled about how this decision would cause him to turn over in his grave if he knew.

Sister Mears agreed to have the funeral at CGT if certain conditions were met. Steve agreed not to speak or have any part in the service whatsoever. Sister Mears felt that Steve and Becky had not only betrayed her, but they had betrayed Brother Mears. Ultimately, her conditions were met and the service was held at CGT. She also decided to bury Brother Mears in the local cemetery.

This would be my last appearance at a church-related visitation. It has sometimes been painful for me not to go and express my sympathy. However, the month following Brother Mears' death, I reached the conclusion that I could no longer visit CGT for any reason other than the loss of an immediate family member. So far, I am thankful to say that I have not suffered such a loss.

26

Disturbing Testimony

In 2005, a year after she confronted Steve about the cover-up surrounding her abuse, Jennifer was having serious problems in her marriage. It was around the same time that Steve became the official pastor and just prior to the financial scandal surrounding Sister Mears. Jennifer was not attending CGT regularly, but she decided to go to the camp meeting in Shepherdsville, where she had a life-changing experience.

The congregation was singing a song about Jesus never letting us walk alone. She closed her eyes and had a vision of Jesus. She explained that she saw Him and heard His voice in this vision. She could not see His face because it was so bright, but she saw His hand extended to her. He took her by the hand and walked with her through particularly painful times in her past life. He emphasized that He had always been there with her, holding her hand, except when she had let go of His. But even then, He never left her. He promised her that He *never would* leave her and that He would see her again. She didn't believe she would see Him again because of the perfection doctrine. She said she reminded Him, "You know me. You know what I'm like. There is no way I will ever be perfect." And He said back to her, "I promise I will see you again." When the vision ended and she opened her eyes, she knew she was saved and that the perfection doctrine was false.

At the conclusion of that service, Steve approached Jennifer and told her that God had spoken to him, telling him Jennifer had "an important work to do." In the following months, Jennifer began to pull away from CGT. Then the meeting about Terry, Janelle, and Sister Mears took place. She didn't go, but when she heard about it she felt so sorry for them and especially their kids. She told me, "My heart broke for their children because I knew what was about to happen to them."

Around Christmastime, Jennifer went to a party at the home of one of the church women. Although Cheryl no longer attended CGT, she had been invited to this party also. It was on this occasion that their friendship began. Jennifer recalls being treated poorly by many of the women in attendance, but Cheryl had stood and talked with her for a long time. During their conversation, they both noticed that the others were watching them. Jennifer remembers going into the bathroom and bawling. By the time she left that day, she knew she was never going back to CGT. She couldn't figure out why she had stayed as long as she had.

By early 2006, Jennifer's marriage had failed, and she began dating a childhood friend, Paul Beita. Paul's family wasn't happy about it and were extremely displeased when they got engaged. Paul's parents wanted nothing to do with her and nothing to do with Paul if he married her. Although Paul and Jennifer were attending another church by this time, Paul initially allowed his daughters to go to CGT when they were with their mother or his parents. However, when his daughters joined the CGT junior band, Paul objected and made them quit. He did not want his daughters to become too deeply involved in CGT. When he took this stand, a family tug-of-war ensued. Paul's ex-wife had recently remarried and returned to CGT. Paul had previously been awarded sole custody of the children, but his ex-wife had liberal visitation. They had worked things out amicably until then. CGT had not been an issue in the past because the girls' mother did not attend. However, for the brief window of time that she did, the relationship became adversarial.

In April of 2006, Jennifer received a surprise visit from the Department of Children's Services. Apparently, she and Paul were reported for neglect. There were serious allegations in the anonymous report to the authorities, so

DCS had to investigate the claims. Many of the claims described horrific living conditions. It just so happened that around this same time, Paul's ex-wife filed a petition for custody of the girls. Ironically, the false allegations that were cited in the petition were the exact same claims in the anonymous report to DCS. Paul and Jennifer believed this all stemmed from loyalty to CGT. Paul's mother had accompanied his ex-wife to the lawyer's office. She planned to testify against her own son in order to take the girls away from him. DCS found no evidence of neglect or poor living conditions in their investigation. The case was dismissed.

Paul's parents wanted to control the spiritual environment of their granddaughters through whatever means available. Paul's father, who is considered part of ministry in CGT, told his son that he was concerned about his granddaughters' souls being in danger if they went to another church. Church affiliation was probably the only reason they aligned themselves with Paul's ex-wife. I believe various members of CGT were backing her simply because she was attending CGT. Paul and Jennifer had not only left CGT, Jennifer had spoken out about her abuse and the way it was mishandled. Many people in CGT were angry with Jennifer and viewed her as bitter and out to get their church.

Jennifer had been speaking out against CGT since February. The reports to DCS and petition for custody were filed in April. Paul and Jennifer were married in May, and the first court date was in June. The attack felt personal and they responded with a letter informing the trustees that they would expose everything that had happened in CGT over the years if the church did not leave them alone and remove themselves from involvement in the custody dispute.

Jennifer is only a couple of years older than my son, and I couldn't say that I knew her well. When I attended the 2004 meeting, I remember wondering why Jennifer remained in CGT considering that Steve had misrepresented important facts publicly after she had informed him of the truth just days earlier. Then I reflected on how long I had stayed even after I had seen the inconsistencies and arrogance. If I believed that God had kept me there for some purpose, perhaps the same was true for her.

It was during this custody fight when Jennifer reached out to those of us who had left CGT. She asked several of us if we would be willing to testify on her and Paul's behalf. She offered to issue subpoenas if that would make it easier for us. She knew that we might suffer unpleasant repercussions for standing with her and Paul in this fight as most of us had family members who were still in CGT. She also anticipated that members of CGT would come to the court hearing to support Paul's ex-wife.

This was a serious request; something I had to think and pray about. I asked Jennifer how my testimony would help since I had never had an opportunity to observe either her or Paul in their roles as parents. We did not hang out together. I barely knew Paul. Jennifer assured me she was not asking me to vouch for them as parents. All she was asking me to do was be willing to tell the truth about CGT if needed, nothing more. She said she would understand if I didn't want to get involved.

John and I talked about the request. He was concerned for me and wasn't convinced it was necessary for me to be drawn into this. However, I could not avoid asking myself why I would *refuse* the request to do *nothing more than tell the truth.* I knew in my heart that if I refused this request, it would be for no other reason than to protect *myself* from any unpleasant consequences of telling the truth.

Perhaps I would lose more friends. Perhaps I would even lose family. No doubt I would come under attack as an individual and experience more character assassination. There was nothing for me to gain personally and many negative repercussions that would come from my testifying. However, the decision came down to right and wrong. I believed that what was being done to Paul and Jennifer was wrong. Their former church was supporting false and malicious claims against them as parents. How could I possibly refuse to get involved on the basis of my own personal comfort? What about them? Would I not hope that someone would be willing to tell the truth for me in the same situation?

I dreaded the personal consequences, but I knew I could not live with a willful choice of self-preservation over doing the right thing. I told Jennifer she could count on me. She had her attorney subpoena me as a courtesy. That way, I could truthfully tell anyone who might question me that I was subpoenaed. Sadly, I was still intimidated enough to think I had to justify my actions.

Cheryl and I had both agreed to testify if needed. There was a crowd of potential witnesses, a number of whom suffered personally. I sat in the courtroom listening to the testimony supporting Paul's ex-wife (which included his mother and sister). When Paul presented his case, those of us who might be called to testify were asked to wait together in a separate room. While there, we listed cases of past abuse that each of us personally knew of just off the tops of our heads. The number of victims within CGT was staggering. We counted more than forty probable cases of sexual abuse over a forty-year period of time.

I remember being very nervous as I arrived for the hearing. I had arrived just before Cheryl and waited for her before going into the courtroom. I saw my brother, Todd, pull into the parking lot. He had been appointed as one of the new CGT trustees. I assumed he was there to show support for the ex-wife and possibly to defend CGT. Cheryl and I both hugged Todd in the parking lot. I will never forget the expression on his face when he looked at me. It was a look of sorrow and pity. I was well aware that he believed I was misguided.

A woman was walking up just behind Todd as I hugged him. Because of the similar hair color and height; I wrongly assumed it was Todd's wife, Sue. Without looking at her closely, I took a step toward hugging her as well. She put her hands up, shook her head and emphatically said, "Oh, no. I'm not that gracious." I realized it was Jennifer's mother and sarcastically responded, "Well, praise God." No sooner had the words left my mouth than I felt conviction. I had used the Lord's name in vain, as sarcasm and a weapon to mock someone. My conscience bothered me the rest of the day. I tried to call Jennifer's mother to apologize and didn't reach her, so I sent her an email asking forgiveness. She responded, telling me I was not Jennifer's friend, and that I was simply using Jennifer for my own self-serving agenda.

I told her that I had tried to be a genuine, caring friend to Jennifer and felt it would not be right for me to refuse to tell the truth. I explained that I did not even know the exact questions I would be asked as I had not been deposed. I wasn't eager to testify. I did not seek this out as an opportunity. I didn't enjoy this stress. On the other hand, if God was using this to expose wrong and He required me to suffer the rejection of family or friends to do what He required of me, I accepted that.

Ultimately, after sparks flew and embers died down, she did accept my apology. After our written communication, she expressed a struggle in her heart about me and even a longing to embrace me. However, she informed me that we remained separated by the stand I had taken against CGT, her pastor and her faith. I was satisfied that the communication at least ended peacefully.

The judge ultimately dismissed the petition after hearing testimony from the principle parties alone. None of the potential witnesses were ever called to testify. The judge ordered the parents to work their differences out through mediation. He pointed out that they had always worked together amicably in the past, and he believed they could do so in the future. I was relieved that I never had to take the stand.

Contrary to the opinions of many, I had never been eager for this or viewed it as an opportunity. I feared the condemnation and rejection of people I loved. However, I had learned to recognize those fears as self-absorption; I refused to be controlled by them. I had to be *willing* to tell the truth no matter what the consequence.

⟨⟩

"The essence of courage is this: Courage is facing your heart's greatest nightmare and saying I'm going to do the right thing, I'm going to do the unselfish thing no matter what."

— Tim Keller

Chapter 27

The Anonymous Post

The summer of 2006 brought turmoil, as well as enlightenment, to my life. I had withdrawn myself from the two message boards I followed. The EX-GAC message board was the one I had spent the most time with and the one I posted to. The second message board I had backed away from was located on the official website of a professional musician who attends CGT. I only browsed that message board until that summer.

Neal was already a successful progressive rock musician when he married someone who had grown up in CGT. My husband, John, had an appreciation for all kinds of music. When I told him I had a musician friend who had achieved a level of success in the U.S., but was quite well known in Europe for his music, he asked who he was. I was very surprised when John said he knew of Neal and his band. He told me that he had three of his CDs in the trunk of his car.

After Neal joined CGT, he resigned from his band to pursue a solo career. He combined his genre of musical expression with Christian lyrics. He began touring to promote his first CD around the same time that John and I were planning our wedding. I suggested that perhaps we could invite Neal and his wife, along with my brother and his wife to have dinner with us some time. Neal and my brother were close friends.

We spent a bit of time together between 2003 and 2006. We enjoyed several evenings together in our home, Neal's home, and my brother's home. We spent Thanksgiving together at Todd and Sue's in 2004. The warmth I felt for Neal and his wife was genuine. I separated my friendship with them from the issues I had with CGT, and we always had a good time together.

John even loaned Neal a vintage guitar to record with and let him keep it for an extended length of time.

Our relationship changed (from my perspective) around the time of the custody battle in 2006. Neal came to court, aligning himself with Paul's ex-wife and her husband against Paul and Jennifer. Neal and Todd sat in one camp. I sat in the other. It was awkward and uncomfortable to say the least. I assumed they didn't think I should be there and I certainly did not feel that their presence was justified. I knew this was going to alter our personal relationships, but I still cared about Neal in the same way that I still loved my brother.

When I decided to stop reading the EX-GAC message board, I had decided it might be a good idea to stop reading Neal's message board also. However, in August of 2006, I heard from a friend that there was an interesting debate on Neal's spiritual discussion board on the subject of Christ's deity and the Godhead. A friend of mine had been participating in the discussion and someone suggested I check it out; so I did. I had never signed up to post on Neal's board, feeling that I should avoid expressing my opinions there due to our personal relationship. I had only read silently, never announcing my presence until August 22, 2006.

I read the discussion of the Godhead with great interest. It was the doctrine I was having the hardest time understanding after leaving CGT. Their belief in a two-person Godhead and a created, rather than eternal, Jesus was still stuck in my head. I was open to whatever truth God had for me, but I was confused. (According to a current member of CGT, Steve Farmer has recently advised the congregation that it is improper to use the term "two in the Godhead," since they believe Jesus is a created Son and not God.)

I had always been taught that Jesus was the Father's first creation. He was a heavenly creature. He had come to earth to live a perfect life, showing us that it could be done. He died on the cross to give us an *opportunity* to live forever *if*, after our initial experience of salvation, we went on to achieve sinless perfection just as He had. I was taught that I had to do what Jesus did and live as perfect a life as He had in order to *merit* eternal life. In fact, I was told that the main difference between Jesus and us was that He was born with the Holy Spirit, and we had to receive it. However, once we did, we had the same power to be perfect residing within us that He had.

It had always been emphasized that Jesus *could* have failed to overcome and live a sinless life. I didn't understand the focus on whether or not he *could* have failed, since He *did not* fail! The reason that was such an important acknowledgment in GAC theology was that if He could *not* have failed, that would mean that He had "an unfair advantage" over the rest of us. Whenever I heard that statement, I would always have the weirdest feeling that I was somehow in competition with Jesus. If Jesus willingly left heaven to come to earth and die for *my* sins, how in the world could I ever view Him as having an unfair advantage *over me*? His mission had been 100 percent sacrificial. It's not as though He had to come down to earn favor from God or that we were all competing for God's love.

At this point, I was not sure what I believed doctrinally. I was searching and asking for truth. I had not fully embraced the concept of God in three Persons, yet I was beginning to see clear evidence for the deity of Christ. I was studying Scriptures about Jesus when I began reading the thread on Neal's board addressing this very subject.

The posters from within CGT (whom I knew) were emphasizing the subordinate role Christ willingly took on when He came to earth as a basis of inequality between the Father and Son. They focused on the words *only begotten* in Luke 1 as a basis for Christ having a beginning just prior to the rest of creation. These points had been real stumbling blocks for me. However, the Trinitarian Christians contributing to the discussion had no problem explaining these Scriptures. This was the first time I heard that the word *begotten* is a translation of the word *monogenes* (only kind or unique) in Greek and that Luke was saying that Christ is of the same essence as God. Certain

Scriptures were quoted in support of Christ's deity that I had never considered. I had read them, but I had not *seen* what they said.

I began to recognize the most obvious problem with the GAC understanding of Jesus. The Old Testament forbids worshiping anyone other than God (Exodus 20:1-4; Deuteronomy 5:6-9). In the New Testament, holy men refused worship (Acts 14:15) and so did angels (Revelation 22:8-9). However, we *worship* Jesus and Jesus *accepted worship* in the New Testament (Matthew 8:2; Matthew 9:18; Matthew 14:33; Matthew 15:25; Matthew 20:20; Mark 5:6; John 20:28). If Jesus is not of the same essence as the Father, to worship Him is idolatry; it is sin.

It was as though a veil was lifted and I finally could see a profound truth. I found myself skimming over the posts from people I knew and devouring the posts defending the deity of Christ. I looked up Scriptures and compared translations. I felt like I was finally *seeing* the true Jesus. One by one I was overcoming the hurdles to my acceptance of the deity of Christ as I read the responses from the Trinitarian posters on Neal's board. I could not stop reading.

The CGT posters were skillfully evading some of the questions directed at them. They did not seem to want to provide the full and direct answers. This bothered me. I, of course, knew how the questions could be asked in a more direct way, making them more difficult to evade. However, I could tell that the Trinitarian posters had no idea they *weren't* getting completely forthcoming answers to their questions. They did not know how to ask the questions because they never experienced the church.

As I read the discussion, I felt concerned for new Christians who might possibly be influenced by reading Neal's board and listening to his music. I hated the thought of Neal planting seeds of deception in new believers, of teaching them that Christ is primarily an example for us and that we must achieve our own perfection in order to be saved. I felt compelled to make a statement to caution his readers. I knew my motive probably would be misinterpreted as malicious and that my posting probably would embarrass my brother, so I decided it would be better to post anonymously. I made up a screen name and wrote the following:

I have read this thread with great interest. I appreciate reading the posts from those who challenge Neal's theology. You have been helpful to me in my search for truth and understanding. I am still searching and learning.

Let me make this clear: I have nothing against Neal personally. I believe he is sincere. And I have enjoyed his music. But I was once in the church he attends and I was taught these doctrines. There is much more to what they believe than what has been brought out in this thread. And I share the concern of another poster who mentioned the danger in Neal promoting these beliefs, in spite of his sincerity. I was troubled when I read that his new album is about the true church. And I feel compelled to say this to those who may listen to his music, since he is going worldwide with his message.

The church Neal attends (and the churches they associate themselves with) professes to be the true church; THE Body of Christ. They believe that everyone else (and I mean Christians who do not believe their truths) constitute Babylon or the false religious world. They sing songs about it, but they don't admit they believe this openly. Only those who have been there know the truth of this. That is of great concern to me because they also say the truth never suffers from investigation.

This group believes you do not go to heaven if you have not spoken in tongues. So they cannot believe in the finished work of the cross. And they believe you have to reach literal perfection in this life (or after you resurrect) to have eternal life. They will not tell you this directly if they can evade your questions. An example of this strategy is the whole story about the "?" on Neal's last album. You may recall that Neal himself related this story of a friend of his (within the church) who told him that to create interest he should be secretive.

Someone earlier made the point about the thief not having any concept of theology, but still being in heaven. They do not teach that the thief went to heaven that day. The thief would have a resurrection and would then have the opportunity to reach perfection, according to their teaching. It was taught that today meant something other than a literal today. One of them can explain this better than I can as it was always confusing to me.

My reason for posting this is not to persecute Neal. I am not even saying whether or not I know Neal. I do not believe that any of us have full truth or a full understanding of God. And I would never speculate about Neal's salvation. I am just giving a heads up to those of you reading and listening to Neal's music ministry. He is promoting the theology of an exclusive group. I think people reading and listening need to be aware and exercise caution. And asking for very direct answers is something you have to do (usually more than once).

I don't plan to continue reading this message board on a regular basis because I don't want to be drawn back to the past. But I am so thankful that there are students of the Bible contributing to this discussion who are not easily influenced and who have taken the time to give Scriptures that challenge these views. I have learned from you. You have been a great help to me. And I thank you for that.

My post was displayed for perhaps an hour or so before it was removed. However, in that brief window of time, many regular readers saw it and copied it to share with others who had not had an opportunity to read it. I was, of course, completely unaware of what was transpiring behind the scenes.

Shortly after my post was removed I received an email from Neal's wife. She wanted to know if I had been the anonymous poster or if it had been Danny. I was anxious at having been found out. I had not wanted my post to be viewed as personal, but I knew I had to take ownership of my words. I responded to her email, explaining that I wrote the post not out of malice but out of a sense of responsibility to give the readers the whole truth. There were a number of emails between us. I made my motive unmistakably clear to both of them, whether they agreed with it or not.

The next thing I knew, Neal's wife wrote a post declaring that the anonymous poster of the deleted message was just an angry, disgruntled, ex-member of the church wanting to attack them. A member of my own family—who didn't even attend CGT but felt compelled to defend it—wrote a post telling the readers that the anonymous poster was a relative of his with a sinister motive. I literally shook my head in disbelief as I read the discussion that followed my deleted post.

One poster spoke on my behalf. She suggested that it would have been more appropriate to address the post rather than simply make it disappear. I had no idea that several contributors to the message board were privately sharing their own concerns about Neal's theology and influence. For some of them, my post was confirmation of what they had already suspected. They engaged in these discussions because they loved Neal and were praying for his deliverance. I had no idea that some of them had developed personal relationships with Neal and others in CGT, or that they had engaged in serious debate challenging the beliefs of CGT privately.

I made contact with the contributor who had challenged the disappearance of my post. She sent me a copy of what I had written in an email. That is the only reason I have a copy of it today. I had not saved it, as it never crossed my mind that it would disappear. The quick removal made it look as if there definitely was something to hide. For that reason, it was hard to believe they had chosen to handle it so mysteriously. However, I certainly understand knee-jerk reactions.

One specific poster had greatly enhanced my understanding through his articulate and thought-provoking posts. His name was Jason. I obtained his email address and wrote to thank him for the time and effort he had invested on the message board. This led to a casual email friendship in which we discussed theology and the beliefs of my past. I learned that he knew my brother, Todd, pretty well and had stayed in Todd's home. It was surreal. I shared with him how hard it was to put these teachings behind me. He put me in touch with other regular contributors to the message board. That was how I got to know some of them online.

Included in a forwarded email containing the copy of my post was a thread of dialogue sharing convictions similar to my own. I read these comments with great interest. One person wrote:

> "I think I am just a little upset about this whole thing. I love Neal's music as much as any other but it cannot go above God himself. I had some warning signs [throughout] the last two albums but chose to ignore them. But this is outright heresy, there is no other way to go with it. I know you are trying not to make waves so you can still be heard but I think we need to be careful when we say all that name Jesus are the same."

I had been crucifying myself for posting because of the fallout. Reading these words, however, confirmed to me that God was at work in this discussion and perhaps I had not done anything wrong. Personally, it was excruciating. I was overwhelmed with self-doubt. I wondered why in the world I had felt that it was *my job* to say these things; although I could not deny an inner prompting and the strong conviction that I was supposed to write that post.

For the rest of the afternoon, I contemplated telling John about this when he got home from work. He had never understood why I remained emotionally engaged with CGT. He would frequently tell me, "You've left, but you haven't really left as long as you continue to engage this way." He longed to see me fully embrace my freedom. Though he would never condemn me, I feared he would not understand my actions and might even be disappointed in me. I anxiously rehearsed the conversation I would initiate with him when he got home from work.

As it turned out, I would not be the one to initiate this conversation. I would not have to. As John was going through the mail, he casually said, "Guess who called *me* today?" I said, "Who?" He proceeded to tell me that he had gotten a phone call from my brother, Todd, informing him of my post on Neal's board. I was floored. I asked him why and thought that Todd was trying to get in my head.

With a raised eyebrow, John said that Todd's explanation for the call was his *concern* for me. From the things that were said, it sounded to me like my brother was trying to explain me and my "issues" to my own husband. My brother had never made a phone call to *me* to discuss my "issues." I believed he called my husband at work to report on me. I felt strongly that if a phone call had been necessary, the conversation should have been directly with me and not about me. In my mind, this was simply a reflection of the familiar view that husbands should control their wives. I had made no secret of the fact that John would prefer I not post on any message boards. Therefore, I thought it most likely that he had reported my behavior hoping that John would then use his influence to discourage me from doing this in the future.

I later learned that Todd was not the only person who phoned John. Neal had called to discuss me with John as well. John had been reluctant to tell me about Neal's phone call at first. He did not want to upset me further (after my reaction to hearing that Todd had called him). He assured me that although he liked Neal and Todd, he was discerning enough to recognize what was going on. There was no need for me to let either call cause me any stress.

I knew that at some point I would need to talk to my brother. However, I waited for my emotions to settle before I did. When I finally communicated my feelings to him, he responded that he had only been trying to help me. He thought that John was in a better position to offer me *the help I needed* and that was why he spoke to John rather than speaking to me. I told him that I did not have the opportunity to tell John about my post myself. I resented that. I felt that it was wrong. He said that it had not occurred to him that I would feel this way. He was surprised that I had been offended. He assured me he did not have any harmful intent and asked me to forgive him.

I forgave him. However, I could not deny that this behavior was a reflection of the way CGT had operated my whole life; no respect for personal boundaries and very little respect for women. He did not comprehend that calling my husband to talk *about me* instead of talking *to me* was a form of disrespect. He did not recognize how his explanation of concern and the suggestion that John could help me with my issues was condescending. It implied that I was the one with the problem. I was the one who so obviously needed help.

In hindsight, it amazes me that the reaction to my post was this dramatic. Just a short time later, there were other posts on Neal's board that took Neal to task in a much more aggressive manner. Neal responded to those posts. Shortly thereafter, Todd called to ask me if I was involved or if I had any idea who this anonymous poster was. I assured him I was not involved. This call led to a lengthy discussion. It was the first time Todd and I had attempted to discuss anything pertaining to CGT issues. During this conversation, Todd asked me a question that shocked me: "Do you remember hearing the name William Sowders very often in church services? As far as I remember, his name might have been spoken once or twice in a whole year." I couldn't believe it. I told him that was not my memory. His name was spoken far more often than that and with great reverence.

He also told me that CGT didn't really have doctrine, because they had not published a written doctrinal statement. I was practically speechless at hearing this. I thought about the CGT Youth in Christ seminar we had where one of the topics had been, "How do we know we are right?" Why was he saying these things to me?

What was Todd trying to prove—or disprove—with these misrepresentations of the truth? I wondered if he even recognized them as misrepresentations of the truth. I pondered this conversation for a long time. Todd had sounded so sincere in everything he had said to me that day. I honestly could not determine whether my brother knew he was misrepresenting the truth or if he had convinced himself to believe these statements were true.

28

Welcome to the Body

Shortly after the anonymous posts, Neal temporarily shut down his spiritual discussion board. When the message board was in limbo, one of the regular posters suggested we form a private discussion group for those of us who wanted to share our experiences with each other. The private discussion group set the stage for my friendship with Eric and Ann. They were invited to participate also. We became acquainted as we emailed and spoke occasionally on the telephone.

After receiving invitations from the person who set up the group, we all introduced ourselves and gave a short personal testimony in this new forum. I was astounded as I read about Eric and Ann's experiences in Tennessee. Eric wrote in an email, "I am a musician that played on [Neal's first Christian] CD, subsequent tour and DVD. To adequately describe how my family and I are involved in this I need to describe how I came to know Neal." Eric went on to explain that in the late eighties Neal had joined a band in California that he (Eric) had been a founding member of. Eric wasn't with the band then. He had left the band in 1981. However, Eric would still sub occasionally, which was how he met Neal. At this point, Eric was a believer and Neal was not.

A few years later, they connected again when Neal formed a band of his own. Neal got in touch with Eric because he wanted to incorporate a string group into a couple of small spots on two early albums. Eric plays violin, as well as guitar. They again worked together briefly. Eric said Neal's progress and musical abilities blew him away, but he still "didn't detect any spiritual bent" on Neal's part. In 2002, Eric heard that Neal had become a Christian and was leaving his successful band to pursue Christian music. Eric called to congratulate Neal and ended up accepting an invitation to tour with Neal to promote his first Christian CD.

Neal arranged to fly Eric to Tennessee in March of 2003 to record. It was on this visit that he began to meet the people in CGT. He told us that he went home to Ann and told her about these wonderfully nice people who were devoted completely to their church and each other. He said, "It sparked my imagination about leaving California and relocating to a simpler environment, living amongst God-fearing people, and committing my talents to playing this incredible progressive rock music in a new Christian ministry." Eric explained in his email: "I assumed by Neal's lyrics a doctrine of salvation by grace, a reverence for Jesus, as well as other orthodox tenets. To be perfectly honest, I had never encountered anyone in my own personal sphere that held any Christian beliefs one would label unorthodox or heretical. My first visits to CGT yielded no warning signs."

Nashville is known as "Music City," but it is also the capital of the Christian music industry. Eric and Ann, both being professional musicians, looked forward to other employment opportunities that could be cultivated by relocating to Tennessee. The real estate market in California was growing red hot, and many families were leaving with their equity to restart their lives elsewhere. Their family could go from living in a tract home in Orange County, California, to a 22-acre estate in Cottontown, Tennessee. As Christians, they were charmed by the "Bible belt." They hoped to raise their kids through the high school years in this "kinder and gentler environment."

Continuing with his testimony, Eric explained that after much prayer, he and Ann decided to move to Tennessee. They sold their home in California, purchased a home in Cottontown, Tennessee, and moved by September of 2003. The tour was being rehearsed and Eric left with Neal and the band for Europe in November.

In subsequent emails Eric and Ann revealed that they were not told anything about those of us who had left CGT. Even after they became friendly with my own family, little was mentioned about me. Ann said that they knew Todd had a sister named Shari, but they never knew I was devoted to the Lord.

During this time, Eric and Ann, along with their two children, began attending CGT and getting to know the people. Ann began sensing that something was amiss. There was a particular service that deeply troubled her. Ann did not know CGT's distinctive beliefs at the time, but she began feeling very uncomfortable during services and asked God why. She said that she heard Steve shout, "Lord, don't let me lose my place!" Ann could not believe what her ears had just heard.

Eric was on tour in Europe at the time; when she told him what Steve had said, Eric thought Ann must have heard him wrong. It seemed inconceivable that Steve would actually believe that God would take away his place and give it to another. Ann said she knew there was plenty of room in heaven for all of God's people, adding, "I knew something wasn't right. I still couldn't put my finger on it." They had been attending CGT for eleven weeks and she was continuing to feel ill at ease.

She thought it was because of so many life changes in a short period of time. She wrote to the group:

> "Our huge move and change of life circumstances were what I originally thought were responsible for my lack of peace. . . . The most troublesome cause of discomfort, though, was the underlying current they conveyed to me; that I wasn't saved. I began questioning my own salvation because of it. In retrospect, they *didn't* think I was saved, I now know. But the truth is I am and was, and red flags began appearing."

> "The sermons made no sense. Eric and I couldn't track the teaching. It was in circles. The women I sat with [distracted themselves] with magazine articles, talking, playing with their kids under the pews and sharing shopping and food ideas. [It seemed] their participation in the services was limited to the uncontrolled emotional displays at the front (which I didn't feel comfortable

participating in because there wasn't Scripture to back up what I observed)."

Ann continued to feel uncomfortable and unable to worship at CGT. She told us that she asked God why she could not worship Jesus in that church. She went on to say, "What came to me rocked me to the very core. Jesus wasn't in those services, and that is why I couldn't worship Him there." She prayed, "But Lord, they say your name . . . they call you sweet Jesus." The truth that came again, however, was the same, "I can't worship Jesus there because He isn't being worshiped there."

Ann shared with me that sometime in December 2003, she decided to attend a church service elsewhere. Because of being in CGT, she was feeling a darkness that caused her to question her own salvation. She was asking herself questions such as, "Why are they so animated emotionally and I'm not feeling anything?" Although she was new to Tennessee and did not know her way around well, she found a Calvary Chapel in Rivergate. She told me that she sat in the back, anonymously, searching her heart for answers and felt filled with God's love and His Spirit. Tears streamed down her face. She realized it wasn't her; it was CGT that was empty.

As Ann shared her experiences, I was amazed at how rapidly she had discerned certain things without anyone spelling out their beliefs. She shared with several of us, "I was (and always have been) wary of emotional-based religion. That isn't meant to disregard all emotions connected with a relationship with the Lord. In fact, not to feel emotions when the Lord touches me would be strange. . . . But, emotions in the absence of the Truth of His Word (written) have always raised my eyebrows."

She also thought it was odd that people consistently said, "If I have done anything to offend anyone here, please forgive me." Ann told us that this affected her negatively. While it is, of course, important to seek forgiveness and repent of your sins, we are supposed to ask our brothers and sisters to forgive us, confessing *specific* sins. Instead, this was a habit of some, and it seemed that they believed by saying those words they were released from their sins. Ann thought it was a cop out.

One of the most disturbing things of all for Ann had been the greeting card given to them when they arrived at CGT. Handwritten inside were the words, "Welcome to the Body." Eric and Ann had been believers for years before attending CGT. Everyone knew they were not new converts. The implication was, "As though we weren't in the body before. Now I know they only believe they are the body and it explains the card. At the time it was perplexing."

In addition to the uneasiness she was feeling in worship services, she did not like the dress codes, the separation of men and women, the pulling apart of her family. She shared that she was troubled by the separatism, the gossip, and the pride displayed by many that she met. She told me personally that she felt she was losing touch with her family as a result of the social segregation within CGT. Men and women seemed to socialize in separate rooms. Kids always went off on their own, apart from the adults. This was not the family atmosphere she had hoped for. Their son had grown weary of the church and wasn't interested in going very often. However, their daughter had been absorbed in her new friendships and all of her Tennessee friends were in CGT. She insisted on attending all of the services.

Around Christmas of 2003, their daughter went to a sleepover with her CGT girlfriends and returned home telling her parents specific stories about Adam and Eve's sin being the sex act as well as other false doctrines. The information shared with their daughter during that sleepover was distressing enough to them as parents that Eric decided to Google the name William Sowders. He remembered the name from talking to a friend in CGT. One of the first listings that came up was "How to get out of the cult, Gospel Assemblies." They were taken completely off guard and knew that they could no longer attend CGT.

As the picture of the Gospel Assemblies began to take shape, Eric understood why Neal was only interested in fellowshipping with these particular churches. Right after the New Year, 2004, they sat down with Neal and told him that they could not attend his church any more. They had hit a dead end and wondered why God had brought them all this way, only to be completely cut off. Without work and being way out in the country, they felt isolated from everything and everyone. Ann describes that as a dark, desperate time. All the people who had welcomed them and enveloped them in so much love disappeared when they decided to stop attending CGT. Their social network quickly evaporated. Ann expressed sadness that she hadn't met any of us former members during that time. We could have offered her such comfort and reassurance. She said, "Eric and I find it incredible that there were others out there who had left CGT living so close by."

Eric and Ann began deep and lengthy studies of Scripture to support why they believed what they believed. They prepared a paper for Neal outlining Scriptures that revealed Jesus' deity, supported the Trinity, that explained salvation through faith and not works and the finished work of Jesus on the cross. They included passages that warned against false teaching, teaching a different gospel. Eric explained the motive and desire that he and Ann shared:

> "[We] took great care to make the doctrinal differences clear using Scripture. As it became obvious that Neal wasn't seeing any validity in our words, I realized that I could not continue in a Christian music ministry alongside him. When we parted ways professionally in early '04, I hoped that my absence would be noted and would prompt questions that would bring his doctrine up for debate. It has always been my desire to see him reconciled to the true Gospel and perhaps generate a revival among the dear people that make up his church. I didn't go public then because I wanted him to have the opportunity to be led by the Lord in his own time and perhaps change course in a manner that would preserve everyone's dignity."

Eric and Ann returned to California and kept a quiet eye on Neal's message board to see if Neal would ever have to openly face the Christian community and proclaim his allegiance to these "special truths." Since Eric had been professionally involved in Neal's "coming out" as a Christian artist, he remained more than casually interested in the progression of Neal's music ministry.

For two years, he and Ann had prayed for more knowledge about CGT to be exposed. Eric has many prayer journals in which he repeatedly asked God for greater understanding regarding their experience in Tennessee. In the limited length of time my post had been visible on Neal's message board, Eric and Ann had seen it. I had no idea that my post was, for them, an answer to prayer and confirmation of what God had shown them while attending CGT. I had known so little about them or the true reasons behind their departure. I was curious about them, but never imagined having an occasion to make their acquaintance once they had moved back to the West Coast.

What I had initially heard was simply that some musician *friends* of Neal's from California had come to visit, fallen in love with CGT and were in the process of relocating so they could join the church. This came through a family member. The excitement was openly shared. Then, less than a year later, I heard that their family was moving *back* to California. However, this was quietly acknowledged, not announced the way their arrival had been. The version told to me was that Eric's wife, Ann, had concluded that CGT was a cult because they did not believe in the Trinity and she convinced Eric they needed to leave. I would only learn that leaving had been a completely mutual decision much, much later.

The brief description Eric and Ann received of me was that I had moved away and I had *issues* with CGT. This statement was true, but extremely incomplete. I had only moved one hour away and I certainly was not the only person who had serious *issues* with CGT. (In my opinion, such dismissive comments were intended to make me sound like I had a problem, not CGT.) Ironically, the comments I heard about *their* departure suggested *Ann had issues* as well. I know through various sources that many people in CGT believed Eric and Ann had done a monumental disservice to their daughter by taking her away from the church and her beloved church friends. This was said openly. There was even corporate prayer for her to find her way back to CGT.

There were a few remarks made about Ann not wanting to conform to their dress standards and such. I imagined that all the rules had played a part in her discomfort. However, I had no idea that Eric and Ann had challenged, in writing, several of CGT's doctrinal positions as well as the calling of William Sowders.

One of the things Eric shared with me was that he felt he had been intentionally deceived. He had uprooted his entire life under a false impression, facilitated by Neal and others in CGT. In all his conversations and time spent with Neal and other CGT members, no one had ever shared the unusual teachings of CGT with him. When he and Ann went to Neal to tell him the reasons they could no longer attend his church, Neal admitted that there had been private discussion about whether or not to share CGT's distinctive beliefs with Eric before he moved his family to Tennessee. However, the decision had been made that Eric was not ready for "meat," but only the "milk" of the Word at that point.

Neal apparently had no idea how arrogant this was. Eric had been a believer far longer than Neal had been. Yet Neal was making a life-altering decision *for Eric* based upon his judgment of Eric's spiritual maturity level and ability to grasp CGT's "deeper truths." It was insulting. But it was worse than that. No one has the authority to play God in other people's lives this way. However, in CGT, they think nothing of this behavior.

I explained to Eric that I did not believe Neal thought he was doing anything wrong or deceptive. He had simply taken on the ways and attitudes of this movement. He was emulating the men he had grown to respect and admire. The arrogance in this movement is unbelievable. Yet this behavior is not viewed as arrogant; it is considered wisdom. Based upon my many years there, I am confident that Neal believed he was exercising wisdom and caution in Eric's best interest. This group sincerely believes they have something unique to offer to other Christians that cannot be found elsewhere, and to reveal the "truths" prematurely might hinder someone from ultimately receiving and embracing "the truth."

I reminded Eric and Ann that Neal had not been a believer prior to his involvement in CGT. That was the only form of "Christianity" he had been exposed to. I told them I did not think Neal had intended to do them harm. Eric described his feelings this way: "Granted, no one intentionally thought they were doing us harm, but they purposely chose to keep us in the dark to their actual beliefs. The *deception* lies in the fact that they *know* the Christian world rejects their *truths*, and they knew our family was unaware of this." He said it was "deceptive and destructive and wreaked havoc" in their lives.

In April of 2004, Eric wrote Neal a letter to give closure to their brief professional relationship. He assured Neal that he did not take any of this lightly and told him that he had never faced a challenge of this magnitude in his entire walk as a Christian. In writing, Eric stated their doctrinal differences and reiterated that these differences separated them, even if only on his part.

Eric stated that Neal, as leader of his music ministry, represented everyone in his organization; therefore, it was Neal's opinions, doctrinal interpretations, church affiliation and voice that would be heard. Eric reminded Neal that he had joined the tour with no knowledge of their beliefs being at such great odds. Now that he *was* aware, he could no longer participate in Neal's music ministry. He asked that questions arising from his absence be answered truthfully and he welcomed Neal to direct inquiries to him if the questions became tedious or Neal was uncomfortable speaking for him.

Eric's absence went unaddressed and his letter ignored. Years later, during a phone conversation, Eric referred to the letter and Neal couldn't even remember it.

꙾

As I reflect on the personal impact of hearing Eric and Ann's experiences, I am overwhelmed. When Eric shared with me that he had prayed for two years for God to provide more information about CGT, more knowledge of their beliefs, and a greater understanding of this part of their journey, I knew God had given me a role in all of that. Not only had I written a post that confirmed what God had independently shown them, in spite of my post being visible for less than one hour, they had seen it. I did not view any of this as coincidence, and it gave me such peace. I had upset a lot of people with that post. I wondered many times if I had been wrong to do what I had done. However, my friendship with Eric and Ann put those questions to rest. Eric and Ann were a gift from God in my spiritual journey.

A very rosy picture had been painted for Eric and Ann. Anything that might have discouraged them from joining CGT had been withheld from them. Based solely on prayer and the leading of the Holy Spirit, Ann had discerned that something was not right in the worship at CGT. God revealed to her the reason she could not worship Jesus in that environment. Then He confirmed this with the documented evidence that Eric discovered by searching for more information. This was a powerful confirmation of all that God had revealed to me personally since I had left. I had come to all of the same conclusions, but my deliverance took years. I was amazed at how quickly Eric and Ann saw through the deception of CGT.

⁓

Ann had expressed how much easier their final months in Tennessee would have been had they only known about all of us and our experiences. That would have given her so much peace. It seemed obvious to me why God had not allowed us to meet sooner. I shared these thoughts with her in May of 2007:

> It is so apparent to me that it was God's sovereign will that you not know about any of us or have any contact with us while you were here. Yes, we would have been able to offer some comfort and support. But we would have tainted your testimony because it would have given the opportunity for everyone there to blame those 'disgruntled ex-members' for contaminating you and influencing you against them. . . . They would have given you no credit for thinking for yourself or being led by God. . . . We would have been the most convenient scapegoats and their explanation of your leaving. But since you never even knew about any of us, much less got to know us during that time, nobody can even go down that road. God preserved you and HE alone sustained you through that time. God gets ALL the glory!

> That is the first time I've heard about the card welcoming you to the Body. . . . That in itself confirms what we have all been saying, that they believe one thing and portray themselves to other Christians in a completely different light. It is so dishonest.

> They don't preach the cross as the means of salvation. They teach that it is our perfection, our overcoming, that qualifies us for eternal life. . . . What [Jesus] did gives us only the opportunity for eternal life. But it is our performance that saves us eternally. However, if you ask them if that's what they believe, they will deny it while at the same time telling all of us who have left that they have not changed on any foundational doctrines/truths. It is constant double speak and it is obvious to anyone who was IN the church.

> I would never have believed I would see the day when CGT would actively pursue the acceptance of other Christians, whom they consider to be the religious world. We did not fellowship

outside the Body and we stayed to ourselves because we had nothing in common with so-called Christians outside the Body.

You were so discerning to see and perceive all that you did in the short time you were there. God has used you and your testimony in such a powerful way in my life—such an undeniable confirmation that God led me out of there. On a personal level, I so wish I could have met you while you were here and we could have shared what we now share. But God's timing is always perfect. God always intended for our paths to cross and for us to share our experiences, but He had a plan first. I am thankful that I didn't lead you to any of your conclusions. God did. And because He has shown you all that He's shown you so independently of what He has shown me, you are another sign post on my journey that points me to HIM.

29

Exposure

After my infamous post on Neal's message board there were many anonymous challenging posts that Neal responded to. The anonymous poster was my friend, Jennifer. She is persistent and posted for about a month or so under different names, pressing Neal for direct answers about his beliefs. Some of Neal's fans thought she should back off. When the moderators blocked her, she just changed her IP address and registered again as a new member. She eventually created the screen name "banned." By this time, everyone knew her identity and she was not attempting to speak anonymously. The exchange between Jennifer and Neal became confrontational.

Neal's position was that Jennifer's presence on his message board was inappropriate. However, Neal was a public person with a public "spiritual discussion" message board. He was about to release a controversial CD with a message about the false church and the true church. The lyrics of his CD spoke directly to—and challenged—the Roman Catholic Church. (He certainly demonstrated a belief in his own freedom of speech.) In addition to all that, Neal had contributed to Jennifer's personal pain by showing up at the custody hearing in support of those who were making false claims about both her husband and herself. Neal suggested publicly that Jennifer had motives other than the ones she was stating. In response to that, she told Neal:

> You all assume you know my motives because of how you choose to view any of us who have spoken out against the church you go to. I have a right to feel the way I do about that place. If what happened to me and many others had happened to your son or daughter, I promise that you would feel completely different [than] you do. There have been so many lies and cover-ups. . . . I am tired

of things being [spun] by them and to me this refusing to be direct about your Doctrine is just another spin. Maybe you should start asking more questions about what went on there before you started attending that church and what has gone on since you have been there. Things were kept from you on purpose at first because they were afraid you would not want to go there if you knew about it.

As if it were completely irrelevant today, Neal ridiculed Jennifer for bringing up abuse that happened to her a long time ago and informed her that they were *praying* for her. Neal called Jennifer's behavior "insane." He charged her with lies. He belittled her with sarcastic remarks about her being "so noble." He made references to persecution. I was surprised by his words and tone. To deemphasize what Jennifer had been through while at the same time suggesting he was being persecuted because of some posts challenging his doctrinal beliefs on a message board was striking to me. He said that she was acting inappropriately by persisting to post, what amounted to, the truth. Jennifer's response was strong, direct and typed in all caps:

WHAT WAS INAPPROPRIATE WAS THAT I WAS SEXUALLY ABUSED BY A MEMBER OF THE CHURCH!!! WHAT WAS INAPPROPRIATE WAS THAT I WAS TOLD I WASN'T ALLOWED TO TELL ANYONE FOR THE SAFETY OF THE MAN WHO ABUSED ME. WHAT WAS INAPPROPRIATE WAS THAT MANY OTHER CHILDREN AT THAT TIME WERE ABUSED AND IT WAS COVERED UP. WHAT WAS INAPPROPRIATE WAS THAT OUR ASSISTANT PASTOR AT THAT TIME WAS A KNOWN CHILD MOLESTER. WHAT WAS INAPPROPRIATE WAS [THAT] YOU THINK THAT BECAUSE MY ABUSE HAPPENED 20 YEARS AGO THAT IT DOESN'T MATTER. WHAT IS INAPPROPRIATE IS THAT THE CURRENT MINISTER IS STILL LYING ABOUT WHAT THEY [KNEW].

Neal advised Jennifer to go to the authorities if there had been criminal behavior, but didn't want her to bring the problem to his message board. Jennifer was relentless, and I understand why Neal felt antagonized by her. What amazed me was that Neal and other CGT members viewed her posts as persecution. For a Christian persecution is defined as *suffering for one's faith in Christ*. To me, Jennifer's pursuit of the truth did not constitute persecution. The antagonism was not directed at Neal *for* his faith in Christ. The antagonism was to get those in CGT to openly reveal all of their distinctive beliefs. Those of us who had left CGT recognized the cagey answers to questions. We knew the things they were not revealing. I never would have felt compelled to post what I posted if Neal had simply answered questions with direct and forthcoming answers. Because of these challenges, Neal *had* to step up and be more open about his beliefs and the beliefs of CGT. No matter what anyone thinks of Jennifer's approach, I don't believe Neal's openness would have happened without someone applying pressure to the situation.

When Neal's new CD was released, he went on tour to promote it. Those of us who knew CGT's beliefs and their "mission" knew that Neal's tour was about more than promoting his music. CGT/GAC has always believed they had something "deeper" to offer other Christians.

Danny felt compelled to inform the churches where Neal was to perform about the heretical beliefs of CGT, and Neal. CGT had never taught salvation through the finished work of Jesus on the cross. That had been labeled as "taking the easy way." Danny felt concerned that Christian churches might embrace CGT ignorantly and innocently, just as Eric and Ann had. His letters and phone calls accomplished little. Apparently, many Christians either weren't convicted about defending the faith or didn't believe Danny. He believed that, in spite of the fact that these fellow believers didn't know him, they should have had a desire to investigate the claims and look into the matter. Danny felt that it was unloving to worship alongside people who rejected the truth of the Gospel, validating their "Christianity" by allowing them to blend into the true Christian community unchallenged. "If we truly loved them, we would challenge them and make every effort to bring them to the truth," he'd tell me. Danny and I had many conversations about this at the time. His boldness sometimes made me uncomfortable.

Danny would not go so far as to say there were no true believers in CGT. He could not know what each person believed in their hearts. However, he insisted the *teachings* of CGT were not Christian. They denied the finished work of the cross and they denied the deity of Christ.

Danny continually emphasized to me the seriousness and the danger of their false teachings. He quoted Scriptures to me about those who would add to or take from the Gospel (Galatians 1:6–10):

> I am astonished that you are so quickly deserting him who called you in the grace of Christ and are turning to a different gospel— not that there is another one, but there are some who trouble you and want to distort the gospel of Christ. But even if we or an angel from heaven should preach to you a gospel contrary to the one we preached to you, let him be accursed. As we have said before, so now I say again: If anyone is preaching to you a gospel contrary to the one you received, let him be accursed.
>
> For am I now seeking the approval of man, or of God? Or am I trying to please man? If I were still trying to please man, I would not be a servant of Christ.

Those Scriptures were strong and bold. He pointed out that they, as a group, were far less dangerous when they stayed to themselves and made no attempts at outreach. However, now that they were actively engaging in reaching out to the unsaved, attempting to be accepted by other Christians, the potential danger was far greater. Danny would point out to me that walking away silently and failing to tell them the truth was not love; it was indifference; it was a sin.

Danny was not indifferent. He contacted churches close by as well as overseas, and he was vilified for his actions. When virtually no Christian church appeared to take his cautions seriously, he was disappointed yet unwavering in the conviction that he had done the right thing. It was his job to alert them. It was their responsibility to investigate and heed the warning.

My dad apparently heard about Danny's actions and saw some of the emails. He was offended. Instead of calling Danny to discuss it with him directly, he called *John* at work. John had nothing to do with anything that was transpiring; he and my dad did not typically have phone conversations. John came home from work and asked the then-familiar question, "Guess who called me today?" I said, "Who?" And he told me, "Your dad." I said, "Really? What did he want?" John explained that he wasn't sure because my dad had not really come right out and asked for anything. He said that my dad had spoken softly and was hard to follow. He mentioned something about Danny going around saying derogatory things about him and he was crushed by it. He mentioned that he knew it was true because he had been shown emails.

John hated to be put in the middle of my family's affairs. I believe my dad and brother, and Neal, all appealed to John because they consider him to be so "level headed and fair." My dad didn't think I could be objective about my own son, but John could. This was also John's impression. The attempts to draw my husband into situations in which he was not involved were offensive and upsetting to me. I felt like my dad was attempting to undermine the relationship between my husband and my son. I did not appreciate this.

John asked me if I had any idea what my dad was talking about. I was clueless and decided to call Danny and let him know what my dad believed he was doing. If Danny was not guilty of speaking disparagingly about my dad, he needed to let my dad know that. If he was guilty of saying something unkind, he needed to repent. However, he could do neither if he was completely unaware. I picked up the phone and called my son. I asked him if he was guilty of this. He said he had not said anything about Grandpa, adding, "I'll just call him and talk to him myself." Not long after that, he called me back and told me that his grandfather was referring to the letters and phone calls warning other Christians about CGT. He said, "When you attack my church, you attack me!" My dad had never mentioned the church in his phone call to John, but instead implied that Danny had run him down *personally*. John was emphatic on that point.

Danny had not backed down to his grandfather's attack. He told him, "Grandpa, I'm telling you the truth *because* I love you. You *are* in a bad place. You *do* need to get out. It *is* a cult. That's *why* I did what I did." His grandfather responded, "You wouldn't have your wife if it wasn't for my church! And your mom wouldn't have John either if it wasn't for the church!" (He was giving CGT credit for bringing us to Tennessee where we met them.) Danny replied, "Joseph wouldn't have been ruler over Egypt if his brothers had not thrown him in a pit and sold him into slavery, but his brothers don't get the credit for that; the glory goes to God." His grandfather said he wasn't interested in hearing his "spin." Just before they hung up, Danny told him, "I love you, Grandpa." There was silence for several seconds, but his grandfather finally said, "I love you, too." That was the end of the conversation.

My dad's health is not good, and I try to avoid any conversations that might cause him stress. Although I continued to have regular phone conversations with him, I never did bring up his phone call to John or Danny's phone call to him. Rather than confront him with my feelings, I chose to let them go. Other than when Danny was a small child, they had never enjoyed a close relationship anyway. After this, I accepted that they never would. I wanted to rise above my feelings in order to maintain some level of relationship with my father.

⌒

I did not realize how much the heat was about to be turned up on all of our relationships. Through a series of events that none of them could have orchestrated personally, four victims of abuse united in purpose.

Cheryl, Crystal (Cheryl's sister), and Lynette (Cheryl's cousin), had all come forward about their abuse at the hands of their grandfather. It had been revealed by another family member that Brother Mears knew of incidents occurring many years earlier. If he had *only* advised family members of this, the granddaughters could have been protected from their abuser. However, not only did he conceal the matter, Brother Mears allowed his brother, Paul, to sit beside him on the platform and preside over services in his absence. Paul officiated at weddings. Paul participated in baptizing people. Paul spoke from the pulpit. He was not on the payroll, but in every other aspect, he performed in the capacity of assistant pastor or minister of CGT when he was not pursuing ministry endeavors in other states.

The only person who had been protected was Paul. The congregation had no idea and the extended family had no idea of any prior violation. After the allegations had been made openly, the greatest concern demonstrated was for the dignity and the legacy of Brother Mears, as I have already stated.

Cheryl, Crystal, and Lynette were victims of their grandfather. Jennifer had come forward about her abuse at the hands of another, but the common thread in each of these cases was that further abuse might have been averted if the former and current pastors had not protected a predator.

Steve, the current pastor, seemed unwilling to acknowledge that or repent for it. Instead, he appealed to people's sympathies by using analogies such as putting butter on a burn. He put victims on the spot with the question, "You don't blame Brother Mears, do you?" It was vehemently denied that Brother Mears did anything other than "not object" to Paul pastoring a church in Phoenix and sitting on the platform of our churches in California and Tennessee. These attempts to rewrite history were not only a means of sidestepping responsibility but preserving the honor and legacy of a man. The victims felt re-victimized by CGT and the current pastor, Steve Farmer.

In addition to their own abuse, they knew of others who had suffered silently, whose lives had been devastated by the way abuse was mishandled in CGT. Jennifer had become involved with an organization that exposed and prosecuted similar abuses within the Catholic Church and other religious affiliations (SNAP). Through that association, she became aware of an attorney in Minnesota. The Minnesota attorney gave her the name of an attorney in California, Joseph George, who specialized in prosecuting such cases. However, up to this point, nothing had really materialized. Jennifer had wanted to talk to Lynette for two years, but had no way of contacting her.

Jennifer was blogging and posting on the EX-GAC message board. She wrote an article on "What is a Cult?" and a link to it was posted on the board. In the article, she mentioned Paul Mears. Lynette was living in California. She did not know Jennifer and she had not been in contact with her cousins Cheryl and Crystal in a long time. One day in late February of 2008, Lynette Googled her grandfather's name to see if anything came up. Jennifer's article appeared; linked to the EX-GAC website. Lynette sent an email to the board moderator, thanking her for posting it. She identified herself as Paul's granddaughter and said, "I have waited for so long for someone to validate all that I have been thinking/saying since I was thirteen years old. FOR THAT I LOVE YOU. I have felt so alone for the longest time. Please contact me if you would like."

The board moderator knew that Lynette's email had been intended for Jennifer, the author of the article. So she forwarded it on to her. Now Jennifer had a way to contact Lynette. Jennifer and Cheryl had prayed for months. They had spoken out publicly. They had waited on God for direction. And they were beginning to think that maybe they had done all they could do when, out of the blue, Lynette found Jennifer. That was just weeks before Lynette's twenty-sixth birthday, the last day within her statute of limitations.

Cheryl had wanted to get in touch with Lynette for so long but did not know how to reach her. The only people who could provide contact information were family members still loyal to CGT. Because she had been vocal in speaking out about the abuse and cover-ups, Cheryl was reluctant to ask any of those family members how to reach Lynette. She knew she would be questioned. Cheryl and Jennifer had been considering their legal options for a while, but they were not sure that was what God wanted them to do yet. This certainly seemed to be an answer to their prayers.

Jennifer asked Lynette if she would be interested in joining them in filing suit. Lynette said yes. The statute of limitations for Cheryl, Crystal, and Jennifer had run out, though new information had come to light that might lengthen their statute in the eyes of the judicial system. Lynette, however, had until her birthday in March before her statute ran out. They made the decision to go forward together.

Jennifer contacted the California attorney, having no idea where in California he was located. She left a message and he returned her call within twenty minutes. He gave her his email address so she could forward information to him. When she received a response from him via email, she saw that he was in Sacramento. His office was only twenty minutes from Lynette's residence. He asked Jennifer to have Lynette meet him at his office first thing the next morning. This was a week and a half before her twenty-sixth birthday. All four of the women would file as close together as possible. However, Lynette was under an extreme time crunch. Her suit was filed the day before her statute of limitations ended.

The decision to move forward with legal action was not one that came quickly or easily. I have been closest to Cheryl, and her struggle is the one I know most personally. For months prior to signing the paperwork, she agonized and prayed over what God wanted her to do (or not do). At times, she thought about simply backing off because the personal stress and consequences would be so great for her if she persevered. However, every time she considered bowing out, something else would happen, leading her to the conclusion that God wanted her to go forward. Every time she prayed and asked for confirmation, it came.

Crystal withdrew her name from the lawsuit because she feared she couldn't withstand the pressure and the personal attacks that would come out of it. She is a recovering alcoholic and has been sober for years. She felt like she needed to protect her sobriety at all cost, and the public condemnation she might experience could have lethal consequences for her. She wanted to support her sister, cousin, and friend from the sidelines. However, once she made this decision, she had no peace about it. She felt convicted that she was making the wrong choice and she would always regret this decision, so she changed her mind.

Many people have assumed these lawsuits were all about money. Nothing could be further from the truth. They were about exposing the darkness and wrongdoings that went unacknowledged for so many years. They were about protecting children from any future abuse. After the lawsuits became public, Cheryl would ask me to give a specific message to other victims because she knew I had relationships with more than one past victim. Her message was simply, "Tell her that we know what she's been through and we are doing this for her as well as all the victims of CGT." When I would relay that message, the response would always be the same. "I know that. Please tell her I said thank you."

30

The Fallout

The lawsuits were filed and the media coverage ensued. Lynette was in California and gave a television interview there. Cheryl, Crystal, and Jennifer gave interviews to the local news in Nashville at Janette's home. The three women shared how abuse was covered up in CGT, and they described the group as a cult, listing specific reasons for their claims. Of course, due to time constraints, only snippets of conversation remained in the final piece.

It was an emotional day for everyone involved. Even though I had not been interviewed I had a lot of anxiety about the upcoming broadcast. In hindsight, I am utterly amazed at the courage it took for these women to stand up for their convictions this way. I believe God had to have given them that courage. I remember thinking that I was not sure I would have the strength to do what they were doing if I were in their place.

In the months preceding the lawsuits, Cheryl and I had discussed all of the potential repercussions of her decision. She never asked me to guide her or help her make the decision. She did not ask me to approve or disapprove (like I probably would have). But she did bounce her thoughts and emotions off of me. She shared specific prayers and Scriptures that had stood out to her as she was seeking God's will and direction. Repeatedly, she received confirmation that God was bringing exposure to this group and He had given her a role in that (whether she wanted it or not).

At the point of signing the paperwork, Cheryl explained that there was no going back. It was a stressful time. We talked again about all the consequences that would come and how unpleasant they would be. We talked about the rejection and the vilification she would experience. She had already become estranged from much of her extended family, but she at least had *some* interaction with old friends at CGT. This lawsuit was going to make the separation complete. She would be viewed as an enemy by most members of the group. People would end up going out of their way to avoid her as though she had the plague. She would be called a liar. She would be openly accused of sinister motives (like monetary gain). I told her more than once that I wasn't sure I could do it if I were in her shoes. I was scared for her. However, she could regret her decision either way. If she backed away from doing what she truly believed God wanted her to do, she would have to live with the knowledge that she had chosen her own comfort and self-preservation. I could never discourage someone from doing what they believed God was directing them to do. I didn't want her to look back with regret. There was just *no easy way* in this predicament. Although it was a decision I couldn't help her make, I assured her that no matter what she decided I would support her 100 percent either way.

Every detail had seemed to simply fall into place. Cheryl had not pursued an opportunity; it had fallen in her lap. In so many ways, it would have been easier to withdraw and offer support behind the scenes. However, for Cheryl, it always came down to her belief that there was a much bigger picture in all of this, and it wasn't all about her. It certainly was not about her personal comfort.

Ultimately, Cheryl signed the papers in March 2008. She told me there really wasn't a decision to be made. God had confirmed again and again that He had a plan, and exposing the abuse was a part of it. She had to give up control and put all her faith and trust in God for the future. She told me that even if her case was dismissed, it wouldn't matter to her. All that mattered was doing what she believed God wanted her to do. The outcome was in God's hands, not hers.

I was determined to do all I could to love and support Cheryl, Crystal, Jennifer, and Lynette. Whenever I became aware of personal attacks on the Internet (which were many), I defended them. I felt extremely protective of these women and all the other victims who, for their own reasons, had not come forward so visibly. I occasionally received open *and* anonymous emails from the quiet ones who wanted these women to know of their support and gratitude. Because I was visible on the Internet, some chose to communicate these feelings through me.

After the media picked up the story, CGT responded with their version of the situation. They published a timeline on their website and called a town hall type of meeting at the church. The media and the surrounding community were invited. There were handouts at this event, including printed copies of the timeline.

I had first watched my sister-in-law and others I loved sharing about their sexual and spiritual abuse on television. The same week, the CGT town hall meeting received media coverage. Through my television screen, I then witnessed another person I loved claiming, "We want to be transparent."

I was shocked to see my brother, Todd, as the spokesperson for CGT. I never could have anticipated that. I guess because he's my brother, I wanted to believe that he was being used, that he *didn't know* what I knew. How could he possibly have chosen to side with CGT against his own sister-in-law if he *did* know? His loyalty was clearly to CGT and to Steve. Cheryl and I wondered if he had been chosen to be the spokesperson because his last name was the same as one of the victims; if one of the goals was to plant the thought in people's minds that even her own family members were not supporting her. It pained me to watch this unfold and, most of all, to see Todd take such a prominent role.

I continued to speak out against the leadership of CGT on the message board and occasionally on my personal blog. What I did not know was that my brother was taking this very personally. Every time I mentioned "the leadership," to him it was as if I was calling his name when in reality I had the pastor in mind. CGT had formed a new board of trustees and Todd had been appointed to a trustee position. I knew that the trustees were technically considered a part of church leadership, and I hated that my brother had accepted this position. However, in all my years at CGT, the pastor had always been the sole leader, from the founding by Reva Mears and continuing with Cornelius Mears and now Steve Farmer, though to a lesser extent. I had never once thought of a trustee as leadership. It was not my intent to personally attack my brother, although I now understand why he perceived it as he did. However, it still comes down to this ultimate priority: I have to be true to God and to my convictions *even if that results in my brother viewing me as his enemy and betrayer.* The Bible says that "They will be divided, father against son and son against father, mother against daughter and daughter against mother, mother-in-law against her daughter-in-law and daughter-in-law against mother-in-law" (Luke 12:53). In this case it was brother against sister. If I altered my stand in order to maintain good feelings within my personal family, I would be a fraud and a hypocrite. Let me be perfectly clear on this. *I would rather be hated.* And in such a serious conflict, I knew that I *had* to come to terms with that early on—*no matter how painful it was.*

In the weeks following the lawsuits being filed, there was the fallout where a lot of information about CGT was getting into the media, and there was a lot of damage control being done by CGT. Several members of CGT gave interviews to local newspapers. In these articles, certain individuals within CGT gave a description of the group and its history that was anything but transparent. *Former* members had made references to the control over our lives and the church "standards" we had been expected to adhere to. *Current* members then laughed at and dismissed these claims, suggesting to reporters there was no control and there never had been. This labeled former members as liars. For those of us who grew up there and experienced the constant oppression, this was a denial of our own lives and histories.

It was disturbing to witness the all-out attempt at rewriting CGT's history while simultaneously claiming, "We want to be transparent." Steve said publicly, "We feel great sorrow" for these women. Yet, he had never repented for CGT's role in their abuse and cover-ups. What victims need most is acknowledgment and repentance. However, Steve continually made excuses for the wrongs of the past. One comment he made on more than one occasion was, "It didn't happen on my watch." Well, that is not entirely true. In the case of Janette's daughter, Steve was acting as pastor. And when it came to the covering up of Paul's first known "inappropriate touching," Steve, by his own admission, had known since 1967. He seemed completely ignorant of the insensitivity of his often-repeated response. It implied that nothing mattered prior to his "watch" as official pastor. It continually reinforced that Steve's priority was avoiding accountability and liability. His words and actions did *not* convey a genuine concern for the victims and their healing.

The local newspaper, *The White House Watch*, quoted Jennifer on June 4, 2008: "I want him [Farmer] to own what's happened to all of the victims, instead of making excuses." Jennifer went on to explain that during the two years she remained in CGT after her alleged abuse was openly revealed all she wanted was for him to apologize without feeling the need to qualify it; she wanted an "I'm sorry," without there being a *but* attached. Steve told the newspaper reporter, "We've not understood how to deal with her." I'm not sure how much simpler Jennifer could have made it for him to know what she needs. How could he not know exactly what she wanted from him? He dismissed Jennifer by implying that she was the one with the problem. I felt he had done the same thing to me, and Ann, and many others. It was subtle and would go unnoticed by the average reader, but it was crystal clear to those of us who had been there and had all been portrayed similarly when we left.

Steve and Becky shared details about financial assistance that had been *offered* to Crystal, one of the victims, soon after she had revealed her abuse. In order to appear compassionate and credible, Steve revealed to the *White House Watch* how they had helped Crystal with her "debt." (Since when does a "church" reveal such a private matter to a newspaper? It was self-serving and it violated a victim of horrendous abuse.) I was appalled. The financial assistance Crystal had received from her own family members (Cornelius Mears was her great uncle) had become a convenient public relations tool in Steve's hand. He told the newspaper that she had been given $4,000 when, according to Crystal, she had been given only $3,000, and he neglected to reveal that there had been an important *condition* put on this "help." Crystal had been required to attend church services at CGT in order to be granted this assistance, and, in fact, Sister Mears had practically insisted Crystal allow them to help her, asking her to *"please* take the money." I remember wondering at the time if they were trying to buy her silence. I knew they were trying to get her back in church.

The same article stated, "According to Farmer, there has been talk inferring the church has changed into a completely different church—an idea he rejects." However, Todd had spoken about the church "evolving" during the town hall meeting. It would be hard for those in the surrounding communities to know *what* the truth was. However, one thing was true; repentance was always conspicuously absent from every conversation, both public and private.

Katie, the woman who had been raped as a little girl by a teenager in the church, told *The White House Watch*, "I want to expose the problem, not get revenge." However, "molestation breeds molesters," she said, and "because the problem was not recognized and called out, it has been allowed to continue in a cycle over the generations." Katie told the reporter that she was not bitter about her childhood and today is "exuberant" about her spiritual life. She concluded her remarks by explaining, "God turned something horrific into something beautiful" (because she has grown closer to Him and has been delivered from the bondage of CGT).

In Steve's public statement to *The White House Watch*, he declared, "The newspaper reports depict us as a church that doesn't care and somehow condones sexual abuse. Nothing could be further from the truth." He went on to say, "Before you judge our church, I hope you will take the time to get to know us. Come to a worship service, or listen to our teachings that are available on our website at [www.cgtchurch.org]. Get to know our members as you see them in the community. You will find transparent men and women of character doing their best to follow the teachings of Jesus."

Nobody to my knowledge has ever said CGT "condones" sexual abuse. It has been said that CGT covered it up and protected the image of the church above the victims. As I have watched the public relations campaign that has been in play ever since the lawsuits became public, I have heard the word *transparent* used a lot. It has become so highly objectionable to me, as well as an emotional trigger. Transparency would be to open up and acknowledge the wrongs of the past and repent to those who have been harmed. Instead, Steve obtained the services of a public relations representative. Excuses, analogies, and denials are not change. Change of direction comes only through repentance. Yes, there have been some very visible shifts in "CGT ways" since the lawsuits were filed, but they appear superficial. They project a continuation of self-preservation and image consciousness. The big difference, in my eyes, is that instead of being image conscious within their own group (the Body), CGT has had to suddenly become image conscious within the community.

Since the lawsuits were filed one year ago, standards (of appearance) that were always so highly revered have simply been tossed out. Women are now wearing pants, short sleeves, earrings, cutting their hair shorter. Men are suddenly free to wear facial hair and dress casually for services. Just five years ago, my friend, Rachel Brady, was told that she could not continue to teach Sunday school if she wore sweats to the ballpark on a cold night. Steve actually suggested to Rachel's husband, Tim, that she wrap up in a blanket, as *his wife* would do, rather than wear a pair of pants in public. Today, however, Steve's wife is wearing pants and capris everywhere.

I do not want to judge Steve's heart, but I do *question* whether any of these standards would have been discarded had it not been for the public scrutiny brought on by the media attention and CGT's desire to appear more "normal" to the community. If Steve suddenly had received the revelation that these rules were a form of legalism and such restrictions should not be imposed by him upon the people, then there are an awful lot of us he needs to repent to for the oppression and personal condemnation of our past. After all, it was falsely claimed, of nearly all of us, that we had left CGT because the standards were too stringent. To be clear on this, it is *integrity* I am looking for; *not* a personal apology.

If these rules are wrong now, they were always wrong. And that is the rub for me and others. I have not heard Steve admit that the rules of appearance, which had always been claimed to be biblical, were a form of legalism and control, that this was wrong in the past. In fact, he has made it a point *not* to acknowledge that publicly in the statements I have read and heard. He emphatically rejects the notion that the church is a completely different church today than it has been in the past. But there is reported division within CGT over the removal of long held traditions. If there was any truth to the claims made by Steve and other members in newspaper articles, why then would *anyone* be struggling with these changes, why would there even be a change in how people dress at all? As someone who spent most of my life there, under the oppression of harsh legalism and the doctrine of perfection, how can I avoid these questions?

Someone on the message board mentioned a CGT service in which person after person got up to repeat back to Steve what they thought he was saying (after he made comments about withdrawing past restrictions). I watched the service on the CGT website, as they archive their video. The people needed to hear specifically that Steve was saying it was okay to choose their own wardrobe. They would begin almost apologetically and then proceed to say, "What I understand you to be saying is . . ." followed by specific descriptions of what was okay like, "If my wife wants to wear a pair of pants to church, that's okay." Steve clearly did not want to say it was okay or it wasn't okay. He said he was being deliberately ambiguous. He wanted people to simply make their own choices and leave him out of it. What a dramatic shift from the past!

As I listened and observed the inner conflict this was causing for some in the congregation, I wondered why people were still willingly sitting there listening. Late one evening following this service, Todd called me wanting to explain Steve's position to me. I had not asked for the explanation, but I listened. We spoke for two hours on the phone. Steve's Sunday night discourse on the removal of standards had been big news on the EX-GAC message board. I had offered my opinion on the subject. And I could only assume that had been the reason Todd had pursued this dialogue.

My conversation with Todd was warm; we both expressed our love for the other. We assured one another that in spite of our many differences, we both wanted a relationship as brother and sister. I viewed it as a positive conversation. Perhaps we were even making actual progress toward one day being closer. I hoped so.

I wanted to believe Todd was sincere; I just didn't understand why he was initiating a conversation *about Steve and CGT* when we didn't have conversations about anything else. Todd and I don't normally call each other on the phone, and we rarely see each other. When we do, it's cordial. However, our interaction is distant and casual. There has always been a barrier between us that I could never quite define. It's hard for me to relax and be myself in his presence. I have often attributed this to our very different core personalities. I have never felt accepted, though I could not specifically say why. While I did not want to be in any way distrustful of his motive, there was one thing I couldn't quite get out of my mind. The impetus for his call had clearly been to represent *Steve* after the service had become a hot topic on the message board. I could not understand why Todd would even care to discuss Steve with me at this point. I had never called Todd to discuss Steve or CGT. I felt perplexed and conflicted about our conversation, but I was thankful for the reassurance that my brother wanted a relationship with me. I decided to focus on that.

Shortly thereafter, I heard that Steve had removed Jesus from the Godhead and wondered if it was true. I didn't want to have a *discussion* of CGT doctrine, so I asked Todd to answer my question via email. I shared openly that I was writing a book and wanted to accurately represent CGT's beliefs. I told him not to feel obligated to answer me (because I knew I might be causing him discomfort). I did not believe he owed me an explanation. But he *offered* the explanation that he didn't want to respond *because it was not in the best interest of our relationship* to continue discussing CGT. Since he had so recently *initiated* CGT discussion in an effort to represent Steve, the *explanation* seemed patronizing to me. This resulted in conflict and Todd revealed resentment he has held in his heart toward me for years. Specific accusations were made, which reopened old wounds. In the pain of the moment, I informed him that I didn't want a relationship anymore. But I regret those words. They reflected my emotion, not the desire of my heart.

It's easy to lose sight of someone else's wounds when you're focused on your own. I have many flaws, but I have always loved my family and wanted closer relationships. At one time, I would have done just about anything to have the love and acceptance of my family. I used to take a lack of connection in my family so personally, as though I wasn't good enough or I didn't fit the mold my family wanted me to fit into. It's such a difficult stronghold to break, but I realize that God does not want me to look to other people for acceptance; including my family members. Instead, I must give my broken heart and broken relationships to God and rest in His sovereignty.

Recognizing my acceptance in Christ has been transformational. God has also loved me through John. Being the recipient of my husband's unconditional love has made it easier for me to live with a void in other relationships. I am less needy than I used to be. Although I still enjoy words of affirmation, I am no longer trying to be filled up by everyone around me.

When the lawsuits became public, I began to have some pretty intense physical symptoms resulting from stress. I first attributed it to hormones, but John insisted it was primarily stress. I was not sleeping well. I started having headaches and night sweats. I cried a lot. CGT stress has wreaked havoc on me.

There were harsh words directed at me for my stand. It has even been widely believed that I was the one behind the scenes *pushing* these women to file lawsuits. I have been repeatedly shocked to learn how many different people have blamed *me* for all of this. This is certainly not true. However, as I became aware that I was getting the credit for instigating and orchestrating all of these events, I began to feel anxiety and even a slight panic that my dad would buy into this collective mindset. There have been many rough spots in our relationship. Though no harsh words had been spoken the last time we talked, we hadn't spoken in several weeks, and I found myself anticipating my dad's rejection next.

I wanted to call my dad, to reach out to him and check on him. However, I thought about my dad's phone conversations with John and Danny. I knew that a stand against CGT represented a personal attack against him, in his mind. I was sure that my dad viewed me the same as he viewed my son. I was afraid just seeing my number on his Caller ID would cause him undue stress in light of the chaos. I did not want him to think I expected him to talk about any of this. On the other hand, I didn't want him to think I didn't *want* to call and check on him. I wasn't sure what to do, so I decided to send him a card.

As I wrote a personal note inside the card, I wept and felt overcome by emotion from the old wounds and past rejection. It was a pathetic attempt to get what I needed from my dad. I was practically pleading with him to tell me that he still *wanted* to hear from me and he would love me no matter what. I read the card to Cheryl and to Danny before putting it in the mail. They both assured me that, in their opinion, there was no way my card could be misunderstood. Apparently it was. My dad never responded. He suggested to someone else that my card caused such discomfort that he couldn't call me now because of it. In trying to look at the situation from his point of view, I have come to terms with the reality that my dad probably cannot handle my raw, honest emotion no matter how heartfelt and sympathetic. He has to protect himself from stress. He is not well physically, and I take all of that into consideration as I reflect on our estrangement. I am not angry. I do not have anything to prove. I just don't know how to fix anything, so I have stopped trying. At some point, it has to be enough to know that God sees my heart even if every family member cannot.

I am *not* suggesting that CGT is to blame for every conflict within my family. All families have problems. But CGT *has* deeply divided our family at a time in our lives when, if not for CGT, I believe we might have been able to grow closer and heal from the wounds of the past. I believe sharing these personal details is important because they illustrate how loyalty to a group can *contribute* to the breakdown of a family. I know of many family estrangements that are a direct result of loyalty to this group. I hope I can help to prevent another family from suffering a similar fate.

When Danny was first dating Rebecca, he spoke to a counselor, Floyd Dawson (the same one I saw during and after my ex-husband's depression), about whether or not he could ever marry Rebecca if she did not embrace CGT. We had always been taught that we should not marry anyone who had not embraced our "vision" of the Body. Floyd told Danny that to choose a group above a relationship was idolatry. His inner conflict had nothing to do with God or Christianity; he was esteeming a group of people too highly. God did not require him to make a choice, since Rebecca was a believer. And any group that imposed that degree of loyalty on him was cultivating idolatry in him. I believe idolatry is contaminating relationships within many families today, including my own.

31

A New Foundation

When you are free from having to protect and defend a particular group, such as CGT, everything takes on new clarity. You can see things for what they really are. I wish everyone attending CGT today could have the vantage point of those of us who have left for even one day. I wish Steve could have *truly* responded to the victims in love and compassion, openly acknowledging the sins of the past, his sins of the past. If only there had been no attempt to protect an image or the legacy of a man. If only there had been repentance and no attempt to dismiss wrong by comparing it to "butter on a burn." If only there had been love and concern for Janette's little girl a few short years ago instead of indifference and contempt. What I would have given if even a *few* people had bothered to dig deeper and discover the truth of that situation. I wanted someone to care and question rather than automatically assume the church was under attack (which was what Steve told them). Instead, there was a complete absence of empathy. It came more naturally for them to label Janette as angry and bitter enough to make up lies in order to hurt old friends rather than to investigate the matter, seeking the truth. Protecting the group at all costs is a cultish mentality.

People who don't feel empathy are usually narcissistic. I have come to see that a group of people can take on the collective trait of narcissism. Everything that happens is primarily about them and their suffering. They have a difficult time getting outside themselves to feel the pain of someone else, even a victim of sexual abuse.

Where there is an absence of empathy, there is usually little conviction for justice. Where justice doesn't matter, the truth becomes something moldable and is often lost in translation. Conversely, where truth is relative, justice has little relevance. I can think of no better example of this than Steve telling Cheryl, "You can believe whatever you want to believe." I have witnessed people with this mindset blatantly rewrite history and distort truth for their own agendas. However, wrong is wrong. Truth does matter; justice does matter; integrity does matter. They matter to God—and they should matter to us as well.

Being built into a group instead of being built into Christ is a dangerous thing. It causes people to lift up and give glory to their group instead of to God without even recognizing that is what they are doing. It will make a person fiercely loyal to the group, but not necessarily to God. It leads to idolatry and pride.

Pride is at the core of all sin. Therefore, if I live in denial of my own pride, it is very easy to think that perhaps I do not sin. But 1 John 1:8–10 tells us, "If we say we have no sin, we deceive ourselves, and the truth is not in us. If we confess our sins, he is faithful and just to forgive us our sins and to cleanse us from all unrighteousness. If we say we have not sinned, we make him a liar and his word is not in us."

One of the things that always stood out to me while I was in CGT was that many who felt they were living up to the standards and doing things "by the book," tended to be proud and unsympathetic to failing people. Those who were not confident in their righteous behavior were humble, but often defeated as well. I was in the latter group. Feeling mercy and compassion for other failing people was never a struggle for me, but I did not feel victorious; I felt like a continual failure. I was never told that Jesus died so that I might have life through faith in Him alone and not through my own merit.

It was my performance that was always emphasized in salvation. I was told that God was going to shake people out or weed people out who didn't "do right." For most of my life, I lived in fear that I might be nothing but a weed in God's garden. I remember wondering if I was a tare among the wheat. If I didn't abide by a standard, it was suggested that I was rebelling against my pastor. There were constant spoken and unspoken judgments based on the most superficial things. It created a Pharisaical spirit in the group.

I remember when a close friend of mine openly expressed disappointment in me for wearing earrings to a formal New Year's Eve party. I was about thirty years old at the time. My boss had given this party for her employees and clients. I indulged myself in wearing a pair of clip-on earrings for the festive evening. Later, I showed my pictures to a friend, not anticipating disapproval. She told me she was disappointed in me. Seeing the look on her face as she commented disapprovingly on my earrings, I knew I had let her down. It bothered me. I apologized for disappointing her.

A few years later, a secret sin in her life was exposed. It was a serious sin; yet she had felt comfortable in her superior attitude toward me. She could only feel that comfort because her own sin was not known. I wonder if that was why Jesus bent down and began writing in the sand when the angry mob called for the stoning of the woman caught in adultery. They had all felt comfortable to expose and judge another, thinking their own sins were well hidden. But their sins were not hidden from God. They had no right to feel superior.

Years later, after her sin was exposed, my friend was convicted of this and brought up the conversation about my earrings, which I had long forgotten. She asked me to forgive her for judging me, especially in light of her own failure. I loved this friend and I still do. I do not struggle with forgiveness. I felt shame for disappointing her rather than resentment about her judgment.

However, the further I get from that mindset, the more I comprehend that this is what legalism and works righteousness breeds in people. As long as your sins are not known, you can live in denial of them as if they do not exist. Jesus, however, showed us it is the sin in our hearts—our pride, our self-righteous attitudes, our lack of love and compassion for others—that is our real malignancy.

At its extreme, the pride that leads to self-righteousness allows a man quite comfortably to occupy the pulpit and preach at others about sexual sin while simultaneously abusing little girls behind closed doors. As long as his sins are hidden, it's as though they do not really exist. It is a horrible malignancy that has the potential to grow exponentially if left unchallenged. I remember my counselor pointing out to me that a dual life was a natural by-product of legalism and perfectionism. Since none of us can actually *be* perfect, the next best thing is to try to *look* perfect.

Unfortunately, looking perfect feeds our pride instead of knocking it down. I will never forget one professor at Lipscomb who spoke to my Senior Seminar class just before graduation. He wrote two words on the chalkboard; *humble* and *exalt*. He had us look at the words for a few moments. Then he said, "As you walk through life, you will have to choose to either humble yourself or exalt yourself in many situations. Just remember that whichever one you choose, God will take care of the other." I knew the concept, but he had put that concept into words that would never leave me.

In one particular counseling session, I had asked Floyd how it was *possible* that a person could attend church four times a week, read the Bible every day, spend time on their knees in prayer, and profess to love God while at the same time treating members of his own family with callous indifference. I genuinely believed the person in question was a Christian. Yet this person's behavior was impossible for me to reconcile with true Christianity. Floyd asked me if I recalled Jesus' rebuke of the Pharisees in Matthew 23, where He likened them to "whited sepulchers." I did. Floyd asked me if I knew what the term for "whited sepulchers" would be in modern language. I felt like I understood the meaning of the passage, but I asked him what terminology he was thinking of. He said, "Jesus was calling them shiny, polished caskets.

They spent a great deal of time shining and polishing what showed on the outside, but what was inside was still dead."

Those words made a lasting impression on me. Because of the insight I gained from Christian books and Christian counseling, I was able to begin looking at my own behavior from a new perspective. Trying to gain the approval and acceptance of others is like polishing your casket. I began to see the idols in my life. For the most part, my idols were (and are) people, and my insatiable need to be loved and affirmed. I realized that I had allowed my most cherished relationships to become idols: things I believed I could not live without. It was not so much that I idolized a particular person. But I began to understand that when something (i.e., being loved) becomes so necessary to my well-being that I think I cannot live without it; when someone becomes so important to me that I literally *fear* their disapproval or rejection, I have created an idol. Rather than seeking satisfaction in God, I have elevated a need or a person to an ultimate place in my life.

I have come to love Proverbs 19:23. "The fear of the LORD leads to life, and whoever has it rests satisfied; he will not be visited by harm."

For the majority of my life, I had been seeking my self-worth through other people instead of finding it solely in God. No wonder I was always empty and trying to fill myself up by earning value in the lives of others. I had been trained to do this through both overt instruction and many implied messages. It had been cultivated in all of my relationships. However, I learned that at the root of all my idolatry was one simple fact: I was not built into Christ. I was built into people. I had to tear down and rebuild.

As I learned the true Gospel, I encountered God's grace. I learned that the Gospel is what frees me from my idols. When I am in Christ, my self-view is not based on a view of myself as a moral achiever. My self-view is not built upon other people's view of me as a good person. In Christ I am simultaneously sinful and lost, yet accepted in Christ. To quote Tim Keller, "I am so bad he *had* to die for me and I am so loved he was *glad* to die for me."

This leads me to deeper humility and confidence at the same time. I am set free to both confess my idols and defeat my idols. No longer do I feel the need to hide or deny my weakness or imperfections. I am loved, accepted, adopted, liberated, and redeemed through the blood of Jesus Christ. He broke the chains and I have been set free.

I am so thankful for the Gospel. I am so thankful for Jesus. I am so thankful for God's provision in my life. Because I am forgiven, accepted, and loved, I can admit to myself *and to others* how deeply flawed and sinful I truly am. I can walk in the light, even though it exposes my darkness. I am not discouraged by my inadequacies because my faith is no longer in me, or other people's perception of me. My faith is now completely in Christ.

In this year's Easter Sunday sermon, my pastor spoke about Pilate's guilt, and his attempt to wash it away with a trickle of water. He demonstrated the inadequacy of this act by spilling a little bit of water on the floor. He then ended the sermon with the sound of Niagara Falls roaring in our ears as confetti streamed over us like a cleansing rain. Amidst the roar of the powerful waters, he focused us on the *power* of God, the cross, to wash away sins. This power is manifested through the shed blood of Jesus Christ. *Only Christ's blood* has sufficient power to cleanse.

> **"We may try to wash our hands of responsibility like Pilate, but**
> **our attempt will be futile, as futile as his.**
> **For there is blood on our hands."**
>
> *— John Stott*

⁓

I did not need a makeover. I needed a new foundation, though I didn't grasp that fully as I was leaving CGT. I often say that the reasons I left are only a fraction of the reasons I would not go back.

32

Believing in My Heart and Confessing with My Mouth

Since no one ever taught me that my salvation was accomplished through faith in Christ alone rather than through my own moral achievement or spiritual maturity level, I have wondered if I was truly a Christian in the past. It's a difficult question to ponder. And the question is personal.

As I reflect on my life, I recognize God's mercy was resting on me prior to leaving this group of people who call themselves the Body. I loved God. However, the core of the Gospel is found in the redemptive work of Christ on the cross and that was not the central message I heard. I was told that if people repented and gave their heart to Jesus and then immediately walked into the street to be hit by a bus, they were not saved based on their faith alone. They still had to mature and meet certain additional criteria. Specifically, they would have to resurrect and meet the requirement of *sinless perfection* before they obtained eternal life. That was the clear and consistent message in all the years I spent there.

I believe there may have been a few individuals here and there who believed privately in their own hearts that salvation was through faith alone in Christ and His sacrifice on the cross. But I don't remember anyone ever *sharing* that saving faith with me. If they believed it, they kept it to themselves rather than challenge the teaching openly.

The Bible tells us in Romans 10:5–11 that Moses describes righteousness by the law, but of the righteousness that is by faith, the passage says:

> The word is near you; in your mouth and in your heart (that is, the word of faith that we proclaim); because if you confess with your mouth that Jesus is Lord and believe in your heart that God raised him from the dead, you will be saved. For with the heart one

believes and is justified, and with the mouth one confesses and is saved. For the Scripture says, "Everyone who believes in him will not be put to shame."

Later, in verses 14–15, the question is posed: "How, then, will they call on him in whom they have not believed? And how are they to believe in him of whom they have never heard? And how are they to hear without someone preaching? And how are they to preach unless they are sent? As it is written, 'How beautiful are the feet of those who preach the good news!'"

This good news of the Gospel was not preached to me or shared with me by anyone in CGT. That reality has left me wondering about the true definition of confessing "with your mouth." What does that mean? Is saving faith something one can privately believe without sharing? How I wish someone who rejected the doctrine of perfection would have shared that with me and told me the good news of the Gospel. But no one ever did. I remember a couple of people saying that they did not think we had it quite right on perfection; that perfection meant something different than a literal moral perfection. However, the implied message was the same; there were additional requirements to faith.

After I left CGT, I remained in doubt about eternity. I believed in my heart and confessed with my mouth, but because of a lifetime of indoctrination that faith in Christ alone was insufficient, I was unconvinced of the Gospel. I was told all my life that Jesus had not "paid it all." My eternity was still in question based upon my yet to be determined meritorious performance. In my own heart and mind I was still uncertain about my place in heaven based on a lifetime of being taught that the whole Christian world had been deceived and we alone had "the truth" on salvation.

As I struggled to believe in the saving faith of the cross, someone pointed me to 1 John 5:13: "I write these things to you who believe in the name of the Son of God so that you may know that you have eternal life." In this passage, it seemed clear that as a believer my eternity was not in question and God wanted me to know that I had eternal life. However, if my former teachers had convinced me of anything, they had convinced me that my eternity remained uncertain. My hopelessness and stagnation had been primary factors in leaving.

I was not able to begin believing with assurance that I would see Jesus in heaven until I renounced my former beliefs. I now believe that saying those words were an essential element in confessing faith in Christ and breaking the chains of my past. I saw that my faith could not be partially in Christ's righteousness and partially in my own. I had to renounce those former beliefs with my mouth in order to embrace the promises of God.

When I did that, I felt like a new believer and a new creation. I immediately experienced the desire to be baptized in water. Though I had been baptized as a child and again as an adult (when I felt the need to re-dedicate my life), I had not heard and embraced the true Gospel at the time of either baptism. I was baptized not believing that Jesus' death on the cross had accomplished my salvation. I did not know that in water baptism, I was buried with Him and raised to new life in Him. I now wanted to be baptized knowing the Gospel of Jesus Christ. I wasn't sure if this was necessary, but I began to question my baptism. Looking back, I remembered how people who had come into our group out of different denominations had been encouraged to be re-baptized (in the Body). I knew that I did not need to be re-baptized because I had changed churches. However, I could not shake the feeling that in spite of viewing myself as a Christian my whole life, I had become a new believer; I had been reborn.

When I began to attend World Outreach Church, I had no particular interest in going to Israel. That had never been a desire. I believed that the Jewish people had a role in God's plan. I believed the prophecy of the Bible that they would one day recognize their true Messiah. But I did not have what I would describe as a *love* for Israel and the Jewish people. I wasn't even particularly interested in what was happening in the Middle East.

My pastor and his family, through their words and actions, demonstrated a deep love for the land of Israel and the Jewish people. Dr. George Jackson and his wife, Betty, had obviously planted this love in the hearts of their children. And through their son, Allen (my new pastor), the seeds of love and interest were being planted and cultivated in me. I watched groups from our church travel safely to Israel and back on a regular basis, and I began to lose my fear of going there as I developed a longing in my heart to make that pilgrimage.

I began to bring up the subject of going to Israel with John. I didn't know when he would possibly be able to make a trip like that in light of his business responsibilities. However, I made it known how much I wanted to go while at the same time trying to make sure I didn't apply too much pressure. I wanted *God* to put a desire in his heart to go.

I was overjoyed the day John told me, "I was going to keep it a secret and surprise you, but I guess I'll just go ahead and tell you; we are going to Israel in November." I was so excited. I didn't care if I ever got to travel anywhere else. After hearing so many of my friends talk about the life changing experience of visiting the Holy Land and walking where Jesus walked, this was the only place in the whole world that I really *longed* to see and experience.

John and I went with our pastor, his wife, and a small group of friends from our church. Rather than going as tourists, we viewed the trip as a spiritual pilgrimage. Allen shared with us that even though he has made many, many trips to Israel throughout his life, he always returns home with his faith strengthened and renewed. I anticipated that for myself.

There were many spiritual high points of the trip. Different settings made different impressions. Because there is such distinctive significance to each location and the events that took place there, it is difficult to have one favorite memory or tag one place as having the greatest impact on me.

I will always have a very special feeling in my heart when I reflect on our time spent on the Mount of Beatitudes, overlooking the Sea of Galilee. I was awed by many sights and inspired by the spiritual applications of many historical events. However, the Mount of Beatitudes was a deeply moving point of worship. We gathered in a quiet spot and sang praises to the Lord. We received communion. Allen ministered the Word to us and talked about the Sermon on the Mount. We had a special time of prayer. If I could only use two words to describe this location, I would choose peace and tranquility. I felt close to God in that setting.

As we took a boat ride on the Sea of Galilee, I was overwhelmed at the thought of Jesus having walked on those very waters and having silenced a raging storm with nothing more than His spoken word. We stood in the very location of the synagogue in Capernaum where Jesus once taught. We looked down over the Jezreel Valley from the top of Mt. Carmel where Elijah and the Lord defeated the prophets of Baal.

Deeply stirring was our ride into the City of Jerusalem, singing "Hosanna!" as we approached, standing on the Mount of Olives overlooking the walls of the old city and the Temple Mount. I now have an enhanced understanding of the significance of each wall and the events that occurred in those locations. I had the honor of walking up the southern steps where Jesus walked as He approached the Temple gates. I stood beside an olive tree in the Garden of Gethsemane that dates back to the days of Jesus. We saw the large stones that had been toppled into the streets when Jerusalem was destroyed in AD 70, just as Jesus had prophesied.

As we looked upon the Sheep Gate, located on the eastern wall, Allen told us about the sheep that were raised for the purpose of sacrifice. They came from Bethlehem and were brought into the Temple through this gate, the same gate that Jesus was brought through on His way to execution as our sacrificial Lamb. I was moved to tears as I thought of the Lamb of God slain for the sins of the world.

We visited the Garden Tomb. As we walked along the path to the tomb, we passed other believers from different parts of the world. That moment will always stay with me. It was so unexpected. As we walked past believers from India (walking in the opposite direction), they were singing loudly and praising God. There was radiance in their countenance. Their joy was palpable.

As we passed one another, they smiled huge smiles, made eye contact, and raised their hands to touch ours. Had I seen these people in any other setting, I might not have even recognized them as Christians. They looked different in appearance, but we shared the bond of faith in a risen Savior. As we passed these joy-filled believers, touching their hands, raising our hands in praise and proclaiming to one another, "He is risen!" I felt the joy of heaven and the anticipation of Christ's return in a way I had never previously experienced. As glorious as this moment was, I knew it wasn't even a fraction of the joy we will share as we gather around the throne of God and the Lamb.

I guess if I absolutely had to pinpoint the most personally significant moment in our trip to Israel, it would have to be my water baptism in the Jordan River. As we rode the bus to the river, our guide told us that we could receive a certificate of baptism. We just needed to let him know if this was our first Christian baptism or a re-dedication. This was a question I had contemplated many times; did I need to be baptized for the first time in the true Christian faith? When I had been baptized previously, I did not believe the Gospel. That had been a sticking point for me. What significance could there have been in my water baptism if I had not even known the Gospel? I had renounced my former belief in salvation through my own perfection. If I had renounced that faith, had I not also renounced my baptism?

I asked Allen on that bus ride if he would consider this a re-dedication or my first Christian baptism. I said, "You know the things I was taught; the things I once believed. You told me to renounce them and repent for believing a false gospel. I don't care about the certificate. I would just like to know the answer to my question." Allen responded, "I would consider this your first water baptism."

We approached a little spot along the Jordan River. One by one, we entered the water for baptism. Several had always wanted to be baptized in the Jordan River, even though they did not question their initial baptism. Although it is an amazing experience to know that you are being baptized in the same river where John baptized Jesus, the location of my baptism was secondary to the reality that I now *knew* what Jesus had accomplished for me on the cross. As Allen plunged me into that cold water, I knew I was being *buried* with Christ. As I emerged from the river, I knew I had been *raised* with Christ to eternal life in Him. At that point I truly believed God's promise that through faith in Jesus' perfect life, his sacrificial death, and glorious resurrection I was saved.

I returned from Israel a changed person. As we went into the Christmas season, I remember a service in which Allen spoke on Romans. He quoted Romans 10:9-10, "That if you confess with your mouth, 'Jesus is Lord,' and believe in your heart that God raised him from the dead, you will be saved. For it is with your heart that you believe and are justified, and it is with your mouth that you confess and are saved" (NIV).

I loved what he said next. And I am sure that after reading my story, you will understand why. I am paraphrasing his comments, which were words to this effect:

> I want you to notice something about this passage of Scripture. There is no mention of me. It is all about Jesus and your faith in *Him*; it's about making Him Lord of your life. It's not about this particular church or me as your pastor. Salvation is through faith in

the Person of Jesus Christ and your confession of Him as Lord and Savior.

❧

I am not at the end of my journey, but I have come to the end of this installment. God has blessed me with His love and mercy, salvation through the cross of Christ, a wonderful church family, and a loving husband I could never deserve. I am thankful for a son and daughter-in-law who are devoted to Christ and to raising their children in the fear and admonition of the Lord. In addition to all of that, God has added and multiplied to me many dear friends, who love, sustain, and encourage me in my continued spiritual journey.

I praise God that my faith is now securely in Christ alone.

❧

"But far be it from me to boast except in the cross of our Lord Jesus Christ, by which the world has been crucified to me, and I to the world."

– Galatians 6:14

Epilogue

Early this summer, my wife and I helped out at a Vacation Bible School in Kentucky. One of the lessons involved a tub of Starburst. I know what you're thinking, but no, it wasn't about what heaven will be like. The lesson consisted of putting the tub of Starburst about ten feet away from a line of tape on the floor. The twenty or thirty VBS students were then told that if anyone could make the ten foot leap to the tub, they could keep all the candy. In less than two seconds, a perky, ten-year-old, athletic looking Pharisee exclaimed, "How about whoever jumps the farthest?" I pointed to her and shouted, "Woe to you, Hypocrites and Scribes!" Not really, but I did turn to the guy next to me and say, "We're all such Pharisees."

There are two types of salvation on this earth. There is the man-made, ladder-climbing, works-based righteousness that always leaves a mess, and there is the salvation God offers through His Son that cannot fail.

I recently met a fellow former Southern Californian in a local Wal-Mart. He noticed my UCLA shirt, and we started talking about Los Angeles and comparing it to our relatively new home in the South. He asked how I ended up here, and I told him I had moved here with a cult. I've heard several replies to that answer, but his was a first. "Good for you," he said. He then proceeded to tell me about Jack Kerouac's novel, *The Dharma Bums*. In the book, Kerouac explains how he believes a person can learn (on this earth) how to live completely free from suffering. It reminded me of the cult my mom and I grew up in. We weren't taught suffering would go away, but we were taught our sin could. Not the guilt of sin. Not the cleansing from sin. But a literal end to the sin in our lives.

Whether it's Zen Buddhism or a Pentecostal cult, the end result is the same: to be free from suffering (or sin) by one's own efforts. Orthodox Christianity could not be more opposite. The story of the Bible is the story of the God who saves. The prophet Jonah sums up God's salvation story with his prayer in the belly of the big fish. *Salvation belongs to the Lord.*

The Bible is God's story, written to tell His people about His salvation plan. His plan for the world overflowed out of His very being. The glorious reality of the Christian God is a God who exists in one substance, yet three in Persons. It's a hard concept to grasp, but He is in relationship with Himself. He is a "community" unto Himself. This community has existed throughout all eternity. God is love because God has always been loving and has always been loved. We are here because God chose humans to carry His image and recreate the fellowship and community of love that He has always been living. When Adam and Eve disobeyed, they violated the Covenant God had made with man. Adam was told that if he obeyed the rule of the tree he would live. Instead, the rule was violated, and we were introduced to the broken world we now know.

C.S. Lewis writes about humanity remembering an embrace we've never actually experienced and how we go to great lengths to recover the embrace. We go on vacations and look at oceans and try to get back to that memory. Joni Mitchell reminds us we are stardust and golden and we've got to get ourselves back to the garden. When Joni Mitchell and C.S. Lewis agree, we should probably pay attention.

After covering Adam and Eve's nakedness, God removed them from the garden and placed an angel with a flaming sword at the entrance. The only way back was through the sword, God's Word, and God's justice.

Jesus is *Immanuel*—God with us. The One in whose image we were made became an image bearer. Not clinging to His equality with the Father, He took on flesh and suffered, bled, and died as a man. Because the violated Covenant was between God and man, the sacrificial atonement had to be God and man. God couldn't have redeemed us with the death of a sinful man because the sacrifice had to be perfect. He couldn't have sacrificed an angel or any other heavenly creation, because the violation didn't occur between God and the angels or another created being.

Jesus, the God-Man, came to earth and lived the perfect image-bearing life. Living the life we should have lived and dying the death believers should have died, Jesus passed through the flaming sword for us. Like Adam, from Gethsemane to the cross, Jesus was obeying the Father's command about the tree. Unlike Adam, Jesus obeyed the Covenant perfectly. The result of His obedience, however, led to death instead of life. Immanuel was willingly cut off from the eternal fellowship of the Trinity in order to bring us back into our original intended place. When He rose from the grave, eternal life was guaranteed to all whose faith was in Him. This is the narrow way of salvation Jesus speaks about. The broad road that leads to destruction includes everything that isn't faith in Jesus, from the blatant rejection of the thought of God to the legalism that poses as the fruit of the Spirit.

The vast chasm between the Holy God and His sinful image-bearers makes a ten-foot jump for a ten-year-old look easy. Sadly, humans have tried to jump the chasm and walk through the sword back to Eden. No one walks through that sword unless they are safely resting in the arms of the Savior, Immanuel.

Like the long-jumping Pharisee, we set standards that we're pretty good at achieving in order to reach, and in turn avoid our need for, God. Cain built a city. The citizens of Babel built a tower. Saul of Tarsus killed Christians and kept the letter of God's law meticulously while ignoring the spirit of the same laws. There are certain "good works" in every culture and religion that are accepted as a means of getting close to God.

Reading *Breaking the Chains* has reminded me of the bondage of my past. The "towers" we built were the length of our sleeves and the number of services we attended. Jesus was reduced to a reachable *example* instead of a gracious *Savior*. It's no different than Muslims who pray five times a day or

Buddhists who refuse to own chairs. It is all an attempt to walk through the sword of God on our own.

Over the past few months, Christian Gospel Temple's sword walking has been visible to a watching community through four lawsuits. Three of them, sadly, were dropped because statutes of limitations had expired. One ended in a settlement. Upon the settlement being reached, the depositions of Christian Gospel Temple's leadership were made public. The lies and cover-ups of the group have been in the newspapers, on blogs, and even on the six o'clock news. My prayer (and I know it is my mom's as well) is that the failed attempt of walking back into God's garden through the idolatry of personal achievement will be forsaken. We pray and hope for a strong deliverance to come for those who have believed a strong delusion. We ask God to open their eyes to the mutilated mess that has been left by those who have been unwilling to repent for wrongdoing. There is rest for the weary. There is forgiveness for the proud man who realizes his need for humility. Joseph Hart wrote, "Let not conscience make you linger; nor of fitness fondly dream. All the fitness he requireth is to feel your need of him."

This book was written with the hope that the members and leadership of Christian Gospel Temple will no longer dream of any fitness that merits reward other than the complete and full fitness freely given to those who are in Jesus Christ. I pray its purpose is accomplished.

Danny Bryant